THE FUTU

Anthropo:
New Millennium

Edited by
Sevak Gulbekian

TEMPLE LODGE
London

Part One, Chapter 1 translated from Russian by Simon
Blaxland-de Lange
Part One, Chapters 3, 5, 9, 10 and Appendix translated from
German by Johanna Collis

Temple Lodge Publishing
51 Queen Caroline Street
London W6 9QL

www.templelodge.com

Published by Temple Lodge 1999

© Temple Lodge Publishing 1999

A catalogue record for this book is available from the British Library

ISBN 1 902636 09 0

Cover by Clairview Studios
Typeset by DP Photosetting, Aylesbury, Bucks
Printed and bound in Great Britain by Cromwell Press Limited,
Trowbridge, Wiltshire

'And in the course of the twentieth century, when the first century after Kali-Yuga has elapsed, humanity will either stand at the grave of all civilization, or at the beginning of the epoch when Michael's battle on behalf of his impulse will be fought out in the souls of those people who, in their hearts, have united reason with spirituality.'

Rudolf Steiner, 19 July 1924

Contents

Foreword

I am preparing myself for this new age that is leading from the twentieth to the twenty-first century—says a genuinely anthroposophical soul—for there are many destructive forces on the earth. All the earth's cultural and civilized life will have to fall into decay if the spirituality of the Michael Impulse does not move human beings and if human beings in their turn prove incapable of bringing about an upturn in a civilization that is bent on decline.

If sincere anthroposophists can be found whose souls are inclined to bring spirituality to earthly life, then things will begin to move in an upward direction. If not, then decadence will continue on its downward path.[1]

Anybody who is prepared to consider even the possibility that Rudolf Steiner was a high-grade initiate and spiritual teacher, will be struck by the certainty and severity of the above quoted words. Indeed—as is well known by any student of his work—Steiner made quite a number of statements in a similarly dramatic vein regarding events at the end of the twentieth century. In summary: humanity would stand at a crossroads in its development, while souls from groups or 'schools' within the spiritual world—connected with Aristotelian or Platonic thought as well as with the spiritual being known traditionally as the Archangel Michael—would incarnate on earth in an unprecedented bid to work together for the future of the human race.

Those attending Rudolf Steiner's lectures will no doubt have been awe-struck by such predictions regarding a time very close to their own. Similarly, throughout the twentieth century many will have read his words in printed form with a matching sense of wonder. And suddenly here we are, at the eve of the new millennium: the future, which so many souls have been so earnestly preparing for, is quite literally ... NOW.

The impetus behind the initiation of this project has been closely connected with the above fact. I am sure that many of those allied to Rudolf Steiner's work—to the modern spiritual science of Anthroposophy—are seriously asking themselves today: Where do we stand in relation to those statements which Rudolf Steiner made around 75 years ago? And yet it has struck me that relatively few people in the anthroposophical movement have seen fit—or felt able—to address such a question. With this in mind, in May 1998 I approached all the authors who have had a book published by Temple Lodge to contribute an essay on the above theme. In my letter I asked them to consider the many statements Rudolf Steiner made about the end of the twentieth century, and to attempt an answer to the following questions:

> ... So where are we now in relation to his vision, and how has Anthroposophy developed over this century? Where do we stand in connection to the battle for the spirit; the meeting of the Platonic and Aristotelian streams; the culmination of Anthroposophy, etc? ... You may wish to write in general terms about these questions, or to pick a specific theme and discuss it in some detail ...

Of the 26 authors I contacted, 19 agreed to take part in the project. Two dropped out, and by the deadline 17 essays had been received and (with the addition of my own) are included in this book.

From the beginning all the writers were assured of the integrity of the project: there would be no attempt to push a particular point of view, subversive or otherwise. My intention was to include a multiplicity of viewpoints—the only prerequisite being an honest and open attempt to tackle the above questions. All participants were assured that they would have the freedom to express their thoughts; and, as promised, only a minimum of editing has taken place.

With some notable exceptions, few of the writers have directly addressed the central questions mentioned above. Rather, many of them have tackled fascinating, but peripheral, themes. (Readers will make of this what they will, but it is clearly significant.) Nevertheless, what we do have in this book is a worthy collection of the considered 'millennarian thoughts' of some of the most prominent writers who are working—in an explicit sense—out of Rudolf Steiner's spiritual philosophy today.

As a consequence of the lack of censorship and the freedom of the writers to express themselves as they see fit, the essays are of necessity a disparate collection. I have arranged them into two sections to give greater continuity and flow: the first dealing more directly with the development of Anthroposophy and its Society and movement, while the second section focuses on individual themes. The essays are not placed in any subjective order of importance.

Sevak Gulbekian, London, May 1999

Introduction
Humanity at the New Millennium and the Future of Anthroposophy

... You have the choice today, either to see reason, to accept what common sense wishes to be realised, or else to advance towards revolutions and cataclysms[1] ... If what I have explained to you as a possible means of salvation does not come about, a series of catastrophes will happen. That which cannot come about through reasonableness will happen nevertheless after great upheavals; for cosmic will requires it.[2]

... [A]ll the catastrophes befalling the world and humanity which we have to experience are due to the fact that the great majority of people still tries to cling to materialism.[3]

This essay is divided into two sections, dealing with separate questions which are nevertheless related. In the second part I will consider the future of Anthroposophy. In this first section my intention is to study the situation facing humanity at the dawn of the third millennium.

Humanity at the New Millennium

Anybody seeking to come to a deeper understanding of our time is led ultimately to consider the question of evil. It could be assumed that the subject is out of place in our materialistic age, but remarkably the word 'evil' is in vogue, as much among tabloid headline-writers and politicians as among religious and spiritual groups. But in what sense is it used today? Certainly, there are many people who still accept the traditional view of evil: that it is a supernatural force which works on and through people via the agency of spiritual beings. More popularly, however, the word has lost any spiritual connotation. While it may be suggested, for example by a journalist, that a person has acted in an 'evil' way, the explanation usually given for his or her behaviour is either that inherited, genetic factors are responsible (e.g. the so-called 'criminal gene'), or that the person's actions are the result of environmental, sociological influences. (Or sometimes a combination of the two.)[4]

While the genetic and sociological explanations of evil are the most popular among the materialistic intelligentsia, the 'supernatural' conception of evil is deeply embedded in popular culture, as is made clear for example by the popularity of books and films in the horror genre. This supernatural or spiritual view can of course also have a more serious grounding, which is seen in the teachings of countless spiritual and religious groups. The movement that has grown up around the work of Rudolf Steiner is no exception. In recent years, particularly in relation to the year 1998 (3×666), a great deal has been said regarding various evil beings and their role in the drama of cosmic and human life. While such conceptions of evil are no doubt important, other significant perspectives from Steiner's work have not been given much attention.

I would like to present one neglected idea—a fresh view of evil—which has a great bearing on the question of the choices facing humanity at the new millennium. This understanding of evil is at once empowering and transformative as it does not encourage the feeling that we are passive victims of external malevolent powers. In order to develop this new perspective, however, it is necessary to put aside all the usual conceptions of evil which we may have. In their place, we can imagine a picture of spiritual forces that work from the cosmos and give us the capacity for further developing our human nature. These forces, while intended primarily for evolving our spiritual self, also give every human being an equal potential to carry out evil acts, although such deeds are a 'secondary effect' of the forces. According to Rudolf Steiner, these powers principally '... are present in the universe so as to awaken in us a propensity, once the consciousness soul has developed, for opening ourselves to the life of the spirit ... We must assimilate them [the 'evil' forces], and by so doing we implant in our being the seed which enables us to have conscious experience of the spirit ... They exist to enable people to break through to the life of the spirit.'[5]

This radical perspective is found in a number of passages in Steiner's work, although always from a slightly different viewpoint.[6] To sum up the basic idea conveyed from these various sources: Evil manifests in human beings when certain forces, that are intended for spiritual development, are not taken up and used in the right way. These forces—which in their primary form are closely connected with the development of the essential core of our being, the human 'I'—are then distorted and appear externally as evil deeds and actions.[7]

This can lead us to the conclusion that the forces working within us, from which the potential for evil arises, are actually 'neutral' forces. They can be used 'positively'—'for opening ourselves to the life of the spirit', for forging the human 'I'—or they manifest 'negatively', as 'outer' evil. Why should these forces manifest as evil? Because, it can be said, human beings must either progress or regress—'sink or swim'; it is not possible to remain stationary. The forces are there and they *must be used*—one way or another. The reality of human freedom is based on this fact. The possibility to *ascend* in human evolution must, of necessity, allow for the possibility to *descend* and sink into decadence.

It now becomes clear why Rudolf Steiner spoke in such stark terms of the choices faced by humanity at the close of the twentieth century. We will stand, he stated quite categorically (see page iii), either 'at the grave of civilization', or at the birth of a new age of revitalized human consciousness and culture. There appears to be no third way. In other words, either we use the forces given to us for their correct purpose, or else these forces will *use us*—by manifesting as evil. On a larger scale, then, it could be said that humanity has the choice of following an archetypal, ideal pattern of development, or else development will be forced upon it by outer evil. I would suggest that on the world stage this 'outer evil' could be understood as war, natural disasters, economic collapse, environmental catastrophe, disease, and so on. (See also the quotations at the beginning of this article.)

I am not suggesting that those who suffer from outer evil 'deserve' to find themselves in such a situation. This simplistic notion of karma would state that if a person or group of people suffer from an outer calamity, they are of necessity receiving 'karmic retribution'. Such a presumption can never be made without exact clairvoyant insight. The reality could be quite the contrary. It is possible, for example, for a person to absorb the karmic consequences of another person's actions as an act of sacrifice.[8] Or perhaps it may be that through a period of suffering in a present incarnation, an individual could be developing a quality for a future incarnation.[9]

The Two Paths

Two paths have been mentioned—one of conscious, free spiritual development, and the other of development forced by outer suffering. Both allow for evolution, but the latter is of course a more tortuous route. Most people can say from personal experience—although often in retrospect—that periods of suffering in their biography have included moments of great spiritual awakening; but such transformation has seemingly been forced through outer circumstance. In our personal biography, and also in the evolution of the human race, perhaps the reality is that we advance through a combination of free, conscious development and development forced by outer circumstance. In other words, the two paths are not mutually exclusive but intertwined.

While this 'intertwining' of the two paths may be a source of comfort when thinking in terms of our own biographies, it should not give us much solace when considering our present, critical times. According to the words of Rudolf Steiner, today—one hundred years after the end of the Dark Age ('Kali Yuga')—humanity *must* awaken from its period of spiritual sleep. The luxury of a prolonged period of ignorance is no longer an option.

So we are left with the following question: Can modern society, with all its entrenched materialism and its sleep-inducing comforts and entertainments, make the advance to a spiritual awakening, or must such a shift in consciousness be forced upon it? With reference to our central theme the question can be rephrased as follows: Can humanity use the forces of spiritual development for their primary function, or must these forces turn on us and act outwardly as evil, as misfortune? (It is often asked why God allows suffering, but from this perspective it must be said that it is humanity that allows the evil and suffering to manifest.)

It is instructive to look back at history and see how this 'law' is illustrated by the catastrophes that have taken place when opportunities for development have been by-passed. For example, in speaking about his attempts to bring about a rejuvenation of social life, Steiner referred his listeners to the attempts of the pastor and author Johann Valentin Andreae to bring about a spiritual awakening in Europe at the beginning of the seventeenth century. There were at that time 'two streams' manifest in human history—Andreae's Rosicrucian initiative (beginning in 1613 with the publication of his *Chymical Wedding of Christian Rosenkreutz* and continuing to 1917) and the events which developed into the Thirty Years' War (1618–48). For various reasons Andreae's attempts to establish Rosicrucianism failed, and so the events leading to the Thirty Years' War took over. With reference to his own time and the social cataclysms and war, Steiner stated the following in 1917:

> Today we again find ourselves within two streams, two possibilities, which must of necessity affect one another. On the one hand there is Anthroposophy with the impulse to further human evolution; on the other hand there is all that which has brought about events similar in nature to those that caused the Thirty Years' War. It depends upon mankind whether once again what ought to happen is prevented from happening. Lethargy, love of ease, might well paralyse the present attempt.

The 'two streams', I believe, are the two paths referred to above. The tragedy is that humanity did revert to 'lethargy' and 'love of ease' in the early part of this century, and the horrendous destruction of the World Wars and their aftermath were a consequence.[10]

While looking back at such historical failures can engender feelings of pessimism, it can also lead to a greater resolution to act and succeed in the present. After all, the concept of the 'two paths' or streams is one which is, ultimately, empowering. The idea that 'destiny is in our hands' liberates humanity from fatalistic interpretations of destiny or karma which have ruled for hundreds of years. Such fixed notions can be found everywhere from Hinduism and Islam ('It is written') to Saint Augustine's teachings about 'predestination', and even in the work of the fashionable New Age writer Paul Coehlo (in his novel *The Alchemist*). Rudolf Steiner's efforts to christianize the teachings of reincarnation and karma hinge on the element of human freedom. The new teaching of karma is that our destiny is dynamic, malleable—it changes according to *what we do*. We create the future.

It is interesting to note that this idea is reflected in the book *Saved by the Light* by Dannion Brinkley—a man whose life was changed by a powerful near-death experience after he was struck by lightning. Brinkley describes how, in the spiritual world, he is shown pictures of coming events, among which are images of a terrible third world war. But the being who is his guide tells him: 'If you follow what you have been taught and keep living the same way you have lived the last thirty years, all of this will surely be upon you. If you change, you can avoid the coming war.'[11]

The 'Son' and the 'Father'

The 'two paths', which offer such different possibilities to humankind, can also be thought of as 'the Path of the Son' and 'the Path of the Father'. In esoteric teachings the individual human soul is known as the feminine principle, while the divine element—God—is spoken of as the masculine form, 'the Father'.[12] Throughout evolution, the 'mother' (the human soul) receives spiritual nourishment from the divine world (the Father). But with the advent of the Dark Age, when human beings lost their instinctive clairvoyance and with it their natural connection to the divine world, the feminine principle became separated from the masculine. The mother—the human soul—was thus 'widowed'. But the widowed mother carries within her the divine seed of the Father, and this seed can be nurtured; the individual human soul can give birth to 'the Son' (or Child), the spiritual individuality or 'I'. (Thus the Christian initiate Mani, who represented the 'I' principle, called himself 'the

Son of the Widow'. Similarly, Christ called himself 'the Son of Man'.)

The path of conscious development, of using the inner spiritual forces for their true purpose, can be spoken of as the Path of the Son (or the Child). The second path, where the forces of spiritual development are reversed and appear outwardly as evil, can be called the Path of the Father.

In our present age, we are given the spiritual forces to develop and evolve freely out of our own individual nature. Dannion Brinkley is told by the beings he meets in the spiritual world: 'Those who go to earth are heroes and heroines, because you are doing something that no other spiritual beings have the courage to do. You have gone to earth to co-create with God'.[13] As has been said, however, if we are not able to develop out of freedom, then evolution is forced on us by outer events. Such occurrences may appear harsh, but they manifest out of a profound wisdom. This is why the 'second way' is referred to here as the Path of the Father—the direct intervention of divine wisdom in earthly evolution. Divine love appears as 'divine wrath'.[14]

The Gospel story of the Prodigal Son juxtaposes the two paths. The son leaves his father and ventures out into the wide world where he falls into vice and decadence. For a time he is lost, but through adverse experiences he awakens to his own self and returns, now out of freedom and knowledge, to his father.

'Freedom and Love' or 'Wisdom and Necessity'
The two paths can further be spoken of as 'the Path of Wisdom and Necessity' and 'the Path of Freedom and Love'. In the period of Earth evolution, said Steiner, we are set the task of transforming Wisdom and Necessity into Freedom and Love. Nature is infused with the most profound wisdom: the graceful spider which spins its intricate web with such

beauty and precision, for example. But it does this out of an instinctive knowledge, for the whole of Nature is ruled by necessity—there is little possibility for free will. A cat does not consciously choose to mother its kittens; a tiger viciously kills another animal but cannot be accused of evil.

It is the task of humanity ultimately to redeem and meta-morphose outer nature. This long process is brought about through the transformation of our own individual inner nat-ure, i.e. through becoming beings of freedom and love. When change is forced through outer adversity—through evil which is allowed to manifest by the Divine world—then we follow the Path of Wisdom and Necessity. But when we begin to take control of our destiny and use our 'I' forces for their true purpose, we follow the Path of Freedom and Love. To what extent humanity has managed to tread the Path of Freedom and Love in our time will, I believe, become apparent from coming world events, adverse or otherwise.

In the first part of this essay I have attempted to outline the profound effects which we—as individuals and collectively—can have on future events, and the choices we face in the present. In the second part I will present some thoughts about the future of Anthroposophy itself.

The Future of Anthroposophy

Among those who follow the spiritual path founded by Rudolf Steiner, there is naturally an ideal to further the work he initiated—to assist in the development of Anthroposophy. But what exactly is meant by 'the development of Anthro-posophy'? I offer the following as my own interpretation of how Anthroposophy can be furthered in the future.

Is Anthroposophy to be a mass movement? Should we expect that Steiner's work might influence millions of people around the world in the way that, for example, Karl Marx's thinking did in the twentieth century? Steiner himself is said to have suggested that the number of souls close to the being of Michael—i.e. those who took part in his spiritual 'school'—consist of some 'millions'[15] (incarnated and excarnated). At present there are around 50,000 members of the Anthroposophical Society, and many others connected to the anthroposophical movement through practical work in education, medicine, agriculture, etc. But could we expect—or would we want—Anthroposophy and the name of Rudolf Steiner to be as widely known and followed as, say, a movement like the Catholic Church? The answer to this question lies, I suggest, in the past...

It is widely believed by anthroposophists that Rudolf Steiner was once incarnated as the Greek philosopher Aristotle (384–322 BC).[16] Although Steiner never confirmed this theory himself—at least not publicly—he is supposed to have hinted at it. Whether or not we accept that Steiner was once Aristotle, it is nevertheless instructive to consider objectively the work of Aristotle as something of an archetype.

Through his philosophy, Aristotle guided an enormous transition in human consciousness. Whereas his teacher, Plato, believed in reincarnation, Aristotle taught that each individual human soul was created by God at conception. With this single thought, he began the process of sweeping away centuries of belief in the pre-existence of the soul (i.e. its existence before birth), and hence also of previous lives on earth. Whereas Plato's conception led the individual's gaze to a vision of eternity—of past, present and future lives—Aristotle's teaching directed attention to the present existence between life and death (with a single afterlife as a consequence of this sole existence). On this foundation was built two thousand years of exoteric Christian thought, as expounded by the Church and its many teachers.

Aristotle's philosophy also had implications and influence beyond the Church. By guiding consciousness to the here and now, he was directing human thinking from the *heavenly* to a new experience of the *earthly*—from above to below. Plato's concept of 'the archetype', or 'forms', looked to the cosmic idea behind physical phenomena. By encouraging people to focus on what is here on earth, Aristotle, in contrast, represented modern scientific thinking. As a consequence of this clear consciousness, human beings began to concentrate fully on what was apparent to their physical perception, and innate clairvoyant capacities began to lose their value.

This is, of course, only the briefest of sketches of vast philosophical and spiritual world-views, but it gives at least an indication of the significant change which took place from the teaching of a master (Plato) to that of his pupil (Aristotle), both of whom have had a tremendous influence on western thought. But in what form has the influence of Aristotle manifested? On the one hand, Aristotle's work has been studied directly by many people over the years, particularly the medieval scholastics such as Thomas Aquinas, and Moorish Muslim philosophers. On the other hand, however, Aristotle's influence has reached far beyond those who have followed him in an *explicit* sense. In an *implicit* sense, his thinking has fully permeated our culture and consciousness, to the extent that it forms the very basis of modern life and the scientific outlook of our time.

By meditating on the enormous change brought about in human history through the philosophy of Aristotle, we may have some inkling of the actual and potential influence of the work of Rudolf Steiner. Whereas it was the task of Aristotle to bring our consciousness to rest on the earthly tasks of the present, Steiner—through his fully scientific, spiritual path—began the long process of respiritualization, of the reascent to the cosmic. The human being can look again to the heavens, but now with a fully developed, clear earthly consciousness. In freedom and knowledge we can turn again to the spirit.

Aristotle's influence has been working on human consciousness for over two thousand years. Rudolf Steiner's work—what he brought to mankind as Anthroposophy—began barely one hundred years ago. His outward influence today is not so great, and not perhaps as great as he may have hoped. Nevertheless, the future task of Anthroposophy is to bring about this enormous transition within human culture and consciousness. This is a universal goal, uniting the whole of humanity. While we may expect, as with Aristotelianism, that many individuals will study Rudolf Steiner's work and identify with Anthroposophy in an outward, explicit sense, we must also expect a much wider influence and manifestation of his impulse. This applies as much to our present time as to the future.

I believe that the challenge facing the anthroposophical movement today—and by this I mean those with an 'explicit' relationship to Rudolf Steiner and his work—will be to recognize true modern spirituality ('implicit' Anthroposophy) when it does not have the words 'Rudolf Steiner' or 'Anthroposophy' stamped on it. This is one of the key questions that faces the Anthroposophical Society and movement at the end of the twentieth century: Will we be awake enough and sufficiently unprejudiced to perceive Anthroposophy in the new forms in which it will inevitably appear? And crucially, on the other hand, will we have sufficient clarity of thought and discrimination to differentiate between true modern spirituality and what is false? The task is hugely challenging!

Over the past century Anthroposophy has been nurtured—cocooned—by relatively small groups of people. Some would argue that this stage in its life was right and necessary. Now, however, at the eve of the new millennium, it is my conviction that it can no longer remain constrained within this form: the new spiritual, scientific consciousness is available to millions of people, many of whom will bring new inspiration with them directly from the spiritual world.

At the very least, we should be aware of the possibility that Anthroposophy will begin to appear in many different forms, and perhaps in the most unlikely places. This does not mean that the present form of Anthroposophy and the Anthroposophical Society should be abandoned. On the contrary, it is all the more necessary that there are groups of people who continue an earnest study of Rudolf Steiner's own books and lectures and continue scientific research, artistic work, etc. But if we are to remain within the dynamic, living flow of spiritual life—the *stream* of Anthroposophy—then we must be alive and alert to what is happening now. As the poet Osip Mandelstam said: 'You're awake! Don't be afraid of your own time, don't be sly.'[17]

SG

Part One

THE FUTURE
OF ANTHROPOSOPHY

1. The End of the Century and the Tasks of the Anthroposophical Society

Sergei O. Prokofieff

As humanity approaches the end of the twentieth century, the question of the 'culmination' of the anthroposophical movement—of which Rudolf Steiner spoke on several occasions in the karma lectures of 1924—is becoming ever more pressing in anthroposophical circles.

However, if one considers this question more carefully it becomes apparent that Rudolf Steiner made the very possibility of this prophecy being fulfilled dependent on the fulfilment of one quite definite condition, which in a lecture of 18 July 1924 he formulated as follows: 'But as everything today depends on free will, this too ... depends on whether the Anthroposophical Society understands how to cultivate Anthroposophy with the right devotion.'[1]

There is, however, a serious problem connected with this condition: can it be said that the Anthroposophical Society has over the course of the twentieth century really cultivated Anthroposophy 'with the right devotion', by which is also meant cultivating the esoteric impulse of the Christmas Conference? Much of what has occurred in its history would indicate that this has not been the case, thus giving cause for highly pessimistic conclusions which, it would seem, are increasingly supported today by real facts: the generally regressive situation of the anthroposophical movement in the world and the deepening crisis in the Anthroposophical Society itself. Thus among anthroposophists the opinion is increasingly widespread that the numerous conflicts, omissions and mistakes that have marked the course of the Anthroposophical Society since the death of its founder testify to the fact that the main condition for the culmination at the end of the century has not been fulfilled, and that it will, most likely, simply not happen.

On the other hand, an opposite opinion is also met with among anthroposophists. According to this, the promised culmination will happen in any case: either as a result of further revelations from the spiritual world or through the great teacher's return to the earth.

However, there are serious objections which can be expressed to such an opinion. Is it possible to imagine that the spiritual world will give human beings access to the next stage of development simply because they have apparently not been able to cope with the previous one? Or can it be supposed that the great teacher will come again* and will begin to speak to people when they have clearly been unable—and in some cases did not want—to accomplish what he spoke about before, when they have failed to pay sufficiently serious heed to his warnings and, most importantly, have not managed to a significant degree to fulfil the spiritual and social tasks placed before the Anthroposophical Society? In other words, is it possible to agree with the thought that Rudolf Steiner will accomplish for us what he entrusted *us* with and which has from the outset been *our* own task?

Finally, there are also anthroposophists who consider that

---

* Here it is necessary to distinguish between a physical incarnation of the teacher, that is, a fact depending solely upon him himself and the laws of the spiritual world to which he conforms, and the possibility of his *outward appearance* to other people, which is dependent in the first instance upon their fulfilment of certain conditions, some of which will be addressed in what follows.

it is necessary to try artificially to hasten the coming of the predicted culmination, for example, through the development of intense outer activity, making use of the Internet and other modern means of communication in order that Anthroposophy might spread as rapidly and widely as possible throughout the world. Inasmuch as Rudolf Steiner, in one of his lectures, associated the culmination of Anthroposophy at the end of the century with the attainment of 'the greatest possible extension of the anthroposophical movement',[2] such an approach to the problem is imagined to be fully justified as far as the representatives of this point of view are concerned.

However, this opinion too turns out, on closer examination, to be completely untenable. For if one is standing for a truly anthroposophical point of view, it is hardly possible to say with any seriousness that the culmination of the anthroposophical movement can be attained by any kind of *outward* means without a corresponding strengthening of spiritual work within the Anthroposophical Society, work that is directed above all towards the fulfilment of its true esoteric tasks.

Does it follow from all this that only the pessimistic answer to the original question is correct? Or is the situation that has arisen not hopeless, and can a way out of it be found? There is indeed a solution, and, I am convinced, only one. But when a real experience of work within the Anthroposophical Society shows the path towards it, despite its obviousness it often turns out to be far from simple and is sometimes associated with almost insuperable difficulties.

In order truly to understand the nature of the problem that arises here, it is necessary to be aware that the prophecy about the culmination of the anthroposophical movement at the end of the century was made by Rudolf Steiner in a quite particular context. Indeed, it forms a kind of climax to what he imparted out of his spiritual-scientific research about the karma of the Anthroposophical Society, which in its turn represents the focal point of the entire cycle of 82 lectures on karma research.

This cycle, which contains the deepest revelations from the realm of karma, was actually begun by Rudolf Steiner in the evening lectures of the Christmas Conference and is therefore inseparable from its spiritual content. Rudolf Steiner himself referred to this relationship in the following words: 'Indeed, through everything that it has become possible to give to the Anthroposophical Society since the time of the Christmas Conference, through the various ways in which I have since that time been permitted to work occultly, it is not so much [that] new facts [have arisen] ... but what has now been added to them is that the demons who have not allowed these things to be uttered before had to be silent.'[3]

What was it that forced silence upon these Ahrimanic demons who had not allowed Rudolf Steiner to speak openly about the theme of karma during the previous three seven-year periods? This was the activity of that *Spirit* who fully revealed himself for the first time at the Christmas Conference and then pervaded the entire anthroposophical movement.

In his lectures of 1924 Rudolf Steiner more often than not referred to this Spirit as an 'esoteric impulse'.[4] However, whenever there were the necessary foundations for this, he would speak directly about this Spirit of the Christmas Conference, thus referring to the esoteric nature of this conference as a Whitsun mystery renewed out of the Michaelic Spirit of the Age.

At the Christmas Conference itself Rudolf Steiner bore witness to the appearance of this Spirit—and also defined the most important task of all members of the newly founded Anthroposophical Society arising out of this fact—in these words: 'Then you will ... bear that Spirit who holds sway in the radiant light of thought around the dodecahedral Stone of Love out into the world, where he shall shed light and warmth for the advancement of human souls, for the advancement of the world'.[5] And when, after the Christmas Conference, Rudolf Steiner was looking back and at the same time showing the Anthroposophical Society a path whereby it might take a step forwards, he again touched upon this central task, calling upon all anthroposophists to do everything they could to enable 'the Spirit whom we tried to summon there [at the Christmas Conference] to be always here, through the good will, devotion and deep understanding of the members [of the Society] for Anthroposophy and for anthroposophical life.'[6]

Turning to the mystery of the origin of this Spirit, Rudolf Steiner pointed to the connection of the Christmas Conference with the destruction by fire of the first Goetheanum, which, as a result of this tragedy, from being 'an earthly concern' became 'a concern of the expanses of the etheric world in which the Spirit lives'.[7] With these words Rudolf Steiner was revealing the mystery of the origin of this Spirit, who 'holds sway in the radiant light of thought around the dodecahedral Stone of Love',[8] in that same etheric world where the Mystery of the Second Coming is now taking place.

Moreover, in the same lecture Rudolf Steiner also referred to the connection of the being Anthroposophia with this etheric sphere. For after the fire 'the concern of the Goetheanum became the concern of the expanses of the ether, where dwells a *Spirit-filled wisdom of the world*'. (Emphasis S.P.) This living 'wisdom of the world', which has been brought to the earth by Rudolf Steiner, is Anthroposophy. And the Spirit who was united with it from the beginning in the etheric world, and who appeared for the first time at the Christmas Conference, has since that time—as a new 'esoteric impulse'—also directly pervaded all its earthly revelations.

Hence it follows that all the karma studies of 1924, with their culmination in the revelation of the mystery of the karma of the Anthroposophical Society itself,* are the direct result of the esoteric impulse of the Christmas Conference. This means that the fulfilment of the prophecy about the end of the century which they contain depends upon the implementation by members of the Society of the spiritual and social tasks placed before them by the Christmas Conference.

Thus the main condition referred to earlier for the coming about of the culmination of the anthroposophical movement, consisting as it does in the need to 'cultivate Anthroposophy with the right devotion', implies above all a cultivation of the spiritual impulse of the Christmas Conference, without which that process of development which was permitted by the spiritual world—and which in turn responded to Rudolf Steiner's sacrificial deed by an even greater stream of revelations, including all the karma lectures—would have been impossible.

Thus the following words of Rudolf Steiner, which serve as an inducement that every effort be made to enable the spiritual impulse of the Christmas Conference to 'enter really deep, deep into the heart, into the soul, into the very conscience' of every anthroposophist and thereby to be preserved for the evolution of the earth, sound forth as a warning call: 'We want to work together with the Spirit who was called to mind at the Christmas Conference in such a way that the impulse that was active at this Christmas Conference among anthroposophists who try rightly to comprehend the

---

* In the lectures devoted to this theme, one is struck by the highly significant fact that Rudolf Steiner again and again spoke in this connection not so much about the karma of the anthroposophical movement as about the karma of the Anthroposophical Society.

conditions of anthroposophical life may *never* cease, ... that this Dornach conference, through what anthroposophists make of it everywhere in the world, may indeed *never* cease.'[9] (Emphasis S.P.) Especially this repetition of the word 'never' makes it clear that what is being spoken of here is one of the most important and most essential conditions for the further existence of Anthroposophy on earth.

If the impulse of the Christmas Conference is not to cease working, it is above all necessary to surmount the central challenge arising out of it (for only if this is achieved will it be possible to take on all the other tasks), namely, that as many members of the General Anthroposophical Society as possible might lay its Foundation Stone in their etheric hearts as the spiritual foundation of a new community of Michael-ites and servants of the living being Anthroposophia.

'Then you will be able to establish here a true community of human beings for Anthroposophia'[10]—with these words Rudolf Steiner was referring to that highly significant fact that the General Anthroposophical Society was founded not only for human beings but also for that *spiritual being* of whom he had already spoken on more than one occasion, most notably in lectures given prior to the Christmas Conference in 1923.[11]

This can shed new light upon a further important task of the Anthroposophical Society, which Rudolf Steiner formulated at the Christmas Conference as follows: 'We must be absolutely clear about the fact that our Society in par-ticular will be allotted the task of combining the greatest conceivable openness with true, genuine esotericism.'[12] This is a challenge which, he said, anthroposophists can respond to only in their hearts ('it is in our hearts that this fundamental problem will have to be solved'), that is, where they have previously laid the Foundation Stone that was formed at the Christmas Conference.

Hence the laying of the Foundation Stone in the hearts of the members is not only the esoteric foundation for the right development of the Anthroposophical Society as a whole but also a guarantee that its fundamental task of combining complete openness (exotericism) with the development of a new social esotericism will be fulfilled.* The fact that the Anthroposophical Society and the anthroposophical movement were united at the Christmas Conference—which gave an opportunity for each member of the Society subsequently to take a conscious part in this process—was to serve as the main prerequisite for the fulfilment of this task. For the Foundation Stone was formed by Rudolf Steiner out of the very substance of the anthroposophical movement, and so its laying in the hearts of anthroposophists, as the Foundation Stone of the Anthroposophical Society, is a guarantee of the connection of the latter with the anthroposophical movement.

The same can be said about the culmination of Anthroposophy at the end of the century. It can come about only if a sufficient number of members of the Anthroposophical Society are able to lay the Foundation Stone in their hearts and then manage to keep it there through intensive inner work upon it with the help of the Foundation Stone Meditation. In other words, only by ceaselessly cultivating it will the Anthroposophical Society be able to maintain its connection with the anthroposophical movement, without which the culmination at the end of the century cannot be achieved.

It follows from this that standing firmly upon the ground of

---

* Here it should be emphasized that, in this context, when he spoke of esotericism Rudolf Steiner had in mind not the School of Spiritual Science, whose First Class was opened by him one and a half months after the Christmas Conference (the first lesson was given on 15 February 1924), but the particular esotericism of the Anthroposophical Society itself (see below).

the Foundation Stone is the *main condition* for the coming about of the culmination of the anthroposophical movement at the end of the century (or at a later time); and if this condition is not fulfilled all outward measures will inevitably be doomed to failure. For we must not forget that the Foundation Stone is really the *esoteric foundation* of the Anthroposophical Society, which without this foundation is merely an outer form which no 'constitution' or statutes, even the most ideal, will be able to fill with content, inasmuch as without the Foundation Stone the Anthroposophical Society simply has no future in an esoteric sense.

On the other hand, intensive inner work with the Foundation Stone can bring about such an intimate connection with the spiritual world within the soul that, under the spiritual world's leadership, it will then be able to view in their true light, and with time solve, all earthly problems, including the 'constitutional' question, but to do this not as invariably happens in the world but in accordance with its knowledge of the Spirit, that is, truly anthroposophically.

It follows from the content of the Christmas Conference that the Foundation Stone, as its inner focus, was formed by Rudolf Steiner in the *etheric* world nearest to the earth. Hence it is a reality not only for the human beings who have laid it in their hearts but also for all the souls in the spiritual world who are connected with the Michael stream and, in addition, for the beings of the higher hierarchies. When, therefore, one is speaking of the meeting on earth of the Aristotelians and Platonists, as the *second* necessary condition for the culmination of Anthroposophy at the end of the century, one needs to be clearly conscious that the spiritual place of their meeting will be the Foundation Stone which has been created *for this*. For it contains within itself essential elements corresponding both to the inner orientation of the Aristotelians and to the inner orientation of the Platonists, and also an all-embracing central element capable of uniting both streams on an esoteric level and, hence, of creating the necessary precondition for their working together, which is to say, for the subsequent culmination of the Michael stream on earth.

Thus the *light of thought* surrounding the Foundation Stone, consisting of universal and human thoughts, is indicative of the essence of the spiritual task of the Aristotelians: forging a path for mankind from human to cosmic thinking, to the universal thoughts of the hierarchies. While the *imaginative form* of the Foundation Stone, consisting of universal and human imaginations, represents the essence of the spiritual aspirations of the Platonists, who have the task of blazing humanity's path from human to the universal imaginations in which the beings of the higher hierarchies live and work.

Both these streams, which are associated respectively with the light of universal thoughts and with the figurative quality of universal imaginations, are harmoniously united in the *substance* of the Foundation Stone, consisting of universal and human *love*. In the twofold character of this substance there lies the path of inner development through which man can gradually rise from human to universal love. In this universal love which Christ brought to the earth by uniting it with the whole of earthly evolution through the Mystery of Golgotha,[13] we have a higher power which is capable of uniting all opposites on both the spiritual and the social plane. 'For where two or three are gathered in my name, there am I in the midst of them.' (Matthew 18:20) 'Name' in this context represents the principle of the ego, in which all the wisdom of world evolution hitherto (that is, both the light of thinking and the figurative quality of imaginations) must be transformed into the purest love,[14] of which the substance of the Foundation Stone consists.

Thus if a person lays the Foundation Stone in his heart he can in our time be led directly to a personal encounter with the etheric Christ in the supersensible world nearest to the earthly world. The *whole* of spiritual science serves this aim. But it found its most concrete and concentrated expression in the spiritual being of the Foundation Stone. 'Christ will be revealed to those people who through spiritual science have been able to rise to an understanding, to a vision of the true Second Coming of Christ.'[15] In these words Rudolf Steiner directs our attention to the two elements (the Aristotelian and the Platonic) of the new appearance of Christ: *understanding* him through the light of a spiritualized thinking, and *beholding* him through developing the capacity for consciously perceiving imaginations.

An understanding of the Second Coming is contained in the being of the Foundation Stone through the fact that its three elements correspond precisely to the three main aspects of the appearance of the etheric Christ. From our time onwards, he—as the Divine Bearer of the *substance of love*—reveals himself to humanity in the *imaginative form* which is perceptible by the new conscious clairvoyance, and which is surrounded by the radiant aura of the *light of thinking*, consisting as it does of all the spiritualized thoughts of human beings, with the help of which they try on earth to comprehend the Being of Christ[16] as he approaches man in a new imaginative form, in the surrounding radiant aura of spiritual light.[17]

As regards the next stage, which consists in a direct beholding of the etheric Christ, its attainment is possible today in that, through his inner work with the Foundation Stone, man is entering consciously upon the path described above, which leads from human to cosmic thoughts, from human to universal imaginations, from human to universal love. Then the twofold nature of the Foundation Stone—

which was formed at the Christmas Conference as a twofold dodecahedron, at once universal and human—comes into effect.

We can understand the esoteric significance of this duality only by taking into consideration the results of the spiritual-scientific research shared by Rudolf Steiner in his lecture on 'The Etherisation of the Blood'.[18] In this he spoke at some length of how since the Mystery of Golgotha there has flowed in *every* human being—alongside the *microcosmic* stream of etherized human blood flowing from the heart to the head—a second, *macrocosmic* stream flowing in the same direction: the stream of the etherized blood of Christ himself. 'A union of these two streams can, however, come about only if a person is able to unfold a true *understanding* of what is contained in the Christ Impulse.'[19] (Emphasis S.P.) A union of these etheric streams is necessary because it alone can lead man to a conscious perceiving of Christ in the spiritual world. Hence the Foundation Stone, which is laid in man's *etheric* heart, that is, where the source of *both* streams—the cosmic Christ stream and the human stream—is to be found, must necessarily have a twofold macro-microcosmic nature. Only because of this can it serve as a bridge or connecting link in the human heart between the two streams which have been described and then become a new heart-organ of perception, opening the way to a direct contemplation of the etheric Christ.

Here the *social nature* of the Foundation Stone is manifested in full measure. True, its laying in the etheric heart can take place only as a result of an individually attained understanding of the esoteric nature of the Christmas Conference and of a free decision taken on this foundation. However, in the human heart it then becomes the Foundation Stone *for a new social community of human beings*. This community is of such a kind that, while remaining wholly within modern civilization, where the Ahrimanic 'prince of this world' reigns, it nevertheless has its source and foundation (community-forming principle) in something originating not from this world but directly from the kingdom of the etheric Christ.

Christ's familiar words, 'My kingdom is not of this world' (John 18:36), here acquire their original meaning. In one of his lectures Rudolf Steiner explained them by saying that Christ came to the earth—where the unlawful 'prince of this world' rules—precisely in order to establish here *his kingdom* squarely within modern civilization, thus offering all people the opportunity in future times of becoming participants within it.[20] These words of Christ may find fulfilment for the first time since apostolic times in the community of anthroposophists, where there is an endeavour to build their entire social life upon the Foundation Stone as an inexhaustible source of *social resurrection-forces*.

Because of this, no forces of opposition are able to approach a community of people who are basing their social life upon *this* foundation. This means that such a community has the possibility—despite all obstacles and temptations—of fulfilling its mission in the modern world and thereby becoming an archetype and guiding star for it in the search for new relationships of both an exoteric and esoteric nature. Such a human community will with justice see its field of activity as lying *within* modern, exoteric civilization, while the source of its esoteric being will be in the resurrection-forces flowing into it from the individual spiritual work of its members with the Foundation Stone and with its meditation, the focus of all its socially-formative forces.

Thus we can experience the spiritual essence of the Foundation Stone on three levels or in three different spheres, in each case not in the aspect of the past but in the aspect of the present and future.* This is possible because the Foundation Stone itself was formed by Rudolf Steiner not out of the stream of outer, historical time but out of the stream of *occult* time which brings the forces and impulses of the future from the higher worlds into the earthly present.†

To summarize all that has been said, one can say: the Foundation Stone of the Christmas Conference is, in truth, the gateway to the temple of the new Mysteries, where, from the end of the twentieth century onwards, three things must take place: firstly, the finding of the path leading to a beholding of the etheric Christ, secondly, the creation of the conditions for the uniting of the Platonists and the Aristotelians, and, thirdly, establishing the beginning of a new Christian community upon which mankind will be able to orientate itself in future.

But there is very little time left for us to carry out these

---

* In this sense there is absolutely no ground for the opinion that everything connected with the Christmas Conference relates only to the past and that those anthroposophists who are trying to reveal its essential spiritual nature are, as it is claimed, wanting to direct the attention of members of the Anthroposophical Society merely to an event which took place over 70 years ago and thus draw them away from solving more pertinent problems. Indeed, such a way of looking at things is none other than a contemporary manifestation of nominalism in our circles. For reasoning in this way is like saying that the Mystery of Golgotha itself has now lost its relevance, inasmuch as it took place on earth nearly two thousand years ago. However, just as the Mystery of Golgotha was and will be for all ages to come the spiritual focus of earthly evolution, so the Christmas Conference *in its esoteric essence* was and will be the spiritual focus of the development on earth both of the anthroposophical movement and of the Anthroposophical Society, provided that the latter wants to maintain its connection with this spiritual source not in words alone but in reality.
† Rudolf Steiner spoke in a lecture of 4 June 1924 (in R. Steiner *The Festivals and their Meaning*) about this occult (spiritual) time which was brought to the earth by Christ and—through the Mystery of Golgotha— united with earthly evolution as a whole.

tasks! For we are already in real earnest approaching that epoch when no earthly community which does not have its foundation in the kingdom of Christ which is not of this world will be able to withstand the ever intensifying onslaught of opposing forces in modern civilization. This onslaught will reach its apogee very shortly indeed, when Ahriman himself, who is to incarnate on earth at the beginning of the next millennium, will enter the world through the breach made by the forces of evil in 1998.[21]

The Anthroposophical Society will be able to withstand Ahriman and his numerous servants within modern civilization only if the Foundation Stone of the Christmas Conference not merely becomes a reality in the souls of its members but also forms the inner centre and focus of all their individual and social activity. For in the very near future the spiritual destiny of the Anthroposophical Society will depend on whether its members have, at long last, managed to begin creating on this foundation a *social house for Anthroposophia*, that is, begin the construction of that supersensible 'building' or spiritual Goetheanum of which Rudolf Steiner spoke at the very end of the Christmas Conference: 'We have here laid the Foundation Stone. On this Foundation Stone shall be erected the *building* whose individual stones will be the work achieved in all our groups by individual [members] out in the wide world.'[22] (Emphasis S.P.)

In this way the foundation will be laid of that future 'temple of mankind' which has for centuries been regarded as the highest ideal in all streams of esoteric Christianity, and above all in the circles of true Rosicrucians.[23] From it the 'Light Divine, Christ-Sun' shall shine forth to humanity into our epoch of the Second Coming. Then this Sun Temple dedicated to the higher powers of our cosmos will become a place to which Ahriman and his hosts will not have access.

This aspiration towards the gradual transformation of the Anthroposophical Society under the influence of the impulse of the Christmas Conference into a 'living seed' of the future temple of mankind is invisibly present behind the many words with which Rudolf Steiner again and again, and from very different aspects, characterized the spiritual-social tasks of the Society. Thus in a lecture of 28 January 1924—directly addressing the heart of each anthroposophist who wants to remain faithful to this central impulse of the anthroposophical movement—he spoke as follows: 'At the same time I want to appeal to every member of the Anthroposophical Society to help to ensure that this Christmas Meeting lays the Foundation Stone of anthroposophical life in the hearts of our members and that it does not cease to develop as a living seed, so that active life may constantly increase in the Anthroposophical Society. If that happens, the Anthroposophical Society will also be able to send its impulse out into the world.'[24]

In these words it is possible to sense again today the spiritual promise of the great teacher, as he appealed to all his pupils and at the same time indicated to them the actual path leading to the culmination of Anthroposophy at the end of the century. In order to embark upon this path, we must first devote ourselves to the esoteric essence of the Christmas Conference and lay in our hearts 'the spiritual Foundation Stone for the Anthroposophical Society',[25] and then, on this foundation, develop in the Society a spiritual life which will eventually become so strong that it will be able to radiate beyond its bounds into the outer world.

If we become truly conscious of the full significance of this spiritual promise of our teacher and today—after the passing of a full cycle of a human life (72 years) since the time of the spiritual founding of the Anthroposophical Society and the laying of its Foundation Stone—turn with all the powers of our soul to the Christmas Conference, as the central 'mystical fact' of its history, the real perspectives of the further development on earth of the Michael impulse will open up before us. For as we have seen, only the Christmas Conference opened the gates for a full flowing of this impulse out into humanity as a whole, through the revelation of the Michael Mysteries in the karma lectures and leading thoughts[26] and also in the founding of the Michael School on earth.

It follows from everything that Rudolf Steiner said about the Christmas Conference that Michael is that hierarchic Spirit who, at the behest of still higher beings of the spiritual world, granted his approval of Rudolf Steiner's deed at the Christmas Conference, an approval which was therefore also extended to that path which the Anthroposophical Society must henceforth follow. And Rudolf Steiner himself was the first who consistently and unswervingly followed this path, thus manifesting to all his pupils a living example of what service to Michael means in our time and of what the spiritual world associated with Michael expects from us. 'What matters now is that the Anthroposophical Society shall take up this, its inner task—a task which consists in not calling in question Michael's rulership of human thinking [which also means not entering into opposition against Michael's intentions as they have been expressed through the Christmas Conference and its consequences]. It is not a question of being fatalistic here. The point is simply that human beings must work together with the Gods, with Michael himself.'[27]

At the Christmas Conference itself, Rudolf Steiner gave a direct indication of this when he called upon all members of the newly founded Anthroposophical Society to carry the following in their consciousness: 'The spiritual world wants [to begin] something with mankind at this particular moment in historical evolution, it wants [to begin] this in the most varied realms of life [the various sections of the Michael School subsequently arose out of this impulse]; and it is up to us to follow these impulses from the spiritual world in full clarity and truth. Even though there might be opposition to start with, in the long run this is the only beneficial [direction]. Therefore we shall cope with our inner problems only if at every opportunity we steep ourselves in whatever impulses can come out of the spiritual world.'*[28]

It follows from these words that only a real understanding of the spiritual tasks originating from our new association with Michael, which arose through the Christmas Conference, and also solid work on their implementation can create the conditions for the spiritual world to continue its leadership of the anthroposophical movement on earth. Naturally, the difficulties which will emerge on this path will be great. For the opposing forces will spare no pains to prevent the further development of this new association between the Gods and human beings, between Michael and the Michaelites. Rudolf Steiner himself emphasized this as follows: 'However, with this [the esoteric consequences of the Christmas Conference] is also connected the fact—and I am looking from the spiritual aspect—that very powerful opposing powers, demonic powers, will unleash an onslaught against the anthroposophical movement. But it is to be greatly hoped that the forces deriving from the bond with good spiritual powers, which we have been allowed to establish through the Christmas Conference,

---

* Immediately after these words Rudolf Steiner gave the first rhythm of the Christmas Conference, prefacing it by reading the three microcosmic parts of the Foundation Stone Meditation, which he characterized as words spoken here 'in accordance with the will of the spiritual world' (26 December 1923).

will be able in future to drive from the field all those hostile powers in the spiritual domain who make use of human beings on earth to achieve their objectives.'[29] In other words, we shall only be able to withstand all the attacks of the anti-Michaelic powers, which will without doubt significantly increase in the immediate future, by doing all we can to preserve and strengthen that bond with Michael and the spirits who serve him which was forged at the Christmas Conference.

And inasmuch as we are living in the epoch of freedom, the very possibility of preserving this bond will, in the first instance, depend on the extent to which we ourselves can come to realize both the full seriousness of the situation in which we find ourselves today and our personal *responsibility*, as anthroposophists, before mankind and the spiritual world, a responsibility which was spoken of in such forceful words in the last lecture of the Christmas Conference.

In this concluding lecture Rudolf Steiner finally unfolded the entire spiritual-historical significance of this Conference, which in its esoteric essence is none other than a *call* of the Guardian of the Threshold to contemporary humanity, a call which must, for the good of earthly evolution, be heard by the group of human beings—however small they may be—who have prepared and joined together for this in the Anthroposophical Society.* It was, therefore, to them that Rudolf

---

* In the introductory lecture of the Christmas Conference Rudolf Steiner referred to how the anthroposophical movement originated 'not from any arbitrary earthly consideration but in obedience to a call resounding from the spiritual world' (24 December 1923). Rudolf Steiner followed this call over the course of 21 years by developing Anthroposophy on earth. However, he revealed the mystery of its origin to the members of the Anthroposophical Society only in the concluding lecture of the Christmas Conference, in order that, by consciously hearing this call, they might embark upon the path which he had himself followed.

Steiner addressed the words with which the spiritual world itself now appealed to them: 'But to those souls who are the souls of anthroposophists it shall be said: Your remaining test is to be that of your courage to bear witness to that voice [from the land of the spirit] which you are capable of hearing because of the inclination of your souls, because of the inclination of your hearts.'[30] For an anthroposophist today needs 'only *one* particular exhortation: In hearing the voice from the land of the spirit you must develop the strong courage to bear witness to this voice, for you have begun to awaken. Courage will keep you awake; lack of courage alone could lead you to fall asleep.'[31]

Do we have the courage to 'bear witness' at the threshold of the new millennium to this call of the Guardian of the Threshold, this voice from the land of the spirit sounding to us from the entire esoteric essence of the Christmas Conference, in order with its help to maintain an inner wakefulness in our destiny-laden time? Do we really want to follow Rudolf Steiner on the path which he opened up to us at the Christmas Conference, in order to become the living witnesses and collaborators of our teacher in bringing about what he himself, viewing the esoteric significance of the Christmas Conference as a whole, called 'the beginning of a world turning-point of time'?

Upon the answer to this question—though not a theoretical answer but one that leads a person to actually laying the Foundation Stone in his heart, thereby transmuting it into a fearless and true guardian of that spiritual treasure entrusted to it by Rudolf Steiner[32]—depends not merely the future of the Anthroposophical Society but also something immeasurably more.

For, if at the end of this century our answer to the call of the Guardian of the Threshold is positive, that is, full of inner strength and a real will for work and service,* this will become the first step towards fulfilling the 'Michael prophecy', with which the destiny of earthly civilization in its entirety is connected.[33] 'If it is possible to work in this way, in the way predestined by Michael, then Europe and modern civilization will emerge from decline. But in no other way than this!'[34]

---

* This work and service also includes active participation in the activity of the School of Spiritual Science (the Michael School), whose content derives directly from that region of the threshold of the spiritual world which was spoken of in the last lecture of the Christmas Conference. Thus the basic demand, placed upon every member of the esoteric School, of being a true representative of the anthroposophical cause (GA 260a, 30 January 1924), means at the same time being a representative in the world of the esoteric impulse of the Christmas Conference.

2. The Global Social Situation at the End of the Twentieth Century

The Emergence of a Threefold Global Society and the Future Tasks of the Michaelic Movement

Jesaiah Ben-Aharon

Viewed from the distance of the moon, the astonishing thing about the earth, catching the breath, is that it is alive. The photographs show the dry, pounded surface of the moon in the foreground, dead as an old bone. Aloft, floating free beneath the moist, gleaming membrane of bright blue sky, is the rising earth, the only exuberant thing in this part of the cosmos. If you could look long enough, you would see the swirling of the great drifts of white cloud, covering and uncovering the half-hidden masses of land. If you had been looking for a very long, geologic time, you could have seen the continents themselves in motion, drifting apart on their crustal plates, held afloat by the fire beneath. It has the organized, self-contained look of a live creature, full of information, marvelously skilled in handling the sun.

Lewis Thomas[1]

The global situation at the end of the twentieth century clearly shows how the one-sided *economic* development of the West/North has predominated for more than a hundred years over basic political and civil human needs and values in the West itself and the world as a whole.

The tendency of modern economic development to predominate over the basic needs of society is inherent in its historical momentum, i.e. in its increasing emancipation from the physiocratic, theocratic and class-binding social forces which held it in check until the eighteenth/nineteenth centuries. This emancipation is, however, not incidental or wrong in itself; it is a necessary and fully justified development if looked at from the perspective of the general emancipation and individuation of human consciousness over the course of time. As such, it is a part of the driving force that leads the independent human soul towards a fuller understanding and utilization of the forces and materials of the physical world.

This development is, of course, not without its dangers. But can we ask for major new developments in human evolution and yet wish to be spared their possible aberrations and risks? Apparently not, and in the case of the maturing world economy today, the aberrations and risks are obvious.

For example, the influence of a global economy on the ecological system of the planet has been thoroughly studied:

> The global output of goods and services grew from just under $5 trillion in 1950 to more than $29 trillion in 1997, an expansion of nearly sixfold. From 1990 to 1997, it grew by $5 trillion—matching the growth from the beginning of civilization to 1950...
>
> As the economy grows, pressures on the Earth's natural systems and resources intensify. From 1950 to 1997, the use of lumber tripled, that of paper increased sixfold, the fish catch increased nearly fivefold, grain consumption nearly tripled, fossil fuel burning nearly quadrupled, and air and water pollutants multiplied severalfold. The unfortunate reality is that the economy continues to expand, but the ecosystem on which it depends does not, creating an increasingly stressed relationship.
>
> While economic indicators such as investment, production, and trade are consistently positive, the key environmental

indicators are increasingly negative. Forests are shrinking, water tables are falling, soils are eroding, wetlands are disappearing, fisheries are collapsing, range lands are deteriorating, rivers are running dry, temperatures are rising, coral reefs are dying, and plant and animal species are disappearing.

'Growth for the sake of growth', notes environmental writer Edward Abbey, 'is the ideology of the cancer cell. Just as a continuously growing cancer eventually destroys its life-support systems by destroying its host, a continuously expanding global economy is slowly destroying its host—the Earth's ecosystem.'[2]

The influence of a global economy on the global economic situation, especially the growing polarization in most economic parameters between poor regions, nations and populations, and the rich ones, is alarming:

Globalization offers great opportunities—but only if it is managed more carefully and with more concern for global equity.

Proceeding at breakneck speed but without map or compass, globalization has helped reduce poverty in some of the largest and strongest economies—China, India and some of the Asian tigers. But it has also produced losers among and within countries. As trade and foreign investment have expanded, the developing world has seen a widening gap between winners and losers. Meanwhile, many industrial countries have watched unemployment soar to levels not recorded since the 1930s, and income inequality reach levels not recorded since the last century.

The ratio of global trade to GDP has been rising over the past decade, but it has been falling for 44 developing countries, with more than a billion people. The least developed countries, with 10% of the world's people, have only 0.3% of world trade—half their share of two decades ago.

—More than half of all developing countries have been bypassed by foreign direct investment, two-thirds of which has gone to only eight developing countries.
—The terms of trade for the least developed countries have declined a cumulative 50% over the past 25 years.

—Average tariffs on industrial imports from the least developed countries are 30% higher than the global exports in industrial nations.

The bottom line for poverty and incomes: The share of the poorest 20% of the world's people in global income now stands at a miserable 1.1%, down from 1.4% in 1991 and 2.3% in 1960. It continues to shrink. And the ratio of the income of the top 20% to that of the poorest 20% rose from 30 to 1 in 1960, to 61 to 1 in 1991—and to a startling new high of 78 to 1 in 1994.[3]

One paramount cause for the almost unlimited power of a global economy over environmental and social interests lies, undoubtedly, in the increased weakening of the realm of equity: the middle sphere of the social-human element, that must have its stronghold in the equity consciousness of human beings, and be implemented by the democratic institutions of the political state which provides law and security and guarantees human rights:

The most disturbing aspect of this global system is that the formidable power and mobility of global corporations are undermining the effectiveness of national governments to carry out essential policies on behalf of their people. Leaders of nation-states are losing much of the control over their own territory they once had ... Tax laws intended for another age, traditional ways to control capital flows and interest rates, full employment policies, and old approaches to resource development and environmental protection are becoming obsolete, unenforceable, or irrelevant ...

But no political ideology or economic theory has as yet evolved to take account of the tectonic shift that has occurred ... [T]he nation-state everywhere faces a crisis of redefinition without a practical ideology that confronts the realities of the emerging global order ... [A]s national economies become increasingly intertwined, nations are breaking up in many different ways, and no alternative community is yet on the horizon.[4]

But are Barnet and Cavanagh entirely right in assuming that 'no political ideology or economic theory has as yet evolved to take account of the tectonic shift that has occur-red' or that 'no alternative community is yet on the horizon'? Our contention is that they are right if they refer to the fact that no new political *ideology* or economic *theory* has arisen, but wrong if they don't notice that an 'alternative commu-nity' is, as a matter of social-historical fact, already emerging. This only means that our political-social and economic ideologies and theories are once again lagging behind a new and significant social evolution that has been occurring dur-ing the course of the twentieth century, producing a new social *reality*.

Civil society comes of age

This most recent social change is but another stage in a continuous process of social emancipation. Just as the new economic forces were emancipated, becoming self-conscious with the dawning of the age of imperialism, capitalism and scientific/industrial progress, and just as, after the French and American revolutions, a democratic state became the place in which human rights-consciousness awakened to self-consciousness, so now a third, new social force is beginning to become conscious of itself, beyond the economy and the state. This is the sector of the new civil society, in which forces of moral freedom and free responsibility for the earth, human rights and free culture are emerging.

The decline of the state and its power to protect the environment and human rights is, in itself, not reversible. Nor should we hope that it be—not in its traditional forms. Both human rights consciousness and the economy need a fresh infusion of forces from a new source, that can only be the moral-spiritual motivation of free human souls and spirits.

This means that the possibility for true social transformation lies in the spiritual revitalization of the first two social sectors by means of the new and younger forces of a *third sector*: the emerging global social sector of free civil initiative and action.

Only by means of free, independent moral-social responsibility and action, which strives to influence the handling of economic activity and to reawaken awareness of human rights, can a new relation be established between the equally justified needs of 'capitalism' and 'socialism'. The middle sector of law and human rights which is the true domain of the democratic state, and the economic sector which administers production, trade and consumption of goods— these can gradually be regained by the *whole* human individuality and by the interests of society as a *whole* only if mediated and permeated by the new third sector. A more mature and evolved tri-part social structure is emerging to replace the old, exhausted bi-part structure that cannot cope with the new dilemmas created by economic globalization, and environmental, human and cultural degradation.

This is the main difference between a tri-part concept of society and the traditional bi-part social concept. Yet aware though they are of the above-mentioned recent weakening of the state, most critics of globalization, when challenged to advance from criticism to truly new and creative social alternatives, merely come up—again—with yet more proposals for stronger state intervention, more or less in the established socialist or social-democratic political traditions of the past hundred years.

The historical paradox is obvious. While most socially active non-governmental organizations (NGOs) and individuals are representatives of a newly arising 'third sector' of society, i.e. civil society itself, many of them are not yet self-consciously cognizant of their own new social sector.

More often than not they still look back to the political sector, embodied in the state, as the answer to all difficulties. We have witnessed this repeatedly. When those activists are eventually elected they become part of the old bi-part social structure of economy-versus-state, and more often than not they realize that they are forced to repeat the same compromises and mistakes because they have no new, creative social solutions to the same unresolved old dichotomy, the struggle between 'capitalism' and 'socialism'.

Nevertheless, the third sector, or social member, *is* becoming increasingly influential, revealing itself through many NGOs and active individuals the world over, *precisely because* it represents the principle of freedom: free civil, social, moral/spiritual responsibility is manifesting as a new source of social initiative that must be distinguished from state/government and economy/business. The significance of this third social sector is also becoming better understood by social science which is beginning to recognize the existence of a third member of social life beside the economic and political:

> We understand 'civil society' as a sphere of social interaction between economy and state, composed above all of the intimate sphere ... the sphere of associations ... social movements, and forms of public communication. Modern civil society is created through forms of self-constitution and self-mobilization.[5]

This quotation expresses a growing readiness on the part of social science to acknowledge the existence of a 'threefoldness', a trilateral structure of 'division of labour' within the body social. And it is not only a theoretical change that is in process, for a real social change is occurring, as indicated above. The powerful impact of a more confident and self-conscious third sector, civil society, has already made a difference in central global economic and trade policy, especially in connection with the recent negotiations about a Multilateral Agreement on Investment. So powerful, in fact, was its impact that leading circles in the financial-political American establishment had to take its activity into account. In doing so they demonstrated their well-established historical and social alertness to emerging trends in the spiritual-cultural life of modern humanity. In their study and immediate efforts for co-optation of the emerging civil society and its organizations, they were absolutely up to date with current social affairs. They understood what they called a social-political 'power shift' of global proportions far ahead of most anthroposophists and—with the notable exception of the originators of the *Philippine Agenda 21* (discussed below)—of the General Anthroposophical Society itself.

The power shift

In an article with this title in *Foreign Affairs*,[6] Jessica Mathews, a leading senior fellow at the Council on Foreign Relations, wrote: 'The end of the cold war has brought ... [a] novel redistribution of power among states, market, and civil society.' NGOs, the driving powers of civil society,

> deliver more official development assistance than the entire UN system. In many countries they are delivering the services—in urban and rural community development, education, and health care—that faltering governments can no longer manage ... increasingly, the NGOs are able to push around even the largest governments.

Mathews points to the place and time in which she believes civil society, via its NGOs, irrevocably entered the power structure of global society. This happened at the Earth Summit in Rio de Janeiro in 1992:

NGOs set the original goal of negotiating an agreement to control greenhouse gases long before governments were ready to do so, proposed most of its structure and content, and lobbied and mobilized public pressure to force through a pact that virtually no one else thought possible when the talks began ... As a result, delegates completed the framework of a global climate accord in the blink of a diplomat's eye—16 months— over the opposition of the three energy superpowers, the United States, Russia, and Saudi Arabia. The Treaty entered into force in record time just two years later ... with potentially enormous implications for every economy.

An even more remarkably successful campaign of NGOs in the years 1996-8 led to the abolition, at least in their original and draconian form, of the largely secret dealings of the leading world financial institutions and corporations to achieve a Multilateral Agreement on Investment (MAI). This great battle took place far away from commercial as well as 'free' media, finding only very rare and belated public expression. Only by linking in to the vast Internet mobilization, in which hundreds of NGOs were actively cooperating and managing the campaign, could one gain an inkling of the enormity of the efforts, and counter-efforts, being undertaken.

The second major mouthpiece of the Anglo-American establishment, *Foreign Policy* magazine, dedicated a special study to the new phenomenon in its autumn 1998 number, under the title 'Global Impact—NGOs in the field'.[7] Its editor wrote:

Witness the 'victory' that NGOs recently achieved when they stymied efforts by the Organization for Economic Cooperation and Development, a group made up of the world's 29 major industrial countries, to draft the MAI, a treaty setting common standards for the treatment of foreign investment by host countries ... Hundreds of NGOs of all stripes, sizes, nationalities, and interests rallied against the MAI, using one of the most important drivers of globalization, the Internet, to derail an initiative designed to facilitate another of globalization's most powerful forces, foreign investment.

More positively, we read in *International Herald Tribune*:

> They [the NGOs] are called the third sector, alongside the state and private sector. They offer a new channel to introduce both social responsibility and a democratic approach where either government or commerce has always dominated ... [T]hey are an energetic force in the conduct of international relations and the spread of civil society across borders.

Here we see that what we described above, the growing awareness of a 'third perspective' on social questions, is gaining ground:

> There are things that need to be done that governments cannot do or will not do, and things that they should not do, but which the spontaneous but organized NGOs can achieve ... The NGOs have arisen to fill this gap. They both prevent great concentration of power and encourage the focus of power on specific problems.[8]

In her inaugural speech as chosen Carnegie Endowment President (Washington DC, 15 June 1997), Mathews gave concise expression to her worries that the 'power shift' in global affairs might weaken the Anglo-American establishment's hold on global power structures. She remarked that it is essential to 'understand what an NGO can do in this day and age, because that terrain, too, is shifting dramatically under our feet'.

The terrain is indeed shifting dramatically under our feet. Could we point to a similar awareness and readiness for action in the anthroposophical movement, if not in society at large? The fact that we can do so is thanks to many years of effort by Nicanor Perlas and his co-workers in the Philippines.[9]

Philippine Agenda 21

The following passage is taken from an interview with Nicanor Perlas conducted by the economist and writer David Korten (well-known author of the book *When Corporations Rule the World*) on 5 September 1996, one day after the successful completion of a major national NGO Conference which Perlas had convened with the co-sponsorship of six major NGO networks on 'Civil Society; Creative Responses to the Challenge of Globalization'. This passage shall serve as an introduction to the truly remarkable and for too long little known anthroposophical and civil career of Nicanor Perlas in the Philippines.

Korten: When I left the Philippines in 1992 you seemed totally focused on promoting sustainable agriculture. Your current focus on economic globalization seems quite a departure. What happened?

Perlas: It all started with my participation in a conference on biotechnology and sustainable agriculture held in Malaysia in July 1993. That is where I first learned about the General Agreement on Tariffs and Trade (GATT), including its provisions increasing the toxic residues allowable on food for human consumption to a level that would effectively wipe out the protections of the bans of use of toxic pesticides to which I had devoted 20 years of my life. There was also discussion of the GATT provisions on intellectual property rights that would tighten corporate control of the food system by creating farmer dependence on patented seeds.

I became so concerned that I spent much of the next year studying the agreement and exploring its various implications. Only once I had read the whole document did I begin to see its full implications. It would undermine the work of virtually every civil society group in the Philippines: the church, women, coops, fisherfolk, farmers, labor, everyone. The damage to our economy and social fabric could well be irreversible. In August 1994, I began a five-month effort to convince the Philippine Senate to reject the ratification of the GATT agreement. By 1995 I found myself with a few others at the center of the GATT debate in the Philippines.

This is the background, only a very partial aspect of it, that led to the civil struggle culminating in the above-mentioned conference in 1996 on 'Civil Society; Creative Responses to the Challenge of Globalization'. This conference actually sealed the human, civil and spiritual bonds that made Philippine Agenda 21 (PA 21) possible.

One way to approach PA 21 is to quote some of the words spoken by the former Philippine President Fidel V. Ramos in the speech he made on 26 September 1996 in which he announced the public launching of PA 21. All the quotations below are taken from *Philippine Agenda 21 Handbook*:[10]

> In my State of the Nation Address last 22 July 1996, I mentioned that we do not intend to 'grow now and clean up later'. But do not misunderstand me. Given the many demands of development, this 'cleaning up later' not only refers to the economy and the environment. It also means that we will clear up all other facets of Philippine life, including our policies and our culture.
>
> When I say 'we clean up' in terms of our culture, we intend, for example, to grow and develop with our spirituality and sterling Filipino values intact. *I do not want Filipinos to succumb to a materialistic consumerist lifestyle. I do not wish to see our world-renowned Filipino spirituality and social sensitivity being sacrificed at the altar of economic advancement.* (Emphasis added.)
>
> Cleaning up as we grow in the realm of culture to me means to harness Filipino creativity, values, talents and skills to create a new model of development, one that is not only democratic, environmentally friendly and cost-effective, but also celebrates the vibrancy of our diverse cultures as well as respects and develops the tremendous potential that resides in every one of us. This, after all, is what being *maka-Diyos, maka-tao, maka-kalikasan, and maka-bayan means in real terms.*

This is not the place to retell the most dramatic, courageous, and indeed, in the truest sense of this formulation, ground-breaking process, by means of which a strongly united front of the Philippine NGOs, expressing a vital and popular civil society, succeeded, under the leadership of Nicanor Perlas and his collaborators, in actually bringing a reluctant government and resisting business community to agree upon and then draft together the PA 21. But this highest policy document of the Philippine government, signed and approved by presidential decree, is not only *about* a threefold social order *concept*, but has arisen through an intense threefold social *process*, in which, for the first time in human history, representatives of the 'third sector', civil society, achieved an equal social standing at the table of negotiation with the government (polity) and business (the economic sector), thus bringing about a threefold reality already in the negotiation process. In the words of President Ramos:

> Economic growth, unleashed by capitalism, has also been accompanied by other forms, less desirable forms, of growth. The United Nations Development Program reminds us that, if we are not careful, economic growth can lead to jobless, ruthless, voiceless, rootless, and futureless growth...
>
> The growing awareness that *economic growth is a means, not an end in itself*, has influenced most of the countries of the world today to pine for 'another development', one that retains the useful features of capitalism without falling prey to its excesses. (Emphasis added.)
>
> Philippine Agenda 21 envisions a better quality of life for all through the development of a just, moral, creative, diverse yet cohesive society characterized by appropriate productivity, participatory and democratic processes, and living in harmony within the limits of the carrying capacity of nature and the integrity of creation.

On a number of occasions, President Ramos has made it clear that Philippine Agenda 21 is the highest document among the various policy frameworks and social plans. In Memorandum Order 399 he directs that

> All government agencies, departments and instrumentalities ... to adopt and translate the principles and action agenda contained in the Philippine Agenda 21 in their respective work plans, programs and projects and report of their progress and impacts ...

Most important is also the presidential declaration given on the eve of the international APEC Leaders Meeting. In his speech entitled 'APEC, Civil Society and Sustainable Development', Ramos assured an international civil society delegation that PA 21 governs the Philippine Individual Action Plan for Trade and Investment Liberalization and Facilitation in APEC.

Finally, in his speech 'PA 21: Towards Sustainable Development', the President said the following, which must be especially important for those oriented towards Anthroposophy to hear and understand:

> ... Philippine Agenda 21 is *one of the most consultative policy documents produced in the history of our nation* ... This is a document that the future leadership of our country must take to heart as expressing a basic ... deep mandate for sustainable development among the vast majority of Filipinos. (Emphasis added.)

(In the coming Gothenburg Conference we shall have the opportunity to hear from Nicanor Perlas on further developments in the Philippines under the presidency of Estrada, and the first practical steps now under way with the implementation process of PA 21 and the threefold social order in a chosen locality.)

The Manila Conference October 1998

As illustrations in the Manila Conference catalogue show, 'today 352 billionaires enjoy an income level equivalent to what 2.4 billions (2,400,000,000) of the most poor people of the world have.' And further: 'Of the largest 100 economies of the world, 51 are Transnational Companies (TNCs). These TNCs are economically larger, in terms of turnover, than over 140 countries of the world.' It is also stated that in various ways a couple of hundred TNCs control 70–80% of world trade.

TNCs like Monsanto, specializing in genetically manipulated plants, are developing serious attempts to gain control over agriculture, for example through seeds producing good harvests but lacking fertility, so that farmers will be forced to buy new seeds before sowing. These TNCs are striving for control over production and maintenance of the world's food supply.

TNCs are increasingly governing national states: The Multilateral Agreement on Investments (MAI) was designed to transfer the decision-making power from national states to international business life, which in the last resort means to the TNCs, in the interest of the Western Brotherhoods and their outlets in the Anglo-American establishment.

With such concerns in mind and heart, engaged anthroposophists met together for a conference in Tagaytay City, near Manila City, in October 1998. This conference, 'Shaping the Future: Globalization, Anthroposophy, and the Threefold Social Order', was organized and carried through by the dedicated and inspired friends of the Anthroposophical Group in the Philippines, supported by the National Anthroposophical Societies of the Asian-Pacific region (Australia, Canada, Hawaii, India, New Zealand, Taiwan, China, Thailand, Vietnam, USA).

The proceedings of this conference, with all the related materials, will be published later, and then an objective assessment, worthy of the true spiritual and social significance of the event, will be attempted. For the time being only preliminary elements are presented below, in order to invite readers to join in further discussion and participation in the ongoing international continuation of this important social anthroposophical impulse. In accordance with the evolving, life-giving and inspiring powers that lead the true Michael Movement and School, a future plan concerning its development is currently in work, leading to two more conferences, in Gothenburg, Sweden, at the end of 1999 and beginning of 2000, and in Cape Town, South Africa a year later.[11]

In the text above we have already covered much of the social world situation which provided the motivation for PA 21 and the 1998 conference in Manila. Especially pertinent for anthroposophists at the end of the twentieth century could be remarks concerning the state of the Anthroposophical Society itself when studied from this point of view. The invitation to the Manila Conference reads as follows in this respect:

> *Whither the global Anthroposophical Society in the age of elite globalization?* The global anthroposophical movement should be, theoretically, in the best position to facilitate a global appreciation and implementation of threefolding world-wide. After all, Rudolf Steiner, the founder of Anthroposophy, gave the first comprehensive articulation of the threefold social order. But what is the current situation?
>
> *Problematic lack of awareness and isolation.* Unfortunately, the vast majority of anthroposophists is barely aware of the reality of elite globalization. And to accentuate this lack of awareness, scholars and actors outside Anthroposophy not only have more understanding of the external aspects of threefolding and its necessity. They are also doing more to make threefolding,

especially through the liberation of civil society, the key actor in culture, into a global reality.

Because of this lack of awareness, there are few, if any, creative and concerted global strategies to address the problem of elite globalization. Furthermore, anthroposophists are missing out on the opportunity to form strategic alliances with friends outside the movement, an absolute necessity given the sophisticated networking and strategic mergers being rapidly built up by the spiritual powers and institutions behind elite globalization.

Thus the global anthroposophical movement stands at the end of the century: an important agent for utilizing globalization as a stepping stone for building a Michaelic civilization but isolated and bordering on ineffectivity.

In contrast, the proponents of elite globalization are alive, healthy and very active. In addition, they are continuously scheming for ways to magnify and project their power and control through various forms of alliances and networks.

Anthroposophists are in a key position to provide this stimulus. The different anthroposophical institutions can create the necessary cultural resurgence to transform the forces of elite globalization ...

The Need. There is therefore a need for the global anthroposophical movement to take stock of itself in the light of these urgent planetary developments. Then it has to explore ways by which it can develop a global vision of responding to the challenges of elite globalization and create operational strategies to turn this vision into reality.

This brings us to the next step, the continuation of this struggle to awaken anthroposophical awareness among our own circles in order to link with all those active and creative 'Michaelites' working in the world of emerging global civil society. However, in order to work with the expansion of awareness and action horizontally, to reach the world's social periphery, we need to deepen our roots in the centre of the living, now flowing Michael Inspiration, and learn to create the forms of social-esoteric work, of modern freedom in spiritual life, and of community of free striving human souls and spirits. As a next step, the Conference in Gothenburg would like to facilitate a first, humble, but also courageous opportunity in this direction.

Future tasks of a timely Anthroposophical Society and School of Spiritual Science

With the preparations now under way for a continuation of the Manila Conference in Gothenburg's Northern Conference in Sweden and Cape Town's Conference in South Africa,[12] both supported, as was the Manila Conference, by diverse national anthroposophical societies, it seems plausible to assume that some intimations of global change have recently begun to be registered also within the Anthroposophical Society, initially at the periphery. We believe that we have a chance to begin an essential exploration of fundamental anthroposophical questions and issues that might prove—provided it becomes a sincere and prolonged effort—to be a valuable contribution to the Michael Movement in the future.

This future movement has a twofold gesture, both parts of which should be put into practice simultaneously. On the one hand it must gather into itself as much as possible from the achievements of anthroposophists over the course of the twentieth century. On the other hand it must open the horizon to the future in order to support the instreaming new Michael Inspiration. The ability to do this depends on finding those anthroposophists who carry within them the fruits of the century's work, and who are truly seeking and open to the future impulse that is coming from the same sources out of which anthroposophical work started at the beginning of the century. Such people must consciously understand that everything achieved in this twentieth century was due to the original impulse given by Rudolf Steiner

himself in the course of his earthly life, and that we must be
aspiring today for an honest renewal of a direct connection
with the spiritual worlds out of which the same inspiration
and guidance has already been seeking us for a long time.
Will we have the courage to be available to this Michaelic
guiding power, or shall we continue to block its way to us by
ever and again quoting and repeating what this source gave
almost a whole century ago? Are we interested in exploring
what is really meant by Freedom of the Spirit, a community
of free human spirits and souls? Are we really ready to
understand that Michael and his true pupils can only work
with people aspiring to and practising free spiritual and
social activity?

What most anthroposophists seem to be unaware of is a
central spiritual-scientific fact of evolution, which must be
applied also to the Anthroposophical Society and the practical movements originating from Anthroposophy. We must
see that this 'horizontal' spiritual transmission of what
Rudolf Steiner gave physically is bound to become weaker
from one generation to the next, and that this is happening
notwithstanding the question of the significance of any
individual contribution offered along the way. This is so
because of the operation of an important spiritual law that
governs the natural spiritual decline in the vitality and
fertility of any spiritual inheritance in the physical world.

This law works in such a way that a spiritual impulse on the
physical plane can only maintain its—already declining—
inner vitality over the course of three generations. After
three times 33 years—a century—the physical ability to
transmit a spiritual impulse ceases entirely. Then any
spiritual movement finds itself at a crossroads. It has only two
possibilities before it. Either it becomes purely traditional,
carrying forward things past in an old and hence increasingly
irrelevant form, or it is able to break through to the *at present*

living supersensible sources out of which its inspiration came in the first place.

Until now in human history, no spiritual movement that had created for itself a physical-social form of organization has succeeded in this. Every such movement has chosen to remain bound to its physically organized body and use its teachings to keep that dead body in a semblance of life, thus being entirely separated from its founding spirit, which obviously continues to develop, creating for itself new forms of manifestation on the physical plane. Will the Anthroposophical Society be the first to break this tradition of all traditions? Eventually, perhaps already in the course of the present Michael Age, but if not then in the course of the present fifth cultural epoch, a spiritual society on earth will achieve this goal. But is it the *present* Society that will be able to achieve this, or one of its future manifestations in the coming century or centuries? This is the question that must increasingly engage the attention and true heart forces of anthroposophists.

The physically transmitted life of Anthroposophy and its carriers, the Anthroposophical Society and the School of Spiritual Science, has been—since 1998—entering into those decisive years that will either enable it to break through increasingly once more to the truly living spirit reality of the Michael School and Movement, or cause it to become merely a transmitter of outdated traditional contents and forms. In the course of 1998 it was made clear to me that this choice now exists. Since then it has been possible to take a new courageous step—if we truly dare to take it.

We would like to ask the reader to take the following as it is meant: as a factual statement based on concrete experience, which shows that the anthroposophical esoteric content, if it is truly lived as a reality, i.e. if it actually leads the way to the higher worlds, brings one to the time-place in which Rudolf Steiner and the anthroposophical work was striving to enter rightly into world evolution in 1922/3/4/5. This place-of-time, this very specific sought-for entrance (though not, of course, the eternally relevant *content* of the First Class) is wholly past. Its place has been taken by subsequent esoteric and exoteric history.

The complex and multi-layered historical events, extending throughout the whole century, have never yet become 'anthroposophical history' on the earth, among us. We have not taken the reality of the twentieth century into our common esoteric and exoteric practice. Working with the First Class today, even with the utmost subjective seriousness, is like standing on the edge of the abyss—not today's abyss, but as it was in the early 1920s—without entering the real place of the real event.

What happens if man enters this abyss, crosses its threshold, and arrives at the other side, I have tried to portray in my two books *The New Experience of the Supersensible* and *The Spiritual Event of the Twentieth Century*:[13] *One meets the Higher Guardian of the Threshold, the Christ, in his Etheric Form, and is guided into the inner supersensible activity of the true, currently living Michael School.* For now, suffice it to say that the actual, real, not learned or abstract, abyss situation, the crossing of the threshold of the twentieth century and the meeting with the Christ on the other shore, are to become the central work situation of true esoteric anthroposophical work at the beginning of the twenty-first century.

This means that first this future esoteric anthroposophical work must be centred around a shared study of the experience of the modern Damascus event. A communal, social study of the spiritual scientific knowledge process of the Second Coming, individualized through many human beings in the course of this century, is essential to the formation of a new schooling in the secrets of the living Michael School and its esoteric content.

Secondly, the work of the supersensible Michaelic School itself, with its spiritual guidance, carrying and ever again continually transforming the good and bad work done on the earth in the course of the twentieth century, is centred on bringing each anthroposophist to a spiritual maturity as a freely active participant, in accordance with the spirit of modern times. As my own experience showed me, the new Michaelic Impulse, beginning in 1998, already preparing for great waves and upheavals in the first two decades of the twenty-first century, is looking for people, be they anthroposophists already, or many of those who belong to the movement and are seeking this new guidance.

Both are essential for the coming esoteric work, and in the Gothenburg Conference we would strive to begin humbly with its very first preliminary steps.

As preparation for the coming Gothenburg Conference progressed, it became increasingly obvious that, if we want to remain true and deepen the esoteric roots of current spiritual-social activity within the social world of today and tomorrow, we have to transform the ways of working together. If the fiery 'spark' ignited in the East, in the Philippines and elsewhere, is to be shaped into new social-esoteric, truly Michaelic forms, which can be relevant also to northern and central European anthroposophical work in the future, a courageous, indeed adventurous, spirit will be required.

The northern Gothenburg Conference and the southern Cape Town Conference are planned to complement one another. The first will strive to place more emphasis on the search for new approaches to the esoteric, vertical work needed in order to support the horizontal, global economic, social and civil commitment, and the second will explore the horizontal dimensions of globalization, and the spiritual-moral qualities that are emerging everywhere in global civil society. It will bring to light the immense magnitude of the positive, upbuilding forces active in human society today, especially since the 1960s, and will strive to link them to the deeper vertical spirit-roots of the living Michael School.

3. *Rudolf Steiner's Unwritten Work*

Michaela Glöckler

'The World Building must come into existence.
It must be constructed out of human beings.'
R. Steiner, A Notebook

Rudolf Steiner was not only a spiritual researcher who wrote books and gave several thousand lectures. He was also a master builder in the social realm who worked at questions of community building from 1902 onwards until his death. His work as a master builder in the social realm can be traced in every field of activity to which he turned his hand. The physical building of the Goetheanum was intended merely as a symbol for that actual social building, the Temple of Humanity, of which he laid the foundation stone in the hearts of all members of the General Anthroposophical Society. As members of that Society we ourselves are the foundation on which he wanted to erect that building.

It depends on every single individual

The twentieth century has shown that important progress in human cultural life no longer comes about at the instigation of those responsible for science or politics. Instead, progress is now initiated by the great lay organizations such as Amnesty International with its impulse for a realization of

human rights, Green Peace with its efforts to put into practice new ecological policies emanating from the Club of
Rome, La Leche Ligue in its championing of the right of
infants to be breast-fed, Alcoholics Anonymous with its
urgently needed aid for those diseased by alcoholism. If
sufficient numbers of individuals join forces at the right
moment, either locally or world-wide, decisive progress can
be achieved in cultural life. It may even happen that a
political turning point such as occurred in 1989 can become
a historical event.

The General Anthroposophical Society founded by Rudolf
Steiner was the first such world-wide organization open to
everyone in which people joined together to pursue a goal: to
practise humanity in individual, social and professional life.
At first glance a goal of this kind is perhaps not as fascinating
as the question of human rights or protecting the environment. Nevertheless, it is a goal that is shared more or less
consciously by those other organizations whose aims may be
more immediately obvious. If we can succeed in showing how
these aims for humanity as a whole can prove wholesome and
fruitful in every field of life, then the Anthroposophical
Society, too, will attract more and more people and become a
world-wide community for the promotion of helpful initiatives. Support of this kind is needed not only by the Goetheanum as the centre of the Anthroposophical Society but
also by all the other 'Goetheanum-like' establishments, from
day-care centres for infants via Steiner Waldorf schools and
curative establishments to farms, research centres, training
facilities and clinics. In addition we can also unite with other
associations and institutions to widen the basis on which we
work culturally, as is already happening, for example in the
fields of ethical treatment for the dying, the education of
children, or research in genetic engineering.

Spiritual leadership and esoteric life— in the Anthroposophical Society

When he re-founded it at Christmas 1923/24, Rudolf Steiner gave his Society a form that will remain up-to-date for many centuries:

> Human relationships in the truly esoteric sense can provide the only foundation for the Anthroposophical Society. In the future, therefore, everything must be based upon real human relationships in the widest sense, upon concrete, not abstract, spiritual life.[1]

The Foundation Stone Verse given for this Society depicts the human soul in its relationship with the hierarchies, with the Trinity, with the elemental beings. Then, in the fourth part, comes concentration on that Being who is united more than any other with the cosmos and all its entities. This is the Christ Being. In the fourth part of the Foundation Stone Verse Christ himself is strongly brought into a relationship with the life and work of our Society. In speaking those final words:

> *That good may become*
> *What we from our hearts would found*
> *What we from our heads would direct*
> *In conscious*
> *Willing*

we as members utter something like a vow to serve the Christ. What makes us so free is the fact that we can serve and follow Christ regardless of our religious background or national attachment. To serve and follow Christ is thus to span the world and establish tolerance.

I have asked myself many times why Rudolf Steiner, who

loved the German language so much, chose the Greek word 'anthroposophy' as the name for the Society he founded. The conclusion I have now reached is that this arose not only because this word is used in the New Testament whenever reference is made to the human being but also because it is the general name given to Christ, who calls himself 'the Son of Man': νός τον ἀνφρώπον.

The manner of working indicated in the Statutes of the Anthroposophical Society leaves the greatest possible leeway for individual initiative and for the form in which one individual relates to another. Members are totally free to associate with one another in branches or groups on any local basis or subject orientation. Everyone has the right to launch an initiative in any direction, no-one is answerable to anyone else, and no person has to be asked for permission or agreement. The only important aspect is that human beings meet to work or set up initiatives, to do something that promotes humanity in whatever form. It is up to every one of us to make this come true.

—in the School of Spiritual Science

In the third volume of karma lectures we read about the Michael School which has existed in the spiritual world since the fifteenth century and in which human souls not yet incarnated receive pre-natal instruction. It is the task of the Archangel Michael, Time Spirit in our age, to lead human beings to Christ. The Michael School established on earth through Rudolf Steiner—the School of Spiritual Science— serves the same aim. From the very way it was established it is clear that its purpose is to serve the Anthroposophical Society and teach human beings to become active for, with and through this Society. During the Christmas Foundation Conference it was in this sense that Rudolf Steiner called the

School 'the soul of the Anthroposophical Society'. In the autumn of 1924 he also said:

> It was in accordance with the nature of what formed itself out of the Christmas impulse—an impulse with which I was united— that the Free School of Spiritual Science, with its various sections, should constitute the esoteric kernel of all that was once again intended to become effective as esoteric substance within the Anthroposophical Society.[2]

Conditions attach to this spiritual service rendered to the Anthroposophical Society and its task in the world—conditions that apply to every member of the School:

1—to take the schooling path seriously;
2—to remain linked with the other members of the School or, as Rudolf Steiner also put it: to be faithful to the Goetheanum;
3—to be a representative of Anthroposophy in every detail of life.

The *working principle of individual initiative* as cultivated in the Anthroposophical Society is thus joined by the *principle of interest and brotherly understanding* about which Steiner said in the 'curative course' that it would work like a corrective within the Society.[3] There are no boundaries of nationality and no autonomous groupings in the Michael School; it is a worldwide brotherly community working with the spirit. Our task for the twenty-first century is to make this real with increasing earnestness and energy.

—in the Sections

During the Christmas Foundation Conference Rudolf Steiner sketched on the blackboard the new form he had given to the Anthroposophical Society.[4] He showed *horizontally* the levels on which the General Anthroposophical

Society and the three Classes of the School of Spiritual
Science were to work. With *vertical* lines he drew the direction and form of work in the Sections. They were to be active
at all levels, but the direction of their work was to have a life
in which daily work required Inspiration and Intuition from
the spiritual world. This means that the Sections are also
obliged to collaborate with the general social set-up that
surrounds them.

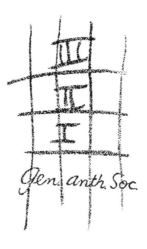

Rudolf Steiner also used the horizontal lines to clarify the
new relationship between Society and School. Prior to the
First World War an Esoteric School had already existed side
by side with the Anthroposophical Society, but the two had
had no direct contact. The institutions founded after that war
also existed in isolation: the Waldorf school, the Christian
Community, the Clinic, the medicine manufacturers, the
publishing houses and others. None of these was integrated
within the life and work of School and Society. A patho-
logical threefold situation had arisen: an Esoteric School, a
Society organizing lectures, and anthroposophical establishments concerned primarily with their own affairs. This

changed when the Society was re-founded during the Christmas Foundation Conference. A network came into being, linking Society, School and the establishments. It is for us to make this network come true through the way we take ourselves seriously and work with others.

The three community-building impulses

The three forms of community building initiated in Society, School and Sections bring us once more to the three conditions that obtain regarding membership of the School. The first condition, to take the schooling path seriously, is in the end every individual's path to Christ; this condition is connected to the nature and task of the Anthroposophical Society. The second condition, to maintain one's inter-relatedness with the other active members, corresponds with the nature of the Michael School, where it is a matter of brotherly relations with one's contemporaries. The third form, that of cultivating community building through the esoteric aspect of one's profession, fits the third condition, which is to realize and represent Anthroposophy in every detail of life in the various professions. In connection with this task of being representatives it is thus valid to enquire after the guiding beings who inspire and accompany the educational, the priestly, the agricultural, the artistic, the scientific or the medical work. How do these beings live in our thoughts and feelings? How do we enable them to accompany our activities?

All over the world we are only in the early stages of realizing this unwritten part of Rudolf Steiner's 'collected works' in our daily lives, this task of building community or erecting the Temple of Humanity. It is exceedingly important that all of us who encounter and love Anthroposophy should feel responsible for being a part of this unwritten work. Such responsibility can give us a sense both of great seriousness and of tremendous enthusiasm.

Doubts about the legitimacy of our own work in Society and School

Members of the Anthroposophical Society periodically appear who doubt whether the karmic relationship entered upon by Rudolf Steiner in connection with this Society continues. Or were the links untied through his premature death? I cannot share these doubts. Would Rudolf Steiner, the teacher of reincarnation and karma, really have withdrawn from those with whom he united so trustingly during the Christmas Foundation Meeting? It is impossible for me to assume that he should have reversed this decision when crises appeared, mistakes were made and difficult social situations arose. Throughout his life he always reacted to problems and difficulties with positive initiatives. How can this be different now? It is we who cut ourselves off from spiritual guidance through our doubts, fears, destructive criticism and lack of confidence. Such guidance can only be effective and experienced by us if we have the courage to seek it out in freedom and turn with initiative to the tasks and goals of our community. In the Appendix to his schooling book *Knowledge of the Higher Worlds*, Rudolf Steiner wrote: '*A book such as this should be taken as a conversation between the author and the reader.*'[5] We have permission to call on his readiness to converse with us.

I hope that the debate on the structure of the General Anthroposophical Society, which is at present causing so much emotional turmoil, will take an energetic inward turn and that it will become a question about inner structuring, an initiative that genuinely speaks to each and every one of us.

If the three forms of work—the principle of personal initiative (work of the General Anthroposophical Society), the principle of social competence (work of the School of Spiritual Science), and the principle of being culturally creative through one's professional activity (work of the Sections)—can be united within us, then there will arise an overall 'consciousness of working together' at building the Temple.

What we need is an entrepreneurial attitude

What can happen to enable the Anthroposophical Society to fulfil its task better in the future, promoting instead of hindering the spread of Anthroposophy? First and foremost it seems to me that every member must have a feeling of being an active co-entrepreneur in the Anthroposophical Society, and especially in the School. What we need is an entrepreneurial attitude. In my experience, those members of our Society who spend a great deal of time criticizing and reproaching others—especially those in prominent positions—about their shortcomings and mistakes are suffering from a paralysis or blockage of initiative. They project their thwarted creative will on to those around them, preventing their work while they themselves often do not achieve anything exemplary either. Behaviour of this kind has a paralysing and obstructing effect, and above all it repels those who are enthusiastic about Anthroposophy and cannot understand why similar enthusiasm is so often lacking in connection with the Society.

If people would begin to use their own initiative in taking up the tasks and goals of the Society or of the establishment in which they work, then a positive work climate could arise that would be attractive to others. If people make full use of their own inner and outer space for work, then forces are freed that are needed for life and work. And something else can happen as well. If people achieve their best not only for themselves or for a specific institution, if they begin to see this as a service to our common task of bringing Anthroposophy out into the world, then both the Society and the School in their relation to one another will become ever more visible and outgoing in the world. Then it will become true that the Goetheanum is not only localized physically in Dornach but also works spiritually all over the world. Why should a good-quality training for teachers in a particular country not show its links with the Education Section at the Goetheanum? Why cannot an interesting result in medical research be made public in a manner that tells the academic world of a researcher at the Goetheanum who has discovered something important? If we all do the best we can achieve in the name of our colleagueship in the worldwide spiritual Goetheanum, the picture of that Goetheanum which arises will differ from one which comes about if we each work only in our own name and are then surprised by there being 'so little achievement stemming from the Goetheanum'. We are all promoters and colleagues of the Goetheanum and in this each one of us can give his or her best.

Review of the twentieth century and tomorrow's tasks

The twentieth century has been the century of world wars and of an awareness of the reality of evil never as yet experienced to this extent.

It has been the century in which the idea of development, the idea of individual freedom and emancipation has taken centre stage. The idea that every human being has the right to retain his dignity has been worldwide since the ratification by most countries of the human rights promulgated in the middle of the century.

It has also been the century in which materialistic methods of thought and research have come to dominate the realm of the living, leading to new techniques in medicine and technology that we must learn to understand, evaluate and assess.

Furthermore it has been the century in which Anthroposophy has entered human evolution as a decisive cultural factor.

It will be our task in the coming century to face up to the battle with evil by learning to recognize ever more clearly our own tendencies for evil and begin to tread the path of self-knowledge and self-development. Peace can only take hold *when the inmost human soul has become the battle's stage*, when war has been internalized and begins to serve our purification and soul-development—in our battle with ourselves.

Liberation of the individual must be joined by respect for the freedom of others. One's actions must be managed in ways that prevent them from interfering with the actions of others, thus leaving their freedom unimpaired. This is the art of destiny and it is the most important task for the coming century: to attain social competence.

Furthermore, the twenty-first century will need something else as well: more Anthroposophy, much more anthroposophical study, energetic work in developing thinking so that materialistic thinking and research can be countered by spiritualized thinking that takes the divine into account. It will also be necessary in the work we set ourselves that we depend not only on people within our own ranks but also on our allies amongst all people of good will. Anthroposophical ideas are needed everywhere. The more modestly we represent them, the more discipline we apply in waiting until we are asked, the more consciously we work at developing a language and ways of expressing ourselves that are generally comprehensible, and the more interest we generate towards the cares and worries of our fellow human beings—the more we shall achieve.

4. The Synergy of Individual Work and Cosmic Thought

Nick Thomas

Rudolf Steiner's research revealed that in the most recent Gabriel period an organ was being developed in the brain which would in the future enable people to remember their past incarnations.[1] In the Michael period beginning in 1879 a different organ has been under development, but not in the physical brain. Steiner makes it clear that humanity as a whole acts like a brain for the spiritual hierarchies.[2] This can be understood if we compare it with the function of the physical brain in relation to consciousness and thinking, for the brain acts as a reflector of our thinking and thus engenders consciousness of our spiritual activity when we think.[3] The activity of humanity as a whole may then, if compared with a brain, be seen to reflect to the hierarchies the activity of *their* spiritual deeds. We are concerned here with mighty spiritual deeds, and a thought of the hierarchies manifests itself in the destiny of a human being as it plays itself out in one incarnation.[4] Indeed we may infer that the level of divine thought involved relates to the span of such a destiny, whether within one life or many, so that an initiate for example is concerned with much longer-range divine thoughts.

There are organs and structures within this divine 'brain', represented by groupings of human beings and their shared activity, so that a folk reflects the work of an archangel, for example, or an epoch of time that of an archai. However, there is also a kind of 'schizophrenia' in all this, as besides the progressive hierarchies other spiritual agencies, e.g. Ahriman, have established their organs. Individual human beings play a decisive role and are not confined to the level of 'brain cells', as through their actions they may inter-relate these mighty organs and affect what is reflected to the hierarchies, and how. Through individual spiritual work the activities within Ahriman's organs may be reflected to the Archangel Michael, and thus help to bring about healing.

This brings us back to the organ Michael is developing, for it is an organ within this cosmic brain rather than in the physical one, and is known to us as the Anthroposophical Society. It is a grouping of human beings that is not based on nationality or other outer differences but on the shared karma of those who recognize the new path into the spiritual world brought by Rudolf Steiner. The deeds enacted by and within this organ reflect back to Michael and Anthroposophia the consequences of this new kind of human group, of this new kind of cosmic thinking. How will individuals act when, through recognition of an institution such as the Goetheanum, they become part of this organ of divine thought? That is what is reflected back: the initiative resulting from participation. The richness of the enterprise grows with the diversity of this, a diversity in harmony with it, of course.

The initial form of the organ is the Anthroposophical Society founded by Rudolf Steiner at Christmas 1923, although this was already a metamorphosis of its earlier form. An organ needs a surrounding membrane or skin, which enables it to be differentiated from its surroundings. Within that it grows and develops, and may even change its skin eventually. How will this organ of cosmic thinking go forward into the new millennium? Does it need a change of skin?

The organ in the brain being developed by Gabriel will only be usable by those who have a relation to spiritual science, but will cause illness in others. Spiritual science can only be developed by human beings, and its sum total is essential to the health of the cosmos. The hierarchies need the thoughts reflected by the work of Anthroposophy, and it is the spiritual scientific content of that work which is distinctive. Without that it remains worthy in a general sense, but outside the 'skin' of the organ. By 'science' is meant a search for knowledge based on individual abilities as distinct from one resting on authority. Spiritual science rests upon the development of new individual abilities, both in the realm of thinking and perception. This enables earthly activity to be in harmony with the cosmos, and thus to be a beginning of the renewal of the Mysteries. If through this we are to take part in the cosmic thinking we are reflecting, then spiritual science must be a community enterprise in a spiritual sense so that individual human work and cosmic thought are in synergy. It is this that needs ever further development such that faithfulness to Michael and free individual initiative remain consonant. The challenge of the new millennium for Anthroposophy is to develop spiritual science ever further in this way, and to ensure that its activities of all kinds, both outer and inner, are rooted in spiritual science. What will help in the face of non-recognition is strengthening, not dilution.

It is important that an organ is organically related to the whole if it is to be healthy, but it must not lose its identity. Strength will ensue when spiritual science can ever more embrace what others are doing that is fruitful, while remaining strong in itself. This requires the strenuous development of individual abilities to match the evident level of ability in other circles.

Expansion, contraction and metamorphosis especially

characterize what is living, and that includes Michael's new organ of thought. No matter how we regard the present culmination of Anthroposophy spoken of by Steiner, it marks the end of a phase of expansion and we may expect a contraction to follow prior to a metamorphosis into a higher form, followed by an expansion in a new style. It would be materialistic to regard such a process with dismay, as it is part of life. Renewal requires metamorphosis and that often requires a prior contraction. But metamorphosis also retains what is essential (i.e. spiritual) from the old, otherwise it is merely revolution. It takes the old as nourishment for the new rather than discarding it. Spiritual science is that essential essence of Anthroposophy, and in the next millennium we need to carry this in our hearts in such a way that its fruitfulness may become a blessing for all. Then the cosmic organ of Michael will wax strong.

5. What must Happen if Anthroposophy is to Fulfil its Task in the Next Century?

Peter Tradowsky

In its essence Anthroposophy is like a living human being, albeit one to whom Schiller's famous description would apply: 'Every individual man ... carries in disposition and determination a pure ideal man within himself, with whose unalterable unity it is the great task of his existence, through all his vicissitudes, to harmonize.'[1] Over 200 years ago Schiller sensed this 'pure ideal man' to be that entity who might also be described as 'the being of humanity'. This 'being of humanity' indwells humanity as a whole; it is world-wide and cosmopolitan. Schiller's name for 'humanity as a whole' was 'the State'; today we would call it 'the social organism'. The 'Man in time' can only develop into the 'Man in idea' in a healthy way through 'the temporal Man being raised to the dignity of ideal Man'. In quoting this we point to the path of development described in 1904 by Rudolf Steiner in his book *Knowledge of the Higher Worlds.*[2]

Even Schiller saw that 'being of humanity' as an entity who stands in the centre and is open to attack from two sides. One of those two threats was described by Steiner in the sentence: 'One must be able to confront the *idea* in living experience, *or else* fall into its bondage.'[3] It is easy to see what immeasurable damage has been done in the twentieth century by our fanatical preoccupation with ideas, a preoccupation that both despises and destroys human beings. The second danger lies in the boundless subjectivity and self-determining despotism by which the 'person', as opposed to the growing 'I', seeks to realize itself.

Like the human being, 'Anthroposophy, the Being of Humanity' lives in a threefoldness, in a trinity, in a way of thinking, feeling and will. One can approach the thinking, feeling and will of this being—getting to understand and fathom it—if, for example, one considers it in depth in three spheres. The three spheres chosen for the purposes of this essay are: the development of thinking through spiritual science, the unfolding of the artistic in the sense of anthroposophical aesthetics, and the threefolding of the social organism (this latter being the main item of the threesome).

Nothing appears more important for the future than that spiritual science itself should thoroughly overhaul thinking, for thinking as a will-filled activity of the 'I' is in the gravest danger. On the one hand it has grown rigid in its intellectual forms, so that it cannot become aware of its own spirituality. On the other hand its intrinsic value is misjudged, slandered even, by the way feelings and experiences are more highly esteemed than thinking, while at the same time there is no clarity about the fact that all interpretations actually come about through thinking. This is especially significant in connection with the 'new age' scene. Blind faith in science comes up against a deep mistrust of thinking. The two together lead many to the view that thinking is not the appropriate medium through which to enter the spiritual world.

This double fundamental error blocks the path to Anthroposophy as spiritual science. Rudolf Steiner never tired of emphasizing the 'character of spiritual science' as a *science*, knowing full well that only the scientific method and the development of thinking can give modern individuals the possibility of entering into a relationship with the spiritual world that is free and appropriate for the human being. In the chapter 'Knowledge of Higher Worlds' in *Occult Science* he showed how one can develop a thinking that is free of the senses. 'The surest way to attain sense-free thinking, the way too that lies nearest at hand for the pupil, is to let his thinking take possession of the facts of the higher world, communicated in spiritual science. These facts cannot be observed with the physical senses. Yet the pupil will find that with sufficient patience and perseverance he can grasp them.'[4] This is a clear statement of the conditions—which are all too easily left out of consideration—as well as the goal.

When these conditions are fulfilled one can indeed experience how those spiritual facts become 'the possession' of thinking. This has something to do with the way the kind of thinking which understands and knows itself discovers that it is a member of the spiritual world, that it is not outside but within the spiritual world. 'For his thinking has within it an inner reality of being which has connection with the supersensible world.'[5] Through energetic work we become conscious of this fact of which we are at first unconscious, and this engenders firm trust in the science of the spirit.

This trust protects us from gaining access to the spiritual world by routes other than that of a science filled with thinking. Great danger lies in despising thinking and science when one wants to enter the spiritual world. Mephistopheles confirms this when he says to Faust: 'Despise good sense and science, man's highest power, permit the spirit of lies to strengthen you through works of illusion and magic, and you will be mine without a doubt.' Entry into the spiritual world under such conditions can lead only to hopeless bewilderment; in fact, such an entry into that world would not be real.

Thinking can be deepened even further. 'By continuously apprising ourselves of what spiritual science tells, we grow accustomed to a thinking that does not take its start from outer observation by the senses.'[6] By strengthening thinking, which brings us into the spiritual world, we are led to form thought combinations that are given by that world.

One can, for example, notice that one thinks even while one sleeps, and that through schooling in spiritual science one can bring these thoughts over into one's conscious thinking. Thinking made fruitful by spiritual science becomes both formed and able to give form, leading one from having to feel one's way to being able to see spiritually. This spiritual vision borne by thinking is the very opposite of any kind of clairvoyance.

The path that through spiritual science transforms thinking into an existence within the spiritual world, indeed into thinking that has vision within the spiritual world, is the path that links the human being deeply with Anthroposophy as a thinking spiritual being. Another way of striking out along this path most fruitfully is to embark on an intensive study of *The Philosophy of Freedom.*

Spiritual science—like any other science that has a proper understanding of itself—has the task of researching and depicting the truth. Art as understood by Anthroposophy, on the other hand, has a mission of its own. Spiritual science must concern itself with things from the spiritual world that can be fruitful for human beings; this entails taking hold truthfully of spiritual realities. Artists, though, create a new reality in their works; as creators they implant in the cosmos an original form made by a human being. Goethe in particular lived in this new concept of aesthetics; and Schiller studied this way of art intensely, thus becoming the first to formulate in thoughts the central concept of this aesthetic.

The artist is as closely linked with the world of idea, of form, of shape—in brief of the objective truth of the spiritual world—as he is with the world of matter, of life, of the senses. The more deeply he is domiciled in both these realms of existence, the higher he stands. Each of these realms of existence fills the human being with forces through which it strives to realize itself one-sidedly. Schiller called them the 'form impulse' and the 'material impulse'. Both function of necessity and can allow the human being no freedom. In the nature of the child, however, Schiller discovered the ability to play with form and matter in such a way that all compulsion ceases. For him this became the prototype and ideal of all artistic creation. In artistic production the idea becomes objective and sense-perceptible; what is sense-perceptible is permeated by the idea and loses its material substance. Schiller called this object of the play impulse, entirely made by man, the 'living form', thus using different words to depict the unification of the two realms of existence.

With the 'object entirely made by man' the artist extricates himself from the constrictions of necessity, i.e. freedom is attained through the production of a work of art. In the work of art the artist has fought his way to freedom; the work of art did not exist before, and the artist has worked to achieve it; it is not a gift but an achievement. 'The real artistic secret of the master,' said Schiller, 'consists in his annihilating the material by means of the form'. (22nd letter) This is a way of giving expression both to the creation of the 'living form' as well as to the dual liberation process. The reality of art is equidistant from the reality of spirit and the reality of the sense-perceptible. Schiller called this reality the 'aesthetic appearance' because in it newly created reality appears. 'The reality of things is the work of the things, the appearance of things is the work of Man, and a nature which delights in appearance no longer takes pleasure in what it receives, but in what it does.' (26th letter)

Rudolf Steiner took up and spoke appreciatively of this central concept in Schiller's aesthetics, which broadly corresponds to that of Goethe. 'In comparison to works of nature, therefore, works of art appear to us as mere appearance. But they must be appearance, because they would otherwise not be veritable works of art. As an aesthete, Schiller is unique in his concept of semblance in this connection; he is unsurpassed and unsurpassable.'[7] Steiner explained this concept of appearance in two ways, firstly by answering the question as to 'what is important in art: It is not to embody something supersensible but to metamorphose something that is sense-perceptible and actual'. Secondly he said, 'The creations of art are not founded on what is, but on what is possible.' That which is possible and which the artist incorporates into matter is at the same time that which is spiritual; as spirit it perishes, only to be resurrected again in the work of art.

In his foreword to the 1909 edition of this lecture Rudolf Steiner emphasized that 'the ideas developed in it are a healthy foundation for Anthroposophy'. In its essence the aesthetic developed in the lecture is the aesthetic of Anthroposophy. For the coming century and even perhaps for a more distant future it is impossible to overestimate the importance of this aesthetic, which gives artists a basis for their conscious work of creation. To understand this we need only look at the crisis in which art—its very existence threatened—finds itself today.

Art is being questioned and attacked from two sides. On the one hand there is the boundless subjectivity which over-exaggerates the personality of any more or less gifted artist if he lacks spiritual schooling and does not search for the objective reality of the spiritual world. All artistic creation is rooted in the supersensible; what is objective and true protects the artist from destructive arbitrariness when he submerges himself in the creative process. On the other hand the artistic impulse is being turned into its opposite by the way so many artists make use of modern technology. All the arts speak to the human senses. The 'aesthetic appearance' increases the activity of the senses through the presence of the spirit in the sense-perceptible; sense-perceptions become what might be described as transparent for the spiritual. This process, which culminates in direct contact between the 'I' of the creator and the 'I' of the observer, cannot in truth be brought about by a technological medium. To say this is not to express any animosity towards technology as such. It is simply a matter of understanding the task of art in connection with the twelve senses of the human being. Schiller had an inkling of this when he wrote: 'Beyond question Man carries the potentiality for divinity within himself; the path to divinity, if we may call a path [something which] never reaches its goal, is open to him in his *senses*.' (11th letter)

Artists who want to work in the direction of anthroposophical aesthetics will have the task of cultivating and saving the senses. What Schiller said about artists ('The dignity of humanity has been placed in your hands; take good care of it') will have to be rephrased for the future: The senses are commended to your care; save them. To be able to do this a working artist will have to make an intense study of the senses; this will clarify what can and what cannot be achieved via the various media.

The ever more perfect world of virtual reality created by the media must be countered in that we more and more emphasize the need to create 'aesthetic appearance'. Only the 'appearance' of art can overcome the 'appearance' of the media.

The third aspect of 'Anthroposophy, the Being of Humanity' is one that has special significance for the future; it is the impulse to view the world as being intrinsically threefold, for threefoldness, a trinity, is the universal foundation manifested everywhere we look. Thinking in terms of threefoldness has become almost lost or hidden as far as general awareness goes. A variegated dualism has come to the fore instead, and this is what dominates people's minds. The opposition of good and evil is the archetypal duality, for this opposition, which is no different from the polarity between Lucifer and Ahriman, extinguishes the Being who is in the centre. In contrast with this, one of the most important impulses of Michael, the Spirit of the Age, is to open our eyes once more to the true shape of the cosmos through the principle of threefoldness.[8] A tremendous spiritual battle is being waged around the principle of threefoldness.

Anthroposophy, the 'Being of the Cosmos and of Humanity', lives in threefoldness; it is its element of life. Therefore it is not surprising that Anthroposophy points everywhere to trinities that lead people into realities, allowing them to make contact with the reality of the triformed world of spirit. There is an abundance of trinities that show us the reality of the threefold principle. Significant for an understanding of the human being is a threefold structuring into body, soul and spirit, into thinking, feeling and will, into head system, breast system and limb system. The spiritual world, for its part, lives in the trinity of the hierarchies and, with regard to guiding humanity, in Lucifer, Ahriman and Christ.

The impulse of threefoldness in the social organism is by far the most important for the social future of humanity. Of all the trinities, it remains the least understood, let alone realized. Yet the impulse of threefoldness in the social organism provides the answer to one of the fundamental processes that is taking place for humanity: the crossing of the threshold, i.e. the entry of humanity into the threefold-ness of the spiritual world. Hitherto this process has for the most part been taking place unconsciously, and therefore it has proved not a blessing but a curse. The crossing of the threshold signifies that spiritual beings—those hostile as well as those friendly to man—are gaining a more direct access to the human 'I' than ever before. This is a blessing if the 'I' awakes to its spirituality and knows what spiritual beings it is dealing with. But it is a destructive curse if spirit beings inimical to man force themselves on the human being who in turn does not recognize that he is possessed by demons.

To cross the threshold means for the individual human being that there must be a separating out of thinking, feeling and will, and for humanity at large it means that the ancient, unified state must be unravelled to form the realms of spirit and culture, of rights, and of economic life. It is the Guardian of the Threshold himself who makes these demands, for he wants to ensure that crossing the threshold will bring blessing. Rudolf Steiner once described this process in a way that also emphasized its goal:

> Just as man, the knower, must realize that his thinking, feeling and will separate in a certain sense and must be held together in a higher way, so it must be made intelligible to modern humanity that the cultural-spiritual life, the life of rights, and the economic life must separate from one another and a higher form of union be created than the State as it has been up to now. No programmes, ideas, ideologies can bring individuals to recognize the necessity of this threefoldness of the social organism. It is only profound knowledge of the onward development of mankind that reveals this development to have reached a threshold where a grave Guardian stands. This Guardian demands of an individual who is advancing to higher knowledge: Submit to the separation of thinking, feeling and will. He demands of humanity as a whole: Separate what has up to now been interwoven in the chaotic unity of an idolized State; separate this into a spiritual, cultural life, a rights life and an economic life. Otherwise there is no progress possible for humanity, and the old chaos will burst asunder. If this happens it will not take the form that is necessary to humanity but an ahrimanic or luciferic form. It is only spiritual-scientific knowledge of the passing of the threshold in our present day that can impress the form that befits the Christ on this chaos.[9]

The future of humanity will depend on its ability to bring forth with conscious dignity and strength that form of the social organism which 'befits the Christ'. This has not been achieved in the twentieth century; indeed it is the task of a century, perhaps even of a millennium. At the end of the twentieth century the impulse for social threefolding can only be characterized in contradictory terms: The more impossible it has become, the greater is the urgency for it. One cannot ignore the way consumerism, the media and leisure pursuits have created a society in which it has become exceedingly difficult to impart or awaken social impulses. Indolence, thoughtlessness and egoism have taken possession of souls that nevertheless deep down appear to long for something else. The powerlessness of spiritual life is an expression of this. In almost every field of public life—cultural, political and economic—it is impossible to overlook tendencies that are growing ever stronger and structures that are becoming established and stand like a mighty bastion against a threefoldness of society. We shall here leave open the question as to the origins of these multifarious oppositions.

A current example may be seen in Germany just now. The new Federal Government is trying to turn away from nuclear energy, yet legally binding agreements and astronomical costs are putting this off indefinitely or indeed making it impossible. We do not need prophetic vision to foretell similar reactions to associations being set up in the economic sphere or to the introduction of genuine co-determination in businesses.

In the social realm the future happiness or unhappiness of humanity depends on the impulses of social threefolding. These are 'essentials for life in the present and future', as formulated so pertinently in the German sub-title of Rudolf Steiner's book *Towards Social Renewal*.[10]

Humanity is in the midst of an immense social tragedy, and there is no end in sight. Despite, or perhaps because of, the obvious tremendous obstacles, the immeasurable increase in the sacrifice of human lives cries out to us to maintain awareness of the impulse for social threefolding, for this alone can generate the powers of will needed to bring about a change in direction. Only if some individuals retain their enthusiasm for 'Anthroposophy, the Being of Humanity', only if they dedicate their work to serving the spirit in one field or another, only if they want to school themselves, can Anthroposophy unfold its healing effect; otherwise it will be doomed to ineffectuality, or even lost to humanity.

Nothing is further from Anthroposophy than to be rigid, lifeless or dogmatic. Anthroposophy is a living, developing being who can everywhere home in on human beings and situations, but it can only undertake this if requested to do so. One of its mysteries is that it is not a world view in the ordinary sense; it is a sum of all world views or, better, it has the gift of being able to move amongst all world views, appreciating and understanding each in its appropriate place.

We have here hinted at the all-embracing Being of Anthroposophy in its aspects of head, heart and will. So long as there are human beings who allow their thinking to be made fruitful by spiritual science, what are, in fact, ultimately agnostic sciences will not succeed in stifling spiritual development. So long as there are artists who are keen to gain through Anthroposophy familiarity with the laws of the spiritual world, and who in their creative work want to influence their fellow human beings in their senses and supersensibly through 'aesthetic appearance', no technological developments in the media will be able to lay waste human souls. The technology created by human beings needs to be balanced by artistic activity and works of art that are in keeping with anthroposophical aesthetics. So long as there are individuals who know which form of the social organism is the form that 'befits the Christ' and thus leads to the path of peace, power and violence will have failed to carry off the laurels of victory.

In this sense the future of humanity depends on the free deed of human beings who want to take into their thinking, into their heart and into their will 'Anthroposophy, the Being of Humanity'.

6. Matters of Conscience

Gilbert Childs

Anthroposophical ideals are vessels fashioned by love, and the human spirit is summoned by the spiritual world to partake of their content. Anthroposophy must bring the light of genuine humanity to shine out in thoughts that bear love's true imprint. Knowledge is only the form in which human beings reflect the possibility of receiving into their hearts the light of the world spirit which has come to dwell there, and from thence to illuminate human thought.[1]

Rudolf Steiner was proficient in the art of getting priorities right, and in the above quotation we have a typical example of this capability. The tirelessness he showed in repeating its theme is evidence enough that it was necessary for him to do so throughout his lifetime, and it may be contended with some justification that were he still with us he would find ample grounds for perpetuating the practice. Had it not been the case, more of his expectations regarding the state of society at the turn of the millennium would doubtless have been fulfilled.

It is pointless to try and set about apportioning blame for the present parlous state of national and international affairs, for the causes are as manifold as they are complex, and seemingly as incapable of betterment as they ever have been. It may be argued that sheer human intransigence is responsible for the ongoing state of every kind of conflict, yet constant repetition of the same noble ideals, lofty moral and ethical teachings consistently acknowledged over the centuries is matched only by humankind's stubbornness in failing to live up to them, regardless of worldwide acceptance of their obvious merits. Steiner spoke as would a prophet of biblical times, but as ever his message reaches only those who have ears to hear it. He rarely if ever employed directly imperative terms in his lectures and addresses to his associates, but only the most grossly insensitive of people could fail to detect when a suggestion or piece of advice emanating from such an authoritative source constitutes an 'order'.

He expected all serious enquirers to *study* basic spiritual-scientific literature almost as a matter of course, and not be satisfied with merely reading it as they would a novel. Certainly included would be the book now mentioned:

> Among the various exercises to be found in my book *Knowledge of the Higher Worlds and Its Attainment* you will discover six that are to be practised for a certain definite period of time. One of these is the cultivation of a completely unprejudiced state of mind. Indeed, dear friends, the Anthroposophical Society as a whole needs to cultivate these six virtues, and it is essential that it strive to acquire them. It must be so broadminded that it reaches the humanness of those who turn to it, and so strong that it can meet their needs.[2]

That matters have not changed very much since he spoke these words in 1923 is evidenced by the present overall state of affairs. Steiner himself abstained from criticism or censure, but nevertheless did not hesitate to apply the principle of 'if the cap fits...' His challenge was for us all 'to search our conscience, to become aware of our responsibilities'.[3] Of course, it is a matter of whoever is without sin among us casting the first stone, but generally speaking most 'deficiencies' play their sinister part at a much more basic level of our being. We can't be bothered, we have other things to do, and so on, and perhaps the most common and fatuous of excuses in more ways than one is: *we haven't the time.*

This is the lamest extenuation of all, particularly so in the view of the fact that we have surrounded ourselves with every labour/time-saving device imaginable. Whether this very fact has contributed to a general lack of will-power evident on all sides is debatable. None of us has the time—we've simply got to make it by exercising our flabby determination. Rudolf Steiner cannot be accused of not practising what he preached. Whilst attending conferences, giving courses and on other similar occasions the light in his room burned longer than anyone else's; his was the inkwell that ran dry; he it was who uttered a cheery greeting to the first person, yawning and bleary-eyed, whom he met next morning.

One of my erstwhile tutors who knew him moderately well once told me a story, possibly but not likely to be apocryphal, of an incident during the early years of the first Waldorf School in Stuttgart.[4] Rudolf Steiner had invited Fritz Julius, a biologist by training, to teach chemistry in spite of his admittedly scant knowledge of the subject. Nevertheless, Herr Doktor persisted, persuading him that all he had to do was keep one step ahead of his pupils, and eventually Julius agreed to the task. After some weeks of the first term had elapsed, Dr Steiner asked him how things were going. 'It's terrible,' replied Julius, 'I'm working eighteen hours a day!' 'Well, that means that you've still got another six, doesn't it?' was the cheery response.

Love as the Verity of Verities

The prime virtue of love is not directly listed as one of the 'Eternal Verities', those great ideals of Truth, Beauty and Goodness which we usually associate respectively with our basic human faculties of Thinking, Feeling and Will.[5] The element of love would seem, at first sight, to be associated with Feeling, and indeed this notion accords with popular belief and understanding. But this is only part of the story, for it is also strongly rooted in Thinking and Will, manifesting through these two soul-qualities as Truth and Goodness. Indeed, it may be said that Love, in the final analysis, is seen to bear little relation to the sheer emotion characterized by 'romantic' love—that which it is almost universally taken to be.

Now Rudolf Steiner maintained that Love, pure and simple, has more to do with Truth, and by implication Thinking, than it has with Feeling. However, he was careful to point out that in respect of this correlation, it is crucial for us to grasp the fact that we are here dealing not so much with our ego of earthly consciousness as with our real Ego, or 'higher Self', which resides in the spiritual world. The following meditational verse is worth quoting in full:

> The seed of Truth lives in Love;
> In Truth seek the root of Love:
> Thus speaks thy higher Self.

> The fire's glow transforms
> Wood into warming rays.
> Wisdom's purposeful Will
> Converts work into strength.

> So let thy work be the shadow
> Cast by thine I
> When it is shone on,
> Illuminated by the flame
> Of thy higher Self.[6]

In this verse we may find it difficult, at least initially, to discern that Truth and Love (and this obviously in the sense of *agape*) are virtually synonymous. Steiner argued that the very activity of seeking after Truth in every field of human striving, but notably spiritual and material science, constitutes the best possible training in selflessness. All factors that conform to egotism, such as arrogance, vanity, prejudice, selfish ulterior motives and other manifestations of self-centredness, are invariably revealed for the impediments that they are to character development and moral fortitude. By contrast, self-effacing behaviour which discloses consistently altruistic motives, from common self-denial to self-sacrifice, are sure indications of a strong ego, and by definition a strong will.

The manner in which Rudolf Steiner infers that Wisdom is the inspirer of deeds of Will serves to demonstrate the essential unity as well as the trichotomy observable in our three soul-faculties of Thinking, Feeling and Will which we deploy in terms of Truth, Beauty and Goodness; for it may justifiably be claimed that Truth, expressed as Wisdom which can in turn be described as 'thinking with the heart', gives us the motivation to express Love in terms of Will, namely in deeds of Goodness, or love in action. The correlation between Beauty and Feeling is fairly obvious, for the manifestation of Beauty through Art involves both spiritual content and material form and these are combined in deeds or acts of will.

It may be asserted with considerable justification that every deed we perform is done in response to some need, whether real or imagined. It is but a short step from needs to mere wants, and very soon all kinds of desires make their demands, and so greed, envy, covetousness and an over-riding ambition to fulfil these are engendered. We are all self-centred to some degree, but at the same time there is general consensus that altruism is a praiseworthy ideal, to be practised whenever we feel that we can. Love and its manifestation bears within it both carnal desire (*eros*) and the capability of self-denial to the point of self-sacrifice (*agape*), and altruism, thus exhibiting its dual functions expressible in spiritual-scientific terminology as subjectivity (sympathy) and objectivity (antipathy).

We all experience the struggle between our higher nature represented by our true ego, which is capable of self-sacrifice, modesty and humility, and our lower nature, with its selfish desires, of which we may or may not be fully conscious, and its urge to manipulate the environment to our own advantage. The desire of all self-centred people is to draw whatever they can to themselves, but their 'gain' comes always at a 'loss', in some shape or form, to their fellows. They are under the illusion that they are enriching themselves, whereas in reality the more egotistical they become the more they degrade themselves, for they come to live more and more within a shrinking world of their own devising in which they are the sole inhabitant.

If this becomes the case it is to their ultimate advantage, for then the cosmic law of self-correction begins to work. Rudolf Steiner asserted that whenever egotism in individuals takes a wrong turn the time comes when they become aware of its powers of self-annihilation, and eventually realize that altruism brings its own rewards.[7] If they are able to grow stronger and more conscious of this fact, so will their powers of self-subordination to the benefit of others. They will come to realize that the more they give themselves up to self-love the more barren they become in their inner life. This acknowledgement must in any case occur, whether during their lifetime in the material world or in the spiritual world after death, that human life has no meaning unless it involves significant others within family, community and an even more extensive social organization, which in itself constitutes an organism. The whole matter is characterized by Steiner in his *Motto of Social Ethics*:

A healthy social life is established
Only when in the mirror of each human soul
The whole community finds its reflection,
And when within the community
Live the merits of every single member.

As above, so below?

Whatever occurs below affects whatever happens above, and vice versa. We know that the Christ Being is now as it were resident in the etheric world, and this fact was acknowledged by the gospel-writers, apostles and others who helped to initiate the Early Church. This was not, as might be expected, an instigation prompted entirely from within themselves, but from the Christ himself, who foretold it to them. (John 14) In the following chapter he provided them with a model of how things would be after his departure in his parable of himself as the 'true vine', his followers as the branches which bear the fruit, and his Father as the husbandman. Predictably enough, he extols the supreme virtues of love as well as the necessity of it, implying that only by living and working accordingly would they 'bear fruit'. The whole chapter abundantly repays the effort of close study, even to the final verse.

Rudolf Steiner, concretely rather than by analogy, referred to the being Anthroposophia as a living being who is independent of the Anthroposophical Society, a mother who gives life to her children. Within general society these take the form of the various practical applications of spiritual-scientific principles to various activities, such as agriculture, education, medicine and so on by bringing to them their own particular gifts, skills and aptitudes. He spoke earnestly about the members' and 'children's' great responsibilities to this very real spiritual being, stating that whatever they did also needed to be capable of justification before her, and that they should 'consult her to this end'.[8]

Unfortunately, a certain proportion of zealous, sincere and well-meaning folk, however enthusiastic, energetic or dutiful they may be, cannot see fit to subscribe wholeheartedly to established anthroposophical ethics and therefore may not measure up to optimal requirements for the task. Unfortunate, too, is the fact that some individuals may not even be aware of their particular short-comings in terms of personal qualities and/or vocational proficiency. More unfortunate are those who simply do not possess the necessary will-power or other capability to overcome their particular deficiencies.[9] Most hapless of all, perhaps, are organizations or individuals who show a certain blindness in matters of goodwill, declining to co-operate or share resources, tending to subordinate moral considerations to those of mercenary interests, expediency and so on.

It is no-one's task to be critical or judgemental of any human being but themselves, but the ability 'to see ourselves as others see us' is nonetheless beneficial when cultivated with energy and application. Time and time again Rudolf Steiner exhorted his close collaborators and distant hearers to submit themselves to close and detailed examination, and that in the most critical manner. An obvious opportunity to do this as a regular task is provided by the practice nightly of the 'backward review', during which we subject our actions to as objective scrutiny as possible. Certainly, it behoves us all to realize that we are children of our time; that we have been brought up under certain influences to the point of conditioning, and educated or even indoctrinated in certain ways which have not failed to leave their mark. At the same time a thorough searching of our conscience ensures that we know what our responsibilities are, that we can then strengthen our determination to rise to their demands.

All we need is love

Typically, Rudolf Steiner was concerned for the welfare of everyone equally, and time after time he came back to the same topic. Love is the supreme Christian virtue, and he endorsed everything written about it in the New Testament, which seems to indicate that love is indeed the panacea, that certain cure for all personal and social ills. Paul's eulogy to love (*agape*) to be found in Chapter 13 of his first letter to the Corinthians virtually says it all. Striking a personal note, I contend that Rudolf Steiner could have claimed that it was he who actually said it all!

It is common experience that 'hope springs eternal in the human breast' in spite of seemingly endless discouragement and failure, and this quality is widely regarded to be as important as the qualities with which it is traditionally associated, namely faith (Christian expectation) and charity (*agape*). The nature of love is very complex, and understanding of it so variable as to be individual. So important is it that a thumbnail analysis of this precious endowment, for which the Greeks had at least three words, is warranted here, as there has been some muddying of the waters over the centuries since their time.

The notion of *caritas*, so successfully promoted by St Augustine, is generally taken to arise from a kind of fusion of the Greek notions of *eros* (desire) and *agape* (unconditional love); but the kind of love which involves the laying down of one's life for one's friends is the purest *agape*, and goes far beyond *caritas* (charity). I contend that the notion of *philos* fits in more neatly between *agape* and *eros* than that of *caritas*. It was used to express liking, pleasing to, fondness for and similar concepts, and the prefix *phil-* was pressed into service to indicate a fancy for practically anything, and was extremely overworked. Such usage implies that human soul-qualities were expressed or engaged; that is to say, sympathy as understood in technical spiritual-scientific terminology. At the same time a certain discretion is called for, as exemplified by the word *philadelphia*, which is usually construed as brotherly or sisterly love with implications for family relationships, and not in the sense of *agape*. So here we have a tidy threefold model which links *philos* with our qualities of soul, even as *agape* and *eros* are seen clearly to relate respectively to spirit and body.

The *Paraclete* (John 14:16,26; 15:26, 16:7) as comforter or advocate, is none other than the Spirit of Truth (John 16:13). This in itself speaks volumes, particularly in the light of the contents of several other verses in John 15 and our earlier discussion involving the virtual synonymity of Truth with 'true' love. The correlations between the two are abundantly evident, besides being too numerous to disregard. Another significant element that is frequently associated with these two factors is the concept of *purity*, which is figured with emphasis in several meditations given by Rudolf Steiner.[10]

Truth is pure by definition and the law of the excluded middle: either something is true or it is false. It is unthinkable that Truth can be anything else than perfect and inviolable. In the case of love matters are somewhat different, for it is not an objective abstract absolute but a subjective many-faceted human attribute. At the same time its ultimate virtue is that of expecting nothing in return, even to the point of actual self-sacrifice. What is given in the name of love is indeed given freely, for it will not be rewarded anyway; in the last resort all love that is given represents gifts to the world.[11]

Both truth and love have close connections with the whole concept of freedom, but fascinating as this arrangement is, it is too complex to be discussed here. Suffice it to mention, perhaps, that just as the Godhead of the World outpours its Light without discrimination or favour, so should the godhood of our soul equally freely pour out Love to all that is.[12] Rudolf Steiner often referred to Humankind as the Hierarchy of Love and Freedom, and this with good reason, as we have seen. Certainly, we need always to bear in mind the following:

> As individuals, our value for the world must be seen to lie wholly in deeds of love, not in deeds done for the sake of self-perfecting ... The higher the stage of development reached by individuals, the more does the impulse of love in them increase in strength; wisdom alone is not enough.
>
> ... When, through love, we have found the path to wisdom, we reach wisdom through the increasing power of self-conquest, through selfless love. Thus do we become free individuals ... and only those who are free in the real sense can become true Christians.[13]

Striving as we must towards the attainment of wisdom, we have to take the utmost care to eliminate whatever stands in our way in the manner of self-seeking and all the other ills that attach to sheer intellectualism and cold-heartedness:

> A spiritual science without love would be a danger to mankind. But love should not be a matter for preaching; love must and indeed will come into the world through the spreading of knowledge of spiritual truths.[14]

Christ, he who declared (John 15:15) that 'greater love hath no man than this, that he lay down his life for his friends'—and went on to prove it—described himself as the true vine, a living organism, and this for special reasons. Paul chose to employ the analogy of a living being, declaring in his first letter to the Corinthians (12:12): 'For as the body is one, and hath many members, and all the members of that one body, being many, are one body, so also is the Christ', going on to describe this notion in some detail in the same chapter and elsewhere. In his letter to the Colossians (1:18) he spoke of Christ as 'the head of the body, the church' (*ekklesia*—assembly), and this without any hint of the excessive religiosity which came later and for which he was not responsible.

It is easy and appropriate to extend this notion to a body of like-minded individuals who also acknowledge the image of the Christ as being central to their many and diverse considerations concerning him, an 'assembly' with many sub-assemblies, a society with many groups, the members of which employ their talents in the furtherance of the interests and welfare of the immediate community, and by extension to the benefit also of the greater public whole beyond. Christ himself declared (Matthew 18:20) that 'where there are two or three gathered together in my name, there am I in the midst of them', and Rudolf Steiner affirmed that such gatherings are indeed attended by spiritual beings.[15]

As we know, the 'Christ Impulse' as such was present on the earth for three years, and during this time was incarnated into, and made use of, the physical, etheric and astral bodies of Jesus of Nazareth, for it had none of its own. Furthermore, we know that the Christ Being will remain united with the earth 'even to the end of the Age'. The Christ Impulse endures and will be received into Humanity during the course of earth-evolution. However, this process requires the active co-operation of altruistic individuals who are willing and able to take on the responsibilities attaching to it. Accordingly, these involve the human capacity for love and the attainment of truth, which together engender wisdom, so that we may secure freedom and hence the will for moral behaviour. Rudolf Steiner put the matter in a nutshell:

> You need only compare two facts: firstly, that we shall attain to the highest moral principles and their understanding only at the conclusion of the striving for wisdom, and secondly, that moral and social communities cannot exist without ethics or morals.[16]

At the same time, he was realistic enough to remind members of the Anthroposophical Movement of certain factors which are easily overlooked:

> We are living in a period that calls for us to recognize that our loftiest modern capacities, those for freedom and pure concepts, must be permeated by the Christ Impulse.... modern society suffers from paralysis of the will ... [but] Anthroposophy inspires thoughts and deeds of ethical and moral nature which require strong will-forces.[17]

Wonder, Compassion and Conscience

Rudolf Steiner asserted that whatever manifests as Wonder, Compassion and Conscience that have lived in human beings since the Christ Event, and continues so to live, serves to provide respectively the astral, etheric and 'physical' body of the Christ Impulse itself.[18] In another lecture he stated something similar:

> All acts performed out of wonder—trust, faith and reverence and everything that paves the way to supersensible knowledge— close like a covering over the Christ, and may be compared with the human astral body. The etheric body is likewise formed through our deeds of love, and his physical body through our actions in the world prompted by impulses of conscience.[19]

These three attributes are inevitably part of our experiences of a soul-nature during our sojourn on the earthly plane, and figure large in our 'education' process. He pointed out that the propensity we have for wondering about our own nature as well as that of the universe, our innate urge to understand, or at least make sense of our environment, forms the basis of all philosophical thinking in its broadest sense. Natural Philosophy was taught in universities long before it became Natural Science, which in turn was broken down into the various disciplines of physics, chemistry, biology and so on. Nowadays, knowledge of the spiritual worlds which complements that of the material worlds has been provided to our great advantage by Rudolf Steiner and associated researchers.

Compassion or fellow-feeling, the kind of unconditional, brotherly or Christian love best represented by the Greek word *agape*, belongs not only to the realm of feeling but also to that of will. The Good Samaritan not only felt pity for the traveller who fell among thieves, but he also did something about it. In all our dealings in society we should bear in mind Christ's words of admonishment: 'Inasmuch as ye have done [it] unto one of the least of these my brethren, ye have done it to me.' Concerning compassion, Rudolf Steiner gave this verse:

So long as you feel the pain
Which I am spared,
The Christ unrecognized
Is working in the world.
For weak still is the spirit
Whilst each is capable of suffering
Only through his own body.[20]

It is by dint of compassion that we are able to experience not only sympathy but also empathy with our fellows; not only feeling for them but feeling with them. In short, if we are incapable of active charity we are morally defective.

The third essentially human quality we are exhorted to cultivate is that of conscience, that certain point of reference which we experience in the depths of our being by which we are able to appraise a given situation and make moral judgements concerning it, and to realize the incentive to act accordingly. There is no need to resort to anything relating to casuistry, much less sophistry, in all this. By curbing our self-interest and adopting as far as possible a practical viewpoint we gradually become less selfish and more altruistic. The stirrings of our conscience prompt us to correct any tendency towards unprincipled impulses and any temptation to behave in a self-indulgent manner. In this regard Steiner had this observation to make:

> ... sharpness of conscience [should be] the pre-requisite of any spiritual movement. If we lack this sharpness of conscience, if we do not feel the most intense responsibility to the holiest truth, we shall make no progress on any other path.... it will above all be necessary to have eyes for the quality of love and compassion.[21]

He spoke about these matters with great earnestness, and what he had to say echoes Paul's words, but with added stark words of warning:

> Whatever wrongs are committed in these three realms [wonder, compassion, conscience] deprive the Christ of the full possibility of full development on the Earth; that is to say, Earth-evolution is left imperfect. Those who go about the Earth with indifference and unconcern, who have no urge to understand what the Earth can reveal to them, deprive the Astral Body of Christ of the possibility of full development; those who live without unfolding compassion and love hinder the Etheric Body of Christ from full development, and those who lack conscience impede the development of what corresponds to the Physical Body of Christ ... but this means that the Earth cannot reach the goal of its evolution.[22]

Are we up to the task?

It is time to return to our earlier considerations concerning the will to work[23] and strive ceaselessly to succeed in cherishing Anthroposophy and fostering her children, and the adage *laborare est orare* (to work is to pray) also supports this notion. But having once put our hand to the plough, there can be no looking back, stony as the way may be. Rudolf Steiner gave warning of this:

To us it is given
At no stage ever to rest.
They live and thrive, the active
Human beings from life unto life,
As plants grow from springtime
To springtime—ever aloft,
Through error upward to truth,
Through fetters upward to freedom,
Through illness and death;
Upward to beauty, to health and to life.[24]

Some individuals will plead, like the chemistry teacher in
the first Waldorf School, that they are putting every effort
into their work as it is, and that a modicum of 'ever-present
help of the spiritual world' would be very welcome. Rudolf
Steiner was often asked why so little help seemed to arrive
from that quarter, and he invariably replied that, to put it
crudely, the spiritual world could only match appropriate
effort with appropriate reward, measure for measure. If a
vessel for receiving the bounty has not been fashioned, it
cannot be given. This response is consistent with what he
maintained with regard to people's efforts concerning spiritual development, namely that we shall be 'rewarded' for
our efforts only when we are sufficiently mature to receive
reward. This may constitute cold comfort for those who have
been striving for years towards their goal, but we have no
choice but to accept what is bestowed on us as fair and just.

Steiner gave solemn assurance that the spiritual world is
indeed alive to our strivings, and reminded us that although
we have immediate adversaries we also have allies, unseen
but nonetheless real. Lucifer is ever ready to promote illusions of every kind, to whirl us away into the realms of
daydream and exaggerated expectations, of unrealistic
hopes, wishes and desires. Ahriman is ever lurking in the
nearby shadows to delude and entrap us, to warp our thinking

and sow misapprehension, deceit and lies. However, we have a secure if stern helper in Michael, none other than the herald of and champion of Christ. The closing words Rudolf Steiner spoke at the end of what turned out to be his 'last address' are at once inspiring and encouraging:

> You, disciples of spirit-knowledge,
> Take Michael's Wisdom beckoning,
> Take the Word of Love of the Will of Worlds,
> Into your souls' aspiring, actively.[25]

7. Do Not Disturb![1]

Peter Bridgmont

'The devil lies in the detail', refers not to that medieval character from the old pageants but to a fundamental reality: that the study of the detail involved in any project or thought soon reveals whether either project or thought has substance. I think it is due to inaccurate observation that we as students of Rudolf Steiner's work do not give him credit for the detail he manages to establish in his lectures. The subject of those lectures could so easily become a trap allowing for vast generalizations and assumptions and unnatural fantasies. His careful choice of words and cautious framing of ideas generates trust in him, which is essential if we are to journey along his path as he opens a Pandora's Box of occultism.

I believe that we all too often impress our own careless thinking on Steiner's words, ignoring the minute detail with which he constructs the new images that shape the thinking within the more intense study of mankind introduced by him.

For historical reasons the centre for study eventually came to be established not in Central Europe but off-centre, so that it now lies on the periphery of the action in Europe. This brought about a misalignment between occult science as a study and its place in the field of scientific study and the whirlwind of social, political activity during the early and middle parts of the twentieth century. Perhaps this is a partial cause for an increasingly non-scientific approach to Steiner's detailed and, we presume, accurate observations.

The central building of the anthroposophical movement, rejected by the city of its choice, was forced to flee outside the political action that soon followed. Thus ostracized, the movement from its early days experienced the pain of iso-lationism. This sense of a fortress (Steiner's description of the second Goetheanum building) can encourage a yearning for mutual support; refugees may band together, creating a dangerous field of tension that divides the supporters from the apparent non-supporters. The result is a tribal stance that is both unhealthy and often quite ridiculous.

We have almost become one of those groups that have succumbed to the safety of such political parties, tribes, cults, believers, members, advocates and so forth, united in the belief that such unity creates a positive social mood strong enough to withstand whatever may come to threaten it.

Yet we know that this is the age of the anti-social, an age to stimulate thoughts and a consciousness which provides that which we most desire instinctively at this time: a sense of standing on our own two feet.

Challenging, confrontational, antagonistic it may be, but this anti-social mood is one that belongs to the English-speaking world and instinctively demonstrates a soul mood belonging to the present age. Aggressive it may be, but greater harm has come from a passive attitude that has weakened considerably the society of occult scientists and students gathered around at present. The belief that mutual understanding, that a sharing and caring society is essential for establishing a direction and a purpose towards meeting the karma of the future, is questionable. Steiner himself pointed out that this is a futile ambition and a recipe for failure.

Two towering examples coming out of Europe have loomed over the twentieth century, based on attempts to establish mass agreement. Again and again the festering wounds break out all over the world, in vain and often cruel attempts to establish a common purpose. Again and again it all collapses, bringing intolerable grief to all involved.

In the anthroposophical movement we have not inflicted upon ourselves the laws of social unity but have weakened the possibility of moving forward by our persistent belief that a warm and cosy atmosphere is a pre-requisite for research. Fear of losing the comfort and warmth of mutual friendship has created a parody of study and thus allowed new ideas to degenerate. Helena's speech and the way Johannes reacts in Steiner's first Mystery Play—this epitomizes the danger we are in.[2]

As Steiner pointed out, 'This is not the English style.' We know we have a definitive task for the future which may be in opposition to the distant future but is nevertheless at this time an essential and correct attitude. The English-speaking peoples instinctively possess an attitude towards information, discussion and belief that is right for now. Yet this has been ignored for the past forty years and we have instead the soft culture of the bourgeois of Central Europe rather than the abrasive egoism and individualism that belongs to the Anglo-Saxon.

Unless this anti-social style is quickly recognized as an objective necessity for the future, we must be both damned and doomed by the poison of habitual manners, pandering and phlegmatism that has haunted us for too long.

Steiner would speak of the need for society to be organized in such a way that the (then so-called) working classes could participate fully in it, for without them the destiny of humanity could not continue in the way it should. They should not be seen as a race apart, but the whole of society should be a gathering of individuals. I have seen in Anthroposophical Society meetings people suffering all manner of humiliation and rejection, and growing embittered with the cavorting on stage of lecturers who came and went in a series of brief encounters. I have seen those I speak of weep over the words of Steiner in his book *Towards Social Renewal*.[3] I have heard those who sat silently while others pontificated on the meaning of this or that phrase, suddenly break their silence with the words, 'This man understands us; he understands the working class.' Which left the pontificators, in turn, sitting silently.

Steiner would often address a member who was abrasive and awkward by his or her first name, like a colleague, rejecting the complaints of others about that individual's bad manners and general behaviour. It must have become clear to him that the whole work of research and study was lifting off the ground like a hot-air balloon. This caused him to organize the Foundation Stone meetings and grasp the waistcoats of the workers as he would grasp a brother.

Almost too late? I would not dare to answer! Nevertheless, under the aphorism 'two heads are better than one', grasping the waistcoat of the world and the cravat of knowledge, we may yet find a bridge of understanding that can plant wisdom. This would renew the study of detail, an anathema to the romantics, and force us to observe in the physical world the deeds of the invisible, and ground the study in a truly scientific mood, so sought after by Strader in the first Mystery Play.

8. Anthroposophy in Britain—How Did We Get Here?

Richard Seddon

It seems rash to generalize as to where 'we' are in the development of Anthroposophy, since this surely differs in every location, and indeed in every individual; but a brief comparison with the situation when I joined the Society in the UK over fifty years ago may show where there is progress (or otherwise), and the direction it is taking. Obviously there are always exceptions to every generalization made.

There were then two societies here: the Anthroposophical Society in Great Britain (A.S. in G.B.), entirely separate from the worldwide General Anthroposophical Society (G.A.S.) founded at Christmas 1923; and the smaller English Section (E.S.) of the G.A.S. This separation had arisen from personal loyalties which need not concern us here, but were very deeply and sincerely felt, especially by those who had participated in events before World War II. It seemed at the time that members of the A.S. in G.B., which occupied Rudolf Steiner House in London, worked mainly through lectures and in the practical activities; whereas members of the E.S., which had a small headquarters near the British Museum, were very conscious that the first stage of the Rosicrucian path was 'study'. Attendance at the weekly study groups of the E.S., which in some cases simply heard in reverent awe the reading of a lecture and in others continued animated conversation late into the evening, was therefore a priority commitment, around which personal arrangements had to take second place. The intensity of devotion of those who had heard Rudolf Steiner himself speaking was very marked.

Apart from the basic books written by Steiner, only a few of his lecture cycles had been translated, and there were very few works by other authors. These were consequently well known, and formed a common language amongst members. It was said that if one mastered *Occult Science* to the degree that a concert pianist masters his music, no other book was needed.[1] The proliferation of books today gives a wonderful opportunity for wider understanding, but brings the danger of detracting from the depth of experience.

Souls in the E.S. were nourished fortnightly by the *News Sheet* from the Goetheanum, which carried half an unpublished lecture by Steiner, often chosen for its topicality, and a short essay or 'little myth' by Albert Steffen, which challenged the imagination. A.S. in G.B. members received the *Anthroposophical Quarterly*, with a full lecture by Steiner and scholarly studies of esoteric substance. (That is why today's *Life in the Anthroposophical Society*[2] and *New View*[3], with short articles rightly directed to the general public, nevertheless leave some older members feeling a gap. But it must not be forgotten that the Society, as a charity, exists not for the benefit of its members but for the education of the general public in the work of Rudolf Steiner.)

Membership of both Societies together was less than a third that of today, yet the occasional A.S. in G.B. conference drew about 250 participants, the Exeter conference (1973) even more. The E.S. ran annual lecture series by Hermann Poppelbaum (later president of the G.A.S.) or Paul Schiller, until in 1960 their annual conferences at Leicester began (drawing about 120 participants). Here half the lectures were soon replaced by working groups, and artistic contributions such as eurythmy were specifically related to the conference theme. Gradually the art of conversation developed. There were then none of the small conferences devoted to special interests which—thanks especially to Emerson College and Hawkwood College—today contribute so much to the practical work in many fields. This is a most fruitful development, so long as the connection with the core of Anthroposophy— as exemplified by the Schooling Course—is sustained. It is important for such courses—and indeed *New View*—to be made known wherever English is the first or second language, which thanks to the Internet now means the whole world.

Both societies were led by people who felt inward loyalty to the Class Lessons, although in the A.S. in G.B. these were spoken of as the 'Esoteric Class', an old theosophical term, and not recognized as the First Class of the School of Spiritual Science. Indeed, the School was there misunderstood as separate from the Lessons and thought to exist, if at all, only in Dornach. The Camphill movement was at that time largely independent, with a separate esotericism derived from its founder, Karl König.

After several attempts to bring the two societies together had foundered, it was the formation of a single circle of those responsible for holding the Class Lessons, in which individuals from Camphill also took part, that enabled Cecil Harwood, following the pattern of F. W. Zeylmans in Holland, to take the courageous step of guiding the A.S. in G.B. back into the G.A.S. led by Albert Steffen. This in turn enabled the E.S. to unite spiritually with the A.S. in G.B. (its Trustees forming a single body with the latter's Council members) and to dissolve formally in 1970. Since throughout history spiritual organizations have formed splinter groups, this reunion was of the greatest significance, setting an example not only to the Christian churches but to all religions, which will in future become an absolute demand. It is good to note today the 'Churches Together' movement gaining strength at local level in Britain.

An attempt to bring the constitution of the A.S. in G.B. into a form similar to the principles given by Steiner at Christmas 1923 was dropped, because it was felt that too much energy can be spent on arguing the minutiae of such matters which should be used more creatively elsewhere; and that the present constitution was no obstacle to such creative work.

An Assembly of active members which met at regional centres around Britain served the useful purpose of making members of the newly united Society better known to one another; but it did not then find a further purpose and was also discontinued—although in the more widely-scattered areas occasional regional meetings continue to be fruitful, especially for those who find travel difficult.

The Council has repeatedly agonized as to its true function, beyond the essential minimum as trustees of a charitable organization. It has consciously rejected the idea that it should be a centre of initiative, since initiatives arise from the work of individuals wherever they may be, especially in the work of the School. It has become clear that there are certain things the Council should not do, such as manage the Rudolf Steiner Press, or events at Rudolf Steiner House, and this has been implemented.

The way forward will probably be found in a council each of whose members is chosen as able to be responsible for liaison with those active in a specific field of work. Generalized responsibility, such as results from election, is no responsibility, and does not belong to the spiritual sphere. The fundamental task of the Society, and hence the Council, is the 'furtherance' of research carried out by the School.

Once the First Class was recognized as the centre of the

School of Spiritual Science, fruitful connections could develop between the School and the practical work. In Britain this was first grasped by the Medical Section, which faced enormous problems here in securing legal recognition of anthroposophical medicine, and in the establishment of Park Attwood—undertakings in which support from other European countries was invaluable.

The Education Section soon followed. Fifty years ago there were only five Steiner Waldorf schools in Britain, but teachers nevertheless found time to play leading roles in the work of both Societies, and many belonged to the First Class. Now that the number of schools has increased (though it is still modest compared with other European countries) such people appear thinly spread. The corresponding loss of inner strength, and the weakened commitment to pupils by class teachers for the full period of 8 years, has counteracted devotion to Steiner Waldorf education as such.

This dilution of inner spirituality may also lie behind the fact that the Youth Section has not become regularly established in Britain, unlike Europe, despite valiant efforts on the part of individuals and the meetings at Emerson College for the twelfth classes of the schools. Whilst of course Anthroposophy is not taught in the schools, the enthusiasm for the spirit so necessary to counter the enormous demands of modern life is not yet apparent among ex-pupils.

Despite the work of three eurythmy schools and a speech school, and real achievements such as the presentation of the Mystery Dramas in English as well as other touring ventures, the performing arts have not yet broken through to the degree of public recognition that would make them viable. This may be connected with the fact that the relevant Section is only just beginning to come together here in Britain. Much the same might be said of the visual arts, whose Section has also recently come together.

The Science Section faces a particularly rigid establishment here, which is difficult to penetrate, but the demand for organic produce may provide an opportunity for the biodynamic movement. There is particular need for inter-sectional work by the Science Section in the development of morphology, study of the metamorphosis of form in the realm of nature (as pursued by this Section at the Goetheanum), in the realm of art (for example in the Goetheanum columns), and in that of medicine (in the metamorphosis of the body of one life into the head of the next) through which the process of reincarnation and karma will gain public recognition.

A vague feeling for reincarnation is much more common than it was, but needs the clarity which comes from an understanding of karma, the reality of biography. Much effort has been directed to this in inter-personal group work, which now needs to be directed outwards. Since one task of the Society is to prepare for the sixth age, a further step needs to be taken within it, which can be briefly expressed in the difference between 'awakening to the other person' and 'awakening at the other person'. It involves really experiencing that our true ego lies not within our own skin, but is actually part of all that we see or hear, especially in those around us who have anything to do with us; and the corollary is that within our skin is a world external to our ego that includes part of the egos of those around us.[4] Only when we become 'hollow' in this way do we make space for Christ, too, to dwell within us.

The Social Science Section was the last to be formed within the G.A.S. But Steiner had already set a special task for it in Britain when he met the second group of English visitors to Dornach after World War I. He told them that the British had the responsibility 'to bring real spirituality into the external empire of the economic life ... or else the demise of earthly civilization will be the guaranteed consequence ...

the situation is much worse than one can bring oneself to imagine ... Do not be afraid of opposition, for to have opposition and to speak the truth is one and the same thing today'.[5] Unfortunately, despite the example set by Daniel Dunlop, this challenge lay unpublished and unknown for over 70 years, and the 'threefold idea' did not take root. But meanwhile the Mercury Provident Society (now Triodos Bank) had started its financial activity, one worthy of the human being.

It seems to be from such small beginnings that the foundations must be prepared on which a threefold society may eventually grow, not by decree from above but by demand from below. There are many signs that it is wanted, from demands for alternative medicine to organic food; for social justice and environmentalism; from community development to a state freed from hereditary privilege. All these depend for success on a change in the whole basis of thinking, which Anthroposophy alone can bring.

9. Only Better Thoughts will Create Better Facts

An interview with Thomas Meyer about
his novel *Der unverbrüchliche Vertrag*[1]
(Questions by Rainer Monnet)

*Herr Meyer, how did you come to write a novel with this
particular and somewhat unusual title?*
The novel is a kind of metamorphosis of books I have written
on certain pupils of Rudolf Steiner, in particular W. J. Stein,
L. Polzer-Hoditz and D. N. Dunlop.[2] It arose quite organically from my work on those books. The title refers to a
prophetic 'unbreakable agreement' (R. Steiner) that was
reached in the spiritual world at the turn of the twelfth to the
thirteenth century concerning the end of our present twentieth century [see below]. 'Unbreakable' signifies that the
prophetic contract referred to was one of those quite specific
agreements of a spiritual nature that cannot simply be
overturned in the fashion so common today where agreements made in personal or political life are concerned. Those
special agreements endure with a 'cast-iron necessity'.

Why did you choose the form of a novel?
A novel gives you greater freedom to depict things that can
only be hinted at in a more historically documented
presentation. A novel appeals to the reader's imagination,
and also offers artistic possibilities not available on the same
scale to a historian or biographer. I have been looking for

some time to find means of expression different from those suitable for a biography, which has to abide by the external facts.

Why and to what extent do you consider the subject of this type of 'prophecy' to be artistically presentable?
Let me first explain briefly what is meant by this contract or this 'prophecy'. It refers in essence to human souls belonging to two separate yet complementary streams. On the one hand a number of souls who had until then been oriented more in the direction of Plato's view of the world, and who had been active at Chartres and elsewhere, were to continue their work in the spiritual world until the middle of the twentieth century. On the other hand, allied with those Platonists, there were certain individualities termed Aristotelians who, during the time of the Scholastics, were to help found the sciences. Later, both at the beginning and at the end of the twentieth century, incorporated in earthly bodies, they were to contribute to the spiritualizing of human thinking, which would by then have grown entirely materialistic under the influence of those very sciences. At the end of the twentieth century, soon to be upon us, representatives of both these streams are to meet and work energetically together. This 'agreement', this 'contract' forms the background to the novel.

One part of the 'contract' thus refers to the early reincarnation of Aristotelian souls who, at the beginning of the twentieth century, had already once been pupils of Rudolf Steiner. Another term Steiner used for this part of the 'agreement' or 'contract' was the 'Michael Prophecy'. In a different sense this designation could also be applied to the 'agreement' as a whole. However, since a number of reincarnated persons from the more Aristotelian circle of pupils around Rudolf Steiner figure in it, my novel is more connected with the 'Michael Prophecy' in the narrower sense. The extent to which I may have succeeded in giving artistic expression to these radical events and far-reaching prospects remains to be judged by kind readers. There is no doubt that opinions will differ.

Would you say a few words about the Michael Prophecy and its consequences?

The fulfilment of the prophecy depends, also, on the free will of those pupils of Rudolf Steiner to whom it refers, individuals who heard of it with their own ears in 1924. Some of these pupils of Rudolf Steiner who served as models for the book lived inwardly with the prophecy in a way that showed how extremely seriously they took it. Amongst a number of other matters, the very first sentence in the book, which is repeated at the end, is not invented but was actually spoken by one of those pupils: 'By the way, I intend to collect my notes myself at the end of the century.' This is the point at which the novel begins. I have allowed myself to paint a picture of what it might look like when these pupils reincarnate, taking the prophecy seriously and making it come true through their own free will. I was not concerned to present an occultistic prophecy of external details respecting these incarnations. What I wanted to do through the novel was project into their present, new incarnation something of certain individuals' characteristic ways of inner endeavour that it has been possible to discover by studying their former incarnations.

It is as impossible to foresee fatalistically what the consequences of this prophecy will be as it is to foretell whether it will be fulfilled at all. One thing it will all depend on is whether the anthroposophical movement (not only in the Society but wherever serious efforts are being made to enter into Steiner's works) will succeed in appreciating people who want to work with what you might call potentized anthroposophical impulses. These are the people with whom contact should be sought. Within the Anthroposophical Society, though, the opinion is widely held that such individuals, conversely, would seek contact with today's Society. I regard this as a dangerous degree of unthinking presumption.

The hero of your novel, Harold Freeman, makes his appearance in two ways. On the one hand the narrator writes about him, and on the other hand he himself reflects on the day's experiences in letters to his fiancée Fiona. What was your purpose in presenting him in this way?
It made it possible for me to depict events more from the outside on the one hand, and on the other to present them in the way they are reflected inwardly by a specific individual. It allows for a degree of contrast in that on some occasions Freeman's letters reflect something strongly that has only been briefly touched on by the narrator, while at other times he reflects something only weakly or not at all that might appear extremely important in the external narrative. The ongoing comments by the main protagonist also provided a framework that enabled me to run a thread of continuity through the novel with its many different layers.

Your book is dedicated to all true pupils of Rudolf Steiner. What do you mean by this?
By 'true pupils' I mean all those who are really and truly interested in the being and destiny of anthroposophically oriented spiritual science. This includes those pupils who were already present at the beginning of the twentieth century. These are of course not exclusively members of the Anthroposophical Society. In fact I was actually thinking more of those who for a variety of reasons have nothing or very little to do with this Society although they are concerned for the being and the destiny of Anthroposophy. Since

Anthroposophy is a matter of worldwide importance, the circle of open-minded contemporaries caring for it is by no means restricted to members of today's Anthroposophical Society.

Rudolf Steiner's name is not mentioned until near the end of the novel; for most of the book you call him simply 'the Master'. Why didn't you omit his name altogether?
There was no way I could have suppressed Steiner's name entirely above all because it is a name that certain people frequently misuse, people who are not capable of genuinely defending Steiner when he is attacked. For example pupils of that ilk spread the word that Steiner never put forward any teachings about races, hoping thereby to circumvent the absurd reproach of Steiner having had 'racist' leanings. What ought to be explained to the world in reality is that Steiner's works contain the profoundest teachings about races (and about peoples) that have ever been expounded, and that this has absolutely nothing whatever to do with racism. Yet people steer clear of doing this.

Another reason for including Steiner's name in the novel is the following. Certain people lack appreciation of Anthroposophy because it sets limits to their own boundless aspirations for power. Nothing would please these people more than the disappearance of Steiner's name from the planet. Or, if this can no longer be achieved, they would like to see it mendaciously coupled with racist or other similar ideas.

These are basically my two reasons: firstly the way certain people name Steiner, his works and his concerns without understanding them or with insufficient courage to represent or defend them; and secondly the way some opponents in the occult sense want to hush up his existence altogether or else drag his name through the gutter. By the latter I mean the more Masonic or Jesuitical tendencies which, as we know, are now intermingled wherever you look. Think of Brussels, or of America's famous crucible for diplomats, Georgetown University in Washington.

Isn't your novel intended for anthroposophists only?
What do you mean by 'only'? I wrote the book for any contemporaries who are genuinely interested in following up the prospects and difficulties a movement as important for the world as Steiner's is likely to face at the end of the twentieth century.

You don't spare the present chairman of the Anthroposophical Society some rather harsh satirical criticism, calling him a 'Grand Copht'. Where is the dividing line between fiction and reality if you point in this way to present problems in the General Anthroposophical Society?
I rather hope that the reality of today's Anthroposophical Society is not as bad as the occasionally satirical image of the style of leadership and certain leading personalities presented in the novel. That would certainly be my wish! Readers will have to ask themselves whether the character called the 'Grand Copht' is satirically overdone or not.

You accuse the leadership of the General Anthroposophical Society, as described in the novel, of harbouring leanings towards Jesuitical or Masonic streams either consciously or unconsciously. What do you mean by this? And do you think these streams pose a threat to this movement in actual fact?
Nowhere in the novel is there a blanket accusation of the General Anthroposophical Society being in cahoots with Freemasonry or other similar spiritual streams. In fact I think you will find that a number of representatives or functionaries of the General Anthroposophical Society, for example

the lady who is leader of the branch in Stuttgart, are painted entirely sympathetically. I most certainly had no intention of arousing any overall negative feelings towards the General Anthroposophical Society. It is a fact, however, that some of the leading functionaries of the General Anthroposophical Society, in particular the person described as the 'Grand Copht', quite obviously show a remarkable tolerance towards streams that equally obviously have no genuine interest in allowing Anthroposophy to come, shall we say, into its own in its pure form. I need only draw your attention to this person's overemphasis on Compostella for a number of years now; I have spoken about this phenomenon elsewhere as well.

Your novel has certain figures expressing criticism of the 'Grand Copht'; is this based on actual experiences of your own—unsympathetic or dramatic personal experiences perhaps?
I have taken myself to task very seriously as to whether what the Grand Copht is based on might have been influenced by any personal sentiments of whatever kind. It is not. Honest critics of the book will not find it easy to get to the bottom of this. Whether you like it or not, this high functionary and representative of Anthroposophy's cause displays—in addition to other entirely acceptable traits—certain peculiar leanings that cannot have been motivated by anything fundamentally anthroposophical. These are what have been characterized as 'Grand Copht tendencies'. As far as I am concerned, the actual person behind my description is not the deciding factor in this.

What made you choose the designation 'Grand Copht'?
'*Der Grosskophta*' was the title of the first play Goethe put on at the theatre he managed in Weimar. In this play he

poked fun at the pseudo-occult charlatanism flourishing in certain circles in his day. His model was Cagliostro of whom, though, he did not have as balanced an understanding as that later given to us by Steiner. For Goethe, Cagliostro epitomized the 'pied piper' of the pseudo-occult scene.[3] The play also pokes fun at the unbelievable gullibility with which some people are endowed.

At the end of your novel the protagonist, Harold Freeman, wonders whether and how a writer might or will approach the theme of the book. Is this a sign of irony, or hidden vanity?
Let me frame my reply as follows. The chapter 'Basle' mentions three gentlemen who claim to be the reincarnated personalities D. N. Dunlop, W. J. Stein and L. Polzer-Hoditz. This actually happened; I did not make it up as you might have thought. Three youngish men called on me one day. After we had eaten supper together they first hinted and then declared openly that they considered themselves to be Dunlop, Stein and Polzer-Hoditz. They said I had a right to know this because in my work I had paid so much attention to those individuals. This visit took place at the very moment when my fictitious hero had also arrived in Basle. The three young men had had this illusion served up to them by a clairvoyant. The very fact that they let on about these 'truths' unasked told me immediately that I was in the company of some rather pitiable dupes. This extraordinary coincidence between my inner work and that outer event led to my gaining a deeper motivation for the whole book. I decided to let my fictitious hero hear about this actual happening. He meditates on it, describes it to Fiona in one of his letters, and comes to the conclusion that it might be sensible if some fictional form could be used to point out the *reality* of the situation in which he and those like him find themselves, since illusory *fictions* about them are beginning to appear in external reality.

Are you sure that individualities such as Stein or Polzer-Hoditz have really reincarnated? Who takes Steiner's prophecy about the end of the twentieth century seriously?

As regards your first question I can only say that if you really look into the intentions these people carried within them in the years leading up to their deaths you will find that they had indeed taken the profound and far-reaching free decision to incarnate again at the end of this century. Let me remind you once more of the first sentence in my book, which is not an invention of mine but the actual words spoken by one of them. You have to take it seriously when people of that calibre reach a decision freely. It sufficed for me to begin drafting a description of this 'utopia', this imagined situation, if you like, in which such personalities might find themselves at the end of the twentieth century.

While I was writing I also began to realize, however, that this prophecy is indeed taken very seriously, but not, as one might have expected, within the General Anthroposophical Society. The standard attitude there is, firstly, that Rudolf Steiner united himself with the Anthroposophical Society (in perpetuity, as many members of the Society erroneously believe). Secondly his good and faithful pupils will therefore also have to have dealings with this Society once again because, thirdly, they will want to live and work wherever their Master is living and working. This is the *blanket* manner in which the General Anthroposophical Society treats Steiner's prophecy about the end of the century.

There are signs, though, that this prophecy is being taken extremely seriously in certain other circles, of a Jesuitical or Masonic kind, where it is causing a good deal of trepidation because it involves the arrival on the scene of human beings who already have an incarnation of anthroposophical schooling behind them, and who will therefore not be so easy to control. This is no laughing matter for members of those

circles. They intend therefore either to take no notice of the
prophecy or to cause confusion by means of spreading false
stories concerning those reincarnations. This is where my
three visitors fit in, with their illusions about being reincarnations of the three main figures in the novel. It was that
extraordinary visit with its uncannily accurate timing that
drew my attention to this very grave hidden background. I
realized the scale of the spiritual battle that is actually going
on with regard to the actualization of the Michael Prophecy.

*Do you believe that Steiner himself will also reincarnate at the
end of the century?*
Walter Johannes Stein wrote in his diary: 'Heydebrand[4] says,
"In 1922 at Stratford Dr Steiner said that he would return in
America in 80 years' time".'

   This diary entry is extant. Does it mean he would be active
again then, at the beginning of the third millennium, in 2002?
Or would he be entering a new incarnation then? There are a
number of other utterances which suggest that Rudolf
Steiner intended to reincarnate at the end of the century.
One must presume, as is shown in the novel, that he will then
work quietly, away from the limelight, as the Master of the
'forty-eight', which is of course only a symbolic number
denoting the most loyal of his pupils.[5] He will surely not have
the task a second time round of giving lectures and appearing
in public. His works already exist in the world.

*There is little external drama in your novel; its action lies more
in the narrative, and it has an open ending. What made you
adopt this kind of construction?*
Do you really think there is little external drama when it ends
with the main protagonist about to be murdered, poisoned?
The people involved naturally possess a degree of confidence, perhaps even a certainty that they will win through

eventually. But I believe the novel shows that they are at the same time being menaced by the most terrible threats. As you say, the book has an open ending.

As a junior diplomat, Harold Freeman travels in Central Europe where he endeavours to take on a specific task. Would you say something about this?
In the future it will be important, I believe, for there to be an understanding and a representation of Central Europe in America. Equally in Central Europe an understanding should develop for the more profound possibilities America has to offer; these can be symbolically summarized in the name of Ralph Waldo Emerson. That is why I have also included this layer in the book. It points to the possibility of collaboration between the Central European and the western element, a collaboration that is at present only a possibility existing below the surface without having become fully real. Harold Freeman is like an embodiment of this possibility, since he carries something of both sides in himself.

Will your novel have a sequel?
Heaven only knows!

Postscript by Thomas Meyer

Behind one of the figures in the novel is the individuality of Eliza von Moltke, wife of Helmuth von Moltke, Chief of General Staff who led the German army into the First World War and died in 1916.[6] Not only was Helmuth von Moltke deeply interested in Rudolf Steiner's spiritual science, but Steiner himself was deeply interested in and linked with the destiny of Moltke. An outcome of this was that Steiner not only followed the after-death development of this individuality (which he did in many other cases too) but actually wrote down hundreds of pages inspired by the departed soul over many years. One of the recurring themes in these post-mortem communications is the individuality's new incarnation at the end of the twentieth century and its new world-historic tasks. In fact, seven years prior to the karma lectures,[7] we find here a kind of prelude to Steiner's far-reaching revelations about the reincarnation of early anthroposophists at the end of the century.

Whereas in the ninth century 'Moltke' had to separate the West from the East, thus becoming the great preparer for Central European development in the second millennium, he will in his present incarnation help to reunite East and West on the basis of spiritual impulses. Thus, for instance, we read in the communication of 22 June 1918:

> It will be the opposite task from the one we had in the ninth century ... In the ninth century we pushed back to the East what was of no use for the West and Central Europe. But it continued to live in the East. Since then, it has lived in the souls of the people of the East, but now it is disengaging from the people, and is becoming like an auric cloud rolling from East to West. What is thus rolling like an auric cloud across Europe from the East during the course of the twentieth century will take shape at the end of the century in such a way that it will be our task to take hold of it. Humanity is being prepared more and more for the realization that one cannot be happy with what is to be found solely on the physical plane, though everyone is seeking for it there. People will have to cease looking for this happiness and will have to realize that what comes from the spiritual world must flow into everything that the human being experiences on the earth.

Such are some of the key motifs for the future development of human beings in general and the new relation between West and East at the end of the twentieth century in particular. The present war in Kosovo actually demonstrates what must inevitably happen if instead of a new spirituality mere narrow-minded power impulses are allowed to rule national affairs (as in Serbia) and east-west affairs (as conducted by current NATO war policy).

In a communication dated 2 February 1922 we read: 'Many adversities are yet to come and pass by. But the light at the end of the twentieth century shines brightly before my soul.'

We are in the midst of perhaps the most cruel of all such adversities—and yet we may strengthen our hopes for a more spiritually oriented way of dealing with national and international affairs if we link ourselves spiritually with the present and future task of an individuality such as Helmuth von Moltke. He is not alone but cooperates closely with many other souls reincarnated from the beginning of the century; and all such souls are inspired by their occult master, Rudolf Steiner.

To link our thoughts with such perspectives can be a real contribution towards a peaceful development of individual and social affairs. Such a contribution should not be underestimated merely because it appears to rest only on 'thoughts'. It is precisely the 'mainstream' *thoughts* of the past hundred years or so which have produced the present dead end of almost all of human civilization and culture and led humanity to the dangerous pit of a new barbarism into which it might fall. Only better thoughts will create better facts. Or, as communicated by the Moltke soul in May 1918: 'People on earth must learn from events that thoughts are facts.'

10. The Vision of Avitus[1]

Mario Betti

Hesitantly Brother Avitus entered the cell of his beloved brother and master where documents of many kinds still bore witness to a life of tireless inquiry.

Avitus could scarcely stem his sadness, although Alanus had died some time ago. Everything was more or less as the revered teacher had left it: the simple bedstead upon which the ancient master had spent his last days after a fall; the crock containing earth from his faraway home, brought to him by a friend of his youth; and many of his life's works. The estate left behind by the *Doctor universalis* was comprehensive indeed. It covered theology, poetry, philosophy, the arts. Everything showed his unmistakable style: concise, confident in diction and forceful in style. 'Citeaux is much in debt to Alanus de Insulis,' thought Avitus, 'and Christendom, too, owes him a very great deal.'

Brother Avitus retraced in his mind the steps of that life as told to the monks by the abbot yesterday during the chapter meeting at which they had commemorated the death day of Alanus. There had been long years of apprenticeship and journeying—though nothing like the whole was known—from Hibernia to Italy, from Spain, where he had dwelt among the Arabs and learned much, to the lands that lie in the East. Above all, though, Avitus thought about the time spent on Mont St Michel, that craggy island which had been so crucial for the onward path of Alanus. There the young Alain, tormented by pangs of conscience, had prayed

fervently to Saint Michael, asking whether what he had
learned among the Arabs was really such a sin; for the belief
had been widespread that the knowledge cultivated by the
Arabs was sinful. The Archangel had appeared to him,
handing the young man deep in meditation a sword with a
pommel shaped like a red rose, before saying: 'Follow me,
Alain, for I need companions in arms.' Alain knew that
thenceforward his powers of thinking would be safe under
the protection of Michael.

Learned in theology, Alanus journeyed from land to land,
fighting with the word for the true wisdom of Christianity. He
entered the Cistercian order only later in life. In Chartres,
where he had taught many times, he witnessed the terrible
conflagration of 1194 that caused large sections of the
wonderful church dedicated to Mary to collapse. Alanus, old
now, was said to have taken this as a sign from heaven that a
long period of human history devoted to the service of the
sublime Natura-Sophia was drawing to a close. Human
thinking would soon come to resemble the charred remains
of that house of god: dark, lifeless and arid. He knew this was
the dawn of an age when the spirit would be denied.

Dwelling on all this in his thoughts, Avitus was overtaken
all at once by weariness; indeed, he often spent more hours of
the night than his brother monks in prayer. He sat down on
the simple stool formerly occupied by Alanus as he bent over
his manuscripts and studies. Slowly closing his eyes, Avitus
suddenly felt his soul gently lifted from his body as though by
a beat of wings; he entered realms of light hitherto unfamiliar
to him.

Beneath an immense dome sprinkled with stars and borne
up by twelve pillars that seemed to grow out of the earth,
Avitus saw a multitude of people. In two groups, they
surrounded an altar firmly built below a great window of
stained glass. One group, to the left of the altar, were clothed

as though in white, in garments of soul that had passed beyond death and been rendered shining by pain and inmost love of wisdom. Before this group, near to the altar, Avitus recognized the figure, changed somewhat, of his beloved teacher.

To the right of the altar he saw the other group of human souls, in whose faces, youthful and solemnly festive, he discerned a wonderful clarity of expression. As his capability for understanding grew, Avitus saw they were souls preparing to descend into earthly bodies; clarity of thought and strength of will were their main attributes. On earth they would serve the Logos who had become Man. Their firm resolve to come to earth showed in a darker cloak worn by each of them and clearly distinguishable from the lighter mantles of the other souls. On their side of the altar, looking deeply into the eyes of Alanus, stood a wonderful human figure. His countenance, clear as crystal, was such as Avitus had never yet seen in a human being—or was he more than human?

Before reaching a conclusion about this he saw that Alanus held in his hand a mighty flame of fire through which flashed crystalline forms. Towards him came the other one, bearing the most translucent crystal of quartz in the midst of which a gentle fire burned. Side by side they stood before the altar, laying their gifts upon it. Their offerings mingled and burst into a brilliance that seemed to reach the highest ceiling of the dome.

Avitus had not noticed before that the stained window depicted Michael on the point of conquering a dragon, but now immediately he realized that both those groups of human beings belonged to Michael. The one, led by the man whom later generations would call *Doctor angelicus*, was now preparing to fill earthly culture with thoughts of spirit. Yet this would be no more than a preparation, for Michael's eyes looked far into the distant future.

Avitus saw a time ahead in which the dragon would have subjugated great expanses of the earth. He heard the cries of despairing human beings, and curses denying the spirit; and he saw the dawn of a new millennium. He remembered words spoken by Alanus after the last feast of Michael they had celebrated together: 'The thoughts of human beings will become like the blackened stones after the conflagration at Chartres, dark and barren, unable to rise to heights of spirit. But in times that are not too far distant Michael will seize, from within, the thinking into which the dragon has wormed his way; he will fan the flames of a wonderfully bright fire of truth that will embrace heaven and earth.'

Thus had the master spoken, and Avitus, uncertain at that time, now knew that Alanus had spoken the truth and that Michael would gather those who were his around him when the time came for the battle that would decide the future of the earth. Deep comfort filled his soul as the light on the altar was reflected in all who stood there, uniting them to form a single community.

The sound of the bell calling the monks to prayer brought Avitus to himself. Slowly, stumbling a little, he left the cell in which Alanus had spent his final hour. On its walls the evening sun was tracing wondrous figures.

Part Two

MILLENNIAL ISSUES: MEETING THE CHALLENGE

1. The Idea of the Threefold Society at the Dawn of the Third Millennium

Terry M. Boardman

The second millennium, which gave birth to innumerable dualisms, is about to give way to the third, but the dualism of the waning age remains strong. On the global scale, the growth of Islamic fundamentalism as a reaction to what is perceived to be American neo-colonialism, and the American response to the Muslim world, have opened up the prospect of a new and pernicious spiritual bipolarity to replace that of the Cold War. Meanwhile, the European Union seems set to become the battleground between two different visions: a unitary superstate under Franco-German control (a new Carolingian Empire, with connections to the Vatican) or the European province of a Transatlantic Union of States under the effective control of the USA. In his book *The Tainted Source—The Undemocratic Origins of the European Idea*,[1] John Laughland writes of the conflicting ideas that compete for the future: the Anglo-American or the Continental European, which he largely identifies with the Germanic: 'In contrast to Continental European constitutional theories or practices which assume or aspire to political harmony, the British and American systems realise that conflict is the stuff of life ... the British parliamentary system gives absolute priority to the principle of disagreement by ensuring that there is always an opposition.'[2] Laughland goes on to contrast the Anglo-American and Germanic views of the economy. The latter, he says, quoting the economist Ralf Dahrendorf, 'is based on industrial discipline, the "discipline of rigid organisation, the habit of subordination and obedience which had been the principle behind the training of the Prussian pattern". It requires a bureaucracy to design lines of action and to control their execution.' The Prussian unification of Germany in the nineteenth century by the economic means of the *Zollverein* (customs union) he considers to be the model for what he claims is the current German unification of Europe. The *Zollverein* was based on the ideas of Friedrich List, the Prussian economist who advocated an active (Laughland would say *dirigiste*) role for the state in the development and protection of national economic life. By contrast, the Anglo-American model, Laughland says, 'brings about an optimal result through competition between the interests involved: it requires the game to have rules, and neutral referees to apply them'.[3] Laughland's ideas mirror those of many in the elites of the West.

At the dawn of the third millennium therefore, we see some dangerous and seemingly irreconcilable new polarities emerging in the spiritual, political, and economic realms. At the same time, there is also the phenomenon of new and confusing mixtures of the three spheres. This is evident in the British government's desire—under both Conservative and Labour administrations—to blur the boundaries between the state, education, and the economy by establishing a national curriculum, control of the content and method of teaching practice, and a joint Department of Education and Employment.[4] It is also evident in the collapse of amateur sports and the takeover of football by major corporate interests (see media mogul Rupert Murdoch's attempted purchase of Manchester United, arguably the world's most popular football club).

From both the right and the left of the political spectrum

there are voices demanding that government should step in to control and supervise the rampages of global capitalism or else to manage it more effectively. There are those in the Anglo-American world who, when seeking to attack the philosophical bases of the European Union, laud free market capitalism, yet when that same western model of capitalism runs into trouble, they run for help to the very people they criticize—to politicians, and demand that governments bail out big business. As the world economy seemed to be heading for the rocks in the Autumn of 1998, Suzanne Moore wrote in *The Independent* (11 September 1998) that: 'Globalisation isn't inevitable: we can do something to stop it ... it is not true that governments cannot stop such huge global forces, that there are no alternatives. They can sign up to treaties and deals that limit the power of multinationals. They can intervene, as laisser-faire capitalism does not prove to be the most efficient way of organising things, and it looks increasingly as though they will have to.' Clearly, she had only just woken up to the fact of a global economy some 80 years after Rudolf Steiner was already speaking of it as an established fact. At the same time Anatole Kaletsky wrote in *The Times* (10 September 1998) an article entitled 'Farewell Laisser-faire Capitalism' in which he argued that

> ... political institutions have a legitimate and indispensable role in managing the capitalist system ... Why do most people, like me, believe that capitalism is an incredibly robust system that will survive every conceivable crisis with a bit of help from the Federal Reserve, the European Central Bank and other policy-making institutions? ... capitalist economies cannot always rely on pure market forces if economic stability and political consent are to be preserved. Governments must accept responsibility for preserving stability and managing macroeconomic demand. How exactly governments do this—through interest rates, taxes, currency management or whatever—depends on ever-changing conditions. But the fact that capitalism requires some degree of

external management is impossible to dispute—and fortunately, the imperatives of global capitalism's self-preservation invariably bring to play the forces of political stabilisation when the system as a whole is under threat ... what is certain is that the era of laisser-faire ideology is fading. Capitalism's own incomparable instinct for self-preservation will see to that.

Kaletsky speaks here of the end of laisser-faire, a mode of early capitalist economy that was rising in the 1840s, a time which, according to Rudolf Steiner, saw the peak of individualism and materialism. Yet Kaletsky's solutions repeat the instincts and language of that period: 'The King is dead! Long live the King!' The spectre of Darwinism—itself a philosophy based on British economic models of the late eighteenth century, is clearly discernible behind Kaletsky's words. They are also misleading in that the Federal Reserve and the European Central Bank are not *political* institutions, though the media often present them as if they were. The barrenness of these ideas, from both the social democratic left and the hard 'liberal' right in face of the challenge of modern globalization point to the degree to which so much thinking at the end of the second millennium is still influenced by the spirit of the Eighth Ecumenical Council of AD869 which in effect declared the individual human *spirit* to be anathema and reduced the human entelechy from a Trichotomy to a Dichotomy: the human being was no longer held to consist of spirit, soul, and body, but of body and soul only, the soul having a few spiritual faculties, which, from that time on were to be guided by church dogma and authority, that is, by religious 'experts and specialists' and not by each individual's own insight and initiative. And so, as the current business paradigm seems patently unable to cope with the successive crises produced by global capitalism, the media call plaintively or stridently for government experts and specialists to rush to the rescue. The false dualisms and false mixtures of the three realms which live in this kind of thinking are based on the out-of-date thinking of the 1840s and earlier epochs.

Although the very name 'Third Way' suggests that there is a sense among contemporaries that the way forward into the third millennium has something to do with the number 3, there is little clarity in mainstream media discourse as to what that way really could be. Communism and the Anglo-American model of free market capitalism have both failed to solve the spiritual, cultural, political, and economic problems of the modern world that have arisen as a result of the Industrial Revolution. In the wake of the Cold War, many are wary of relying on any new overarching 'big idea' that can illuminate the right way forward. In this essay, I shall argue that, finally, after 80 years, the time is now ripe for the idea of the threefolding of society, put forward by Rudolf Steiner at the end of the First World War—an idea which could not be realized then due to the failure of imagination of his contemporaries.

The origins of threefolding in Anthroposophy

Rudolf Steiner developed the idea of the threefolding of society during the First World War as an answer from Central Europe to what he saw as the twofold danger that threatened Europe at that time from East and West: Leninism from Russia and Wilsonism from America. By Wilsonism, he meant in particular the idea, rooted in the experience of *western* nations like Britain, France, Spain and the USA, that national polities should be coterminous with linguistic and ethnic communities: one state, one language, one people, and, for the most part, one religion. Claiming to be based on the principle of national self-determination—a nationalist principle Steiner argued was rooted in an Old Testament vision of society as monolingual and monoreligious—

Wilsonism thus ignored the historical experience of more cosmopolitan multi-ethnic states of Central Europe. This cosmopolitanism, which meant living together and getting on with others who are not of the same stock or religion as oneself, Steiner saw as essential for a healthy society in the coming century. Subsequent events have surely proved him right, since the insistence on the right to national self-determination has caused untold misery in the twentieth century and has led to all kinds of abuses and crimes in the name of national pride and glory.

But the idea of the threefolding of society was not just a momentary response to a particular set of historical circumstances. It grew naturally out of Rudolf Steiner's evolving insights into the very being of Man. During the war he realized that Man's three soul faculties of thinking, feeling, and will were rooted in the three physiological systems of the head and nervous system, the rhythmic system of the heart and lungs, and the system of metabolism and limbs, especially the legs. This realization constituted a grounding in thought of the threefold nature of Man into the physicality of the body, whereas previously Steiner had spoken about the overall threefold nature of Man: body, soul, and spirit, and of the threefold nature of the soul (sentient soul, intellectual-mind soul, consciousness soul) and spirit (spirit-self, life-spirit, spirit-man). All of this, of course, was rooted in his view of Man as a microcosm, a reflection of the threefold nature of the spiritual world with its three hierarchies of spiritual beings. Steiner's revelation of the threefold nature of the spiritual world, of society (in the three realms of culture, law, and economy), and of Man are at the Christian and Trinitarian heart of Anthroposophy which stands under the banner of the Archangel Michael who, since 1879, has not only been the Ruling Hierarchical Spirit of the Age, or Time Regent,[5] but has also been rising in spiritual status from the rank of Archangel to that of an Archë. The knowledge of the threefold nature of the Cosmos, of human society and of Man's being, is at the heart of what Michael desires Man should learn about himself in this fifth post-Atlantean epoch. As the anthroposophical historian Peter Tradowsky put it:

> ... in this year [1917] not only did the ahrimanic impulse clearly establish itself on a historical level, but above all, Rudolf Steiner made the threefolding principle available to man's knowledge and incorporated it into the living current of earthly history as a direct expression of Michael's activity.[6]

During the years when he was bringing forward the idea of the threefold society, Rudolf Steiner also began to speak about profound historical phenomena on the earthly and spiritual planes intimately related with threefolding and with our time: about the events of the fourth post-Christian century, notably in and around the year 333; about the events of the seventh century and the year 666; and about the events of the ninth century and the year 869.[7] The threefold social movement which arose out of Steiner's insights failed as a social impulse in the years 1918–1921. He first brought it as *idea* in 1917–18 to representatives of the governments of Austria-Hungary and Germany, but, while they may have seen something of its truth, they failed to act upon it. It then came forward as *deed* in 1919: a campaigning group arose within the anthroposophical movement, but this too failed due to the lack of anthroposophical maturity and imagination among its members. From 1917 Rudolf Steiner spoke ever more about the three opponents of the threefold impulse: in Wilsonian Americanism from the West, thinking was attacked and became materialistic; in Jesuitism in the Centre, the feeling life was attacked and lulled to sleep, while human equality was denied by hierarchy; and Leninism from the

East stimulated the animal-egoistic instincts to rise up and overpower the will.

At the same time as he spoke about these 'three beasts of the abyss', Rudolf Steiner's revelations about the Being of Michael also increased and culminated in the last two years of his life when he spoke of the threefold impulse of Michael in Autumn when awareness naturally arises of the separation of body, soul, and spirit, in contrast with the unitarian mood of Springtime when all tends to become pantheistic.[8] The year 1923 culminated in the great Michaelic Festival of the Christmas Conference heralding the resurrection of the anthroposophical impulse after the disasters of the previous year. At its heart was the threefold mantra, The Foundation Stone of Love, which condensed all Steiner's revelations about threefold Man and Cosmos in mantric form. This was followed by the establishment of the Michael School on earth, the Lessons of the First Class of the School, and the lectures and letters known as the Michael Mystery.

Despite all this, there were those in the anthroposophical movement who thought that the threefolding of society was no longer relevant, after its failure in 1918–21, or that it had been relevant only to the circumstances of those years. Threefolding would have to be 'prepared', they said, by decades or generations of Waldorf education first, or else it would have to be 'modelled' on micro-scale in anthroposophical communities. They forgot that Rudolf Steiner had ever maintained that the impulse to a threefold society was living in the unconscious will of modern humanity. It did not cease to do so simply because of the failure in 1918–21. There is much evidence today that this is correct. In 1989–90 after the Berlin Wall came down there was much talk about whether there was a 'third way' possible between East and West. Francis Fukuyama in his infamous book *The End of History* insisted that there was not and that West was best. In the 1990s we saw the emergence of three giant economic blocs, the European Union, the North Atlantic Free Trade Area, and the Asia Pacific Forum for Economic Cooperation. In the late 1990s we hear of the much-vaunted 'Third Way' of Bill Clinton and Tony Blair. Ferocious battles reminiscent of the fourth century take place on the Internet about the nature of the Trinity. The General Anthroposophical Society has seen increasing controversy over its own nature: is it threefold or not, and should it be?

The structure of history—What time are we living in now?

In Britain, the millennium is going to be celebrated by a huge exposition inside the giant dome that has been specially constructed for the purpose at Greenwich, the site of the determination of global space and time. Tony Blair's New Labour has continued this Conservative Party project and supports it enthusiastically. Tony Blair has said of it:

> This is our Dome, Britain's Dome. And believe me, it will be the envy of the world ... I want every child in Britain to be a part of the millennium experience. I want today's children to take from it an experience so powerful and memories so strong that it gives them that abiding purpose and unity that stays with them through the rest of their lives ... Greenwich is the place the millennium begins ... if it was Berlin Mean Time, don't you think the Germans would do likewise?[9]

It is well known that there have been many American influences on 'New Labour' and that British foreign policy in its essentials has not changed one jot in its principle of partnership with Washington. Tony Blair echoes the words of Michael Heseltine, former Tory Cabinet Minister, when he says that he wants London to be Europe's financial centre. Successive British governments have served the

cause of Americanism, and while it is beyond the scope of
this essay, a clear thread can be shown to exist from the days
of Cecil Rhodes and his vision of a world dominated by an
Anglo-American Empire to today's synchronized Anglo-
American foreign policy and the increasingly symbiotic
relationship between British and American big business.[10]
This global imperialism of Rhodes and his successors is a
corrupted inversion of the Michaelic impulse of *supra*national cosmopolitanism, which is always such a feature of
Michael's period of rulership in history. Another such cor-
ruption is the institution of the United Nations, which was
conceived and created by the American foreign policy elite
to serve the purpose of global imperialism, the establishment of a New World Order that can serve as the temporal
vehicle for the incarnation of Ahriman, the stage upon
which he can act.

Another great centralizer, the Roman Emperor Justinian,
sought during the first Christian millennium, when the
Catholic Church strove to be the One Faith, to unite his
realm in a New World Order by a symbolic architectural
dome—that of the church of Hagia Sophia (Holy Wisdom, or
Holy Spirit), which he had built in AD537. The circle, of
course, like the Round Table or the stars of the EU flag, is an
image of unity, of perfection. It can either be an image of
unity in diversity, or else it can be the image of the monolith,
a dull and numbing uniformity of spirit. This latter is what
Justinian sought: one Church, one people, one Emperor. In
so far as Tony Blair and his colleagues seem content to follow
the American lead in culture, political thought, and business
practice and economic theory, their dome too will be filled
with the spirit of Justinian, of him who codified Roman Law
and whose church pronounced reincarnation to be anathema.
We can, however, hope for other outcomes. Jonathan
Glancey, in *The Guardian* (25 February 1998) wrote:

... the best of British thinking in 2000 and beyond is likely to be somewhere other than at Greenwich. It may even be in the far from hollow heads of young people who, brought up in the age of mass entertainment, branding, and corporate ideologies, wish to think for themselves.

As Rudolf Steiner pointed out on many occasions, since 1899 mankind has been crossing the threshold of the spiritual world, albeit mostly unconsciously. Since the discovery of the application of electricity in the 1780s, electro-magnetism in the 1840s and atomic energy in the 1930s, mankind has been entering deeper into the world of subnature than was possible with the microscope. In 1879, with the defeat by Michael of the Ahrimanic Spirits of Darkness, those spirits were cast out of the sublunar realm of the spiritual world and took up their abode on Earth in human heads, inspiring a tremendous wave of technological development. Then, in 1900, began the reopening of the doors of clairvoyant perception, which had been shut since 3000 BC. Clairvoyance began to recur naturally in increasing numbers of people who were, however, not in a position to understand it. This means that while still in physical bodies, humanity is living increasingly in the conditions of the spiritual non-physical world. After death, there is a separation of the three soul forces of thinking, feeling, and will, which had been bound up together in a 'unity' in the physical body. This can, if it is not understood and worked with in a healthy way, lead to one-sided extremes of behaviour such as extreme intellectualism and abstraction, fanaticism and intolerance in the realm of feeling, and violence, crudeness and cruelty in will activity. We are living in the midst of all this. Since the 1960s especially, all remaining elements of nineteenth-century culture and social behaviour have been rapidly disappearing.[11] A new culture, driven largely by the new technologies, is appearing, one that seems on the surface very confident and capable, and yet

which is also profoundly unsure of itself. It is in many ways a
heroic culture which is fascinated by the forces of evil in
Man—those forces which, unbeknown to most, have been let
loose on the earthly plane since 1879. Heroic—because it
rises to self-awareness by facing and dealing with those
forces.

We are approaching the end of the second millennium, the
epoch of dualism in religion, politics, and economics, and also
the end, in the year 2030, of the second seventh of the fifth
post-Atlantean epoch (1413–3573; like all the Great Epochs
it lasts 2,160 years) which began in 1722. So, on both the
macro- and the micro-historical scale, we are moving from
the number 2 to the number 3. Finally, we are arriving at the
stage of Egohood for the new 'christened' mankind. Each
century consists of $3 \times 33\frac{1}{3}$ years, or three cycles of the etheric
life of Christ Jesus. This new historical periodicity, which
since Golgotha has been written into the Earth's time body,
corresponds to a single year in the life of the individual
human being. This accounts for the significance of the fourth,
seventh, ninth, fourteenth and twenty-first centuries—for
they are the times of the emergence of 'christened' mankind's
physical sense of self, etheric body, ninth-year crisis, astral
body, and ego respectively.[12]

Clearly, the idea of the threefolding of society corresponds
to the deepest needs of the times. Old dualisms such as
capitalism vs. communism have failed, and so many modern
problems are the result of the confusion of the three realms
of culture, law, and economy. The need for a threefolded
society that works with the changed spiritual circumstances
of the times is paramount. The members of the General
Anthroposophical Society, which was founded by the
preeminent Michaelic initiate of modern times to be the
guardian chalice for the Michael Impulse, need to recognize
this fact, rally to it, and bring forward the threefold social

idea in all ways possible. The threefold social order *is* the big idea of our age, but since Rudolf Steiner's death it has hardly spoken its name. Indeed, until 1935, the masthead of *Das Goetheanum* weekly magazine read: 'Das Goetheanum—Wochenschrift für Anthroposophie und Dreigliederung' (weekly magazine for Anthroposophy and Threefolding), but in that year the words 'und Dreigliederung' were removed and have been absent ever since. Whatever reason they may have been removed for, it is high time they were restored, to signal the Society's will to be the banner-bearer of the impulse of social threefolding. But this, of course, can only happen if the members have that will.

How to proceed for future social healing?

How then can Society members bring forward the idea of threefolding? We need to base our actions for social life in general securely on the Foundation Stone, and specifically on the last verse:

Light Divine
Christ Sun
Warm
our hearts;
Enlighten
our heads;
That good may arise
In what we
From our hearts would found,
In what we
From our heads
Would guide
Into willing.

Since Anthroposophy is a path of *knowledge*, we need to shed light on the evolution of consciousness, paying particular attention to the illumination of the events of the fourth (AD333), seventh (AD666), and ninth (AD869) centuries. This means working out of *spirit-remembering*, finding ways to communicate the anthroposophical truths about evolution that we first learned in the supersensible School of Michael and which were first set down by Rudolf Steiner in earthly form in his *Occult Science—An Outline*. Then there is the need to work out of *spirit-awareness*, to find ways to help ourselves and our contemporaries find a path through the confusion of the present times. For this we all need to be as aware as possible of what arises in our consciousness from moment to moment, so as to be able to maintain ourselves in a state of dynamic equilibrium between the efforts of the adversaries Lucifer and Ahriman to mislead us. Here Rudolf Steiner's *Philosophy of Spiritual Activity* can be our best guide. Finally, we need to show how to advance to *spirit-envisioning*, revealing how Anthroposophy can be the basis for a healthier future social life. The future archetypes for this were given to us in the supersensible Michael Cultic Imaginations at the end of the eighteenth century which were 'earthed' by Goethe, Schiller, Novalis and the Idealists of that time, notably in Goethe's 'Fairy Tale of the Green Snake and the Beautiful Lily'. Here Rudolf Steiner's books *Theosophy* and *Knowledge of the Higher Worlds* can help us, for these represent the spiritual ideals of the present and future shining before us.

And just as the Green Snake became illumined from within by the gold she had eaten, so anthroposophical knowledge needs to fill and enlighten the serpentine Beast of our times. Who is that beast? None but the Media, the media that control most of contemporary knowledge and have the tendency increasingly to make all knowledge utterly materialistic. The Media today 'mediate' knowledge into social action, for good or ill, having become a kind of bridge between the two. This beast is not all bad, far from it, but its nature is to crawl on the ground, for it works primarily (even the print medium these days) with the subterranean forces of electronics. If left to go its own way, if the ideas of Anthroposophy do not permeate it, it will inevitably slide into materialism.

In his lectures to the West-East Congress in Vienna in 1922, Rudolf Steiner spoke of Europe-Asia as 'the problem' of modern times and Europe-America as 'the solution'. By this he meant that Europeans were preserving the dessicated remnants of an ancient Asian spirituality in the dusty abstractions of their intellectual, political, and religious systems. The future lay rather with the *will* to create out of nothing. And this willingness he saw in the youthful energies of the Americans. It is no surprise therefore to learn that it is an American anthroposopher, Joel Wendt, who has articulated best this need for Anthroposophy to enter the belly of the Media. Wendt has written:[13]

> What else have politicians, terrorists, single interest groups, businesses etc. been fighting to control and manipulate? Within Media the People come to *common* (equalized) self-knowledge and mutual understanding. Within Media the idea of the State and of the rights and duties of citizenship come to *common* form. Media shines light on the activities of the State, and media personalities (with varying degrees of consciousness and moral integrity) believe they act thus for the People. However we turn our thinking, if we remain pictorially descriptive of the dynamics of social life as these actually play themselves out in the political-legal sphere we will come to the perception of the threefoldness of State-Media-People.

It is a risk, Wendt says, to enter this realm, but a risk that should be taken, a nettle that should be grasped if the Media serpent is not to continue merely to slide in the dust.

> Media, if its present condition is clearly understood, is young; i.e. it is still undergoing formative developments, and functions

today with a kind of moral or spiritual immaturity. In this sense
Media may take one of two different courses of future development. It may become a kind of *moon* center, rigid, arid, not
light-originating, but rather only able to reflect those impulses
which come to it from the outside. Or, it may become a *sun*
center, a source of warmth and understanding, a medium of
creative forces flowing into the social order and carrying both in
deed and in *word* a true image of man as a being of soul and
spirit. I imagine then, Media becoming a *sun*, a true heart of the
heart of the social organism, so that the *common* understanding
of the People will find a renewed vision of the State. In Media a
song can yet be heard, the song of the truly free man, the moral
man. In this way the rigidification, the mechanization, the image
spell-binding of the *word* will be overcome, and a true understanding given to Western civilization of the Idea of the
Threefold Social Organism as a dynamic social form already
latent in human social existence in the West ... There is of
course no predicting how events will proceed, yet it seems clear
to me that this historic moment is pregnant with certain kinds of
potential. Just as there is great risk of a further fall into
materialism, so as well there is much possibility for spiritual
transformation. If we do not blind ourselves with a kind of
threefold dogma (for example, that the first need is to free the
spiritual cultural life), but instead truly perceive the actual
dynamics, then as far as I am able to hold in pictorial thought,
the ripe moment lies in bringing moral transformative forces to
the thinking active within the Media, to bring a song to life just
here in the heart of the heart of the social organism.

Here speaks a true American voice—a voice of idealism and
the will to courage.

The Israeli author and lecturer Jesaiah Ben-Aharon now
lives in America and he has urged us, in this Age of the
Second Coming of Christ, to learn from the experience of the
disciples at the time of the First Coming 2000 years ago.[14]
First their minds were awakened from slumber and ignorance
of what had happened at Golgotha and afterwards by the
tongues of fire at Pentecost. This was for them a festival of

knowledge. What did they then do? They went out into *the market-place* and began speaking to the people *in languages each could understand*. Finally, they set about creating a new community—the community of Christians. We see here the threefold archetype: the spiritual experience of the 'I', the considerate and respectful dialogue of 'I and you', and the social life in cooperation of the 'we'. This, Ben-Aharon avers, is what we in the anthroposophical movement also need to do with respect to the wider world beyond our all-too-narrow confines. Otherwise, the fact of the Second Coming, of the Etheric Christ, might well be ignored by mankind, which would be an unmitigated disaster.

It will be necessary, then, for us to study the idea of the threefold society, understand it, build enthusiasm for it within the anthroposophical movement, and then *realize it within the Anthroposophical Society*. If we fail to do this at least, and put our own house in threefold order, so to speak, we will hardly be in a position to speak to others about social threefolding. Paul Mackay has spoken of the three stages of development within the anthroposophical movement since the Christmas Conference, each of 33 years: 1923—1956—1989.[15] In the first phase, 1923–1956, the individual element was strong; this was the 'angelic' phase, when the movement was signally affected by the karmic relationships between leading members. Then came the 'archangelic' period, 1956–1989, when anthroposophical communities sprang up in profusion and were deepened, but remained somewhat inward, apart from the rest of society—'islands of culture', as it were. Now, since 1989, we have been in the 'archaic' period when Anthroposophy has to broaden to embrace the world and develop a truly global consciousness that can parallel the ahrimanic aspects of the economically and technologically-driven globalization that has been the much-trumpeted mark of the 1990s. This period will last until 2022. During it,

Anthroposophy will have to plunge into the world if it is to have a meaning that is anything other than sectarian.

On 30 November 1919 in Dornach, at the height of his activity to bring forward the impulse of threefolding, Rudolf Steiner said:[16]

> During the first two decades of the anthroposophical movement in Central Europe we could allow ourselves to carry on in the sleepy sectarian way that has been so hard to combat in our circles and is still deeply lodged in the attitudes of those of the movement. But the time is over when we could allow ourselves such sleepy sectarianism. It is profoundly true, as I have often emphasized, that we must be absolutely clear about the world-historical significance of the anthroposophical movement...

Does the anthroposophical movement have no world-significance today, because Rudolf Steiner is not here to lead it in person? Because most people in the world have never heard of it? Or do we feel that those words of 1919 are truer today than ever, and that they need to be answered?

2. The Spirit or the Letter—On Whose Side is the Teacher of Literacy Fighting? [1]

Brien Masters

Imagining myself in the shoes of devil's advocate—which need not be a bad exercise, as long as one remembers how to untie the laces once the exercise is accomplished—I have sometimes wondered what would be the single most effective target to recommend to my 'client', in order that he achieve his evil designs.

Asking a panel of people with different backgrounds—agriculture, medicine, sport, organized religion, genetics etc.—to put themselves into the same shoes (cloven hoofs?) would no doubt result in a revealing catalogue of replies. Being an educationist, I shall attempt in this essay to confine myself to the sphere of education, and, within that very extensive sphere, the theme of *literacy*. From the broader picture of literacy (what has been described as 'cultural memory')[2] to that of its narrower meaning (i.e. in the context of the three Rs), my aim will be to argue that this taken-for-granted acquisition in an educated person's mental portfolio might turn out to have been the spade that has been thrust into the hands of humanity, which it has been systematically yet unwittingly using to dig its own spiritual grave.

*

Of the comparatively few occasions on which Rudolf Steiner spoke specifically of literacy in its narrow meaning, I shall single out and comment on three. These were:

—during August 1919, when speaking to the teachers designate of the first Waldorf School;

—at the meeting with those same teachers, together with other colleagues who had joined the school, on 15 March 1922, i.e. after the Waldorf School had been running for two and a half years;

—in 1924, during the near year-long sequence of lectures to members of the Anthroposophical Society on Karmic Relationships.

The first of these occasions comes as no surprise. One could hardly found a school—which was what Steiner was helping to do at the time—without substantive reference to literacy and numeracy. What Steiner had to say probably strikes the reader more for the *what* than the *whether* or *why*: for it is here that Steiner introduced the well-known Waldorf approach (swimming against what was to become a strong twentieth-century tide) of allowing the introduction to literacy to wait until entry into the Lower School (age 6+/7 years); and even then, going well out of his way to use innovative pictorial methodology while doing so. It does not need a specialist to realize that to swim against that same tide now, as it races at the turn of the millennium, requires even more effort and conviction.

The second occasion is more complex. In March 1922 an inspector had just visited the Waldorf School and had clearly grasped but little of what the school was about. So at odds was his viewpoint with the Waldorf approach that Steiner good-naturedly teased a teacher, who was 'rejoicing over something the school inspector [had] approved of [with]: "You *will* have to pull your socks up." '[3] During the ensuing discussion, two points arose which are particularly relevant here. More than once Steiner emphasized the importance of publishing afresh the distinctive features of the school—and it is clear that he did not simply mean a reprint of old material, but a new and lively way, that today could be classed as good PR.[4] Of these distinctive features, the approach to literacy heads the list.[5] The other significant point was the way Steiner encouraged the teachers to make known the methodology pursued in the school, through giving public lectures. A number of short citations follows that were part of the aftermath of the inspector's visit.[6] 'A lot will depend on the Waldorf School Movement really containing what it should contain.' 'The spiritual aspects [of the education should] be really well represented in the world.' Near the close of the meeting, Steiner ranged widely, summarizing the tasks and indicating effective strategy: 'First of all you have to tell them that something is wrong with the world ... awaken interest in the educational problems of the times.' 'Convince the audience that we know our subject.' 'More intensive use must be made of our work.' 'We must establish a reputation.' 'Increase in interest only increases our responsibility.' In all of these, Steiner seems to be emphasizing the importance of holding fast to what was central in Waldorf education without any trace of being deflected by 'orthodoxy'.[7]

So we have four main points:

a) we have a way of introducing young children to literacy, clearly detailed by Steiner from the outset;
b) we have the fact that, among the distinctive features of the Waldorf School, literacy was high on Steiner's list of unshakeables;
c) looking outward rather than merely into the classroom methodology, we have the fact that somewhere wrapped up in this approach to literacy was an urgency which had to do with the spiritual dimension of Waldorf education; and

d) that this spiritual dimension was sorely needed in general, the lack of it being somehow intrinsically connected with 'what was wrong' with the world. That is to say, the world problem was at root an *educational* problem.

While all this no doubt gave those concerned enough to be getting on with, there remains the lingering feeling that, within the diffuse, discursive and differentiated discussion at that meeting, there is more in what Steiner is saying than meets the eye.

What the 'more' might be leads us to the third occasion that I have singled out for comment: a reference to literacy which seems to be of a very different nature from where we began in August 1919. On that earlier occasion one could take the inclusion of the subject in a basic educational lecture cycle for granted; on this occasion, certainly as regards its context, it could not have come as more of a surprise. Yet the reference (which I shall quote presently) largely appears to have escaped notice hitherto. The fact that Steiner was not speaking about education but something quite different (karmic relationships) may account for this. But why? Such a remark could hardly have been made as an aside or as a mere illustrative allusion: as we shall see, it verges on the epoch-shaking. Could the impact of the *content* of the karma lectures—the members of the Anthroposophical Society hearing, no doubt with souls amazed, of the previous incarnations of prominent figures in history, many not long since deceased—could that content have eclipsed for them the immediate reality, as Steiner postulated it, not to mention its harsh implications? Could a mood of sensationalism, however slight, arising out of the *content* of the lectures, have caused some of the *principles* at work behind karmic phenomena to have escaped notice? Not that this is necessarily anything to be ashamed of: most of us frequently see new implications in 'revisiting' Steiner that evaded us on first reading.

Whichever way it was, I intend to make the reference to literacy that occurs in the karma lectures the main thrust of my present enquiry. Furthermore, as it *is* to do with karma, it seems appropriate to begin by tracing a few of the karmic footsteps that led in this direction.

*

In the early 1960s, shortly after the first published translation of Steiner's lectures on karmic relationships were coming off the press,[8] my work in an anthroposophical curative home for adults led to the innovation in which the young adults in our care were guided during the second half of each morning through an extended course of 'study'. The first part of the morning, between breakfast and coffee, was given over to workshops, but it was felt that some of the morning hours, being manifestly best suited to 'head' work, should be put aside for learning. Thus a 'main-lesson' became part of the daily round, lasting for some two hours.[9]

But what to teach? The ages of the 'young' adults ranged between 14 and 50, so there was no question of peeping over the Waldorf fence to see if the grass growing there had anything juicy to offer.[10] After some discussion amongst colleagues, it was determined that the year should be divided into three (allowing for a break in the summer season) and that one of these 'thirds' should be given over to a biography, if possible led in such a way that it had a karmic ring to it. If Rudolf Steiner had emphasized the importance of studying concrete karma, why should this be confined to the non-handicapped? Through an in-depth biographical study, and given an appropriate methodology, wouldn't it be good, we asked ourselves, to link handicapped and non-handicapped alike with the beings and impulses of 'great' individualities?

Handicap, after all, is only a small segment of an individual's biography, if one looks at the individual through the telescope of reincarnation over millennia. Maybe more of us than we realize, or would outwardly care to admit, are handicapped, anyhow. Certainly one would imagine that comparatively few of us have been able to detect any handicap lurking in the attractive garb of what we normally regard as one of the indispensables of culture: literacy. But this is to beg the question with which we are concerned.

As a result of the above, through research in the wake of Steiner's karma lectures, it came about that an unusually deep and absorbing interest in Giuseppe Garibaldi (1807–1882), the liberator of Italy, was stirred. For, as I was considering *which* biography to take—awed, even daunted, by the reality that there are as many biographies as there are people!—by chance, I acquired a very dishevelled copy of the historian Trevelyan's *Garibaldi and the Thousand*[11] from one of my favourite haunts, a second- (ninth-, tenth-...) hand bookshop in the outhouse of a pub yard in a nearby town. (One cannot expect all biographical paths to keep to salubrious highways!)

But why should the book have caught my eye? By chance, in the late 1940s, I had met a member of the Trevelyan family on a Northumbrian country bus near Morpeth, their family home. The incident happened to be just when I was deep into Trevelyan's *English Social History*; and the memory of a fellow traveller, sitting in the next seat, chatting to me about the famous author, and coming out with remarks like 'Uncle George this; Uncle George that...' remained fresh in my mind. It was therefore the author rather than the subject who claimed attention amongst the peeling spines, the stained covers and the tattered, mildewy bindings of those discarded remnants of auctions, house-clearances and the like.

But I am not yet done with my 'by chances': for the

decision to inaugurate the biographical 'third' of the year's main-lesson with Garibaldi was followed by another 'find'. In my preparatory research, I came across a reference to Garibaldi's autobiography. Some of the details of that discovery *have* faded; whatever diligence I may have had did not always stretch to annotations of that kind. However, the urge that was born to occupy myself with his autobiography, far from fading, was strangely impelling. Moreover, it intensified as my efforts to borrow or purchase a copy drew one inexplicable blank after another—first at the local library; then amongst friends, whose strong connection with the karma lectures I imagined might have led them to acquire a shelf of supportive literature; then at antiquarian booksellers up and down the length of Charing Cross Road in London, which I scoured systematically, all to no avail.

At last, during a summer visit to friends in Cheltenham, I heard (by chance?) of yet another book dealer in the town centre. Off I went and put my question to the proprietor. 'Ga...ri...baldi,' he repeated slowly. After seeming to be steeped for several seconds in reverie, he knelt down on the floor—I remember it being exactly on the spot where he stood at the moment of my asking him the question (though I am willing to grant that this may be artistic license)—removed half a dozen books from the bottom shelf of one of his stuffed-tight, floor-to-ceiling bookcases, ducked over downwards and sideways to take a reassuring look at the back of the shelf, pressed his cheek against the spines of some handsome tomes higher up—very similar to the attitude of a milkmaid hand-milking her Friesian!—extended his hands and forearms into the space he had created and grimaced once or twice, before slowly, but deliberately, drawing forth no fewer than three chunky volumes that proved to be (once the dust of decades had been scattered with a breath) the mysteriously elusive *Autobiografia*.[12] After all those months of enquiring and traipsing round, I felt more like a witness watching a midwife in attendance at a birth than a mere customer buying books! Moreover, this feeling seemed strangely redolent (for those who know the incident) of the mood of coming-from-nowhere, materializing out of the blue, which was so palpable as Garibaldi and his 'noble thousand' descended from the monastery perched on the heights of Gibilrossa, down through the citrus groves above Palermo, much to the consternation of the Austrian militia, the forces of occupation which he was to overthrow.[13]

On the one hand, the above account, the length of which may at first sight seem somewhat indulgent, may appear out of place here—too much of an anecdotal detour. On the other hand, leaving it intact in this way may serve as an example of how the *will* can be discovered to be the partner in a process which, though seemingly entirely under one's control, is simultaneously participating in something that has a larger orbit. Or words to that effect. This, I would suggest, is the aspect of will, albeit in miniature, that was playing into Garibaldi's biography as he walked the breath-taking tight-rope, taut between life and death, upon which the story of his life seemed constantly to be poised, particularly in the 1840s/1850s.

*

Steiner's explanation of this remarkable biographical phenomenon[14] is that Garibaldi had been an initiate in an incarnation that had occurred long before his life in nineteenth-century Italy, and that *some* of the spiritual capacities from that former time filtered through and were evident in his 'madcap' yet somewhat miraculous adventures in his home country and the emerging Republics of South America. But—and this is the crux of the matter—not *all*: some capacities had been filtered out. As a result of that filtering, his spiritual gifts resided principally in the *will* and not in his *consciousness*. But how had they come to be filtered out? In addressing what must have been his flabbergasted audience, Steiner infers that this was through education and in particular through being exposed to literacy at a young age. Indeed, though the theme of reincarnation is no longer as unfamiliar a one as it was in the 1920s, what he had to say then is still astonishing even to the extent, possibly, of having something of a bizarre ring about it for some readers:

> Now I come back [from considering the deeper significance of Garibaldi's path of life] to the question: Where are the earlier initiates? For certainly it will be said that they are not to be found. But, ...—I shall have to say something paradoxical here!—if it were possible for a number of human beings to be born today at the age of seventeen or eighteen, so that when they descended from the spiritual world they would in some way or other find and enter seventeen- or eighteen-year-old bodies, or if at least human beings could in some way be spared from going to school (as schools are constituted today), then you would find that those who were once initiates would be able to appear in the human being of the present day. But just as little is it possible, under the conditions obtaining on earth today for an initiate, when he needs bread, to nourish himself with a piece of ice, just as little is it possible for the wisdom of an older time to manifest *directly*, in the form that you would expect, in a body that has received education—in the present-day accepted sense of the word—up to his seventeenth or eighteenth year. Nowhere in the world is this possible; at all events, nowhere in the civilized world.
>
> When, as is custom today, a child is obliged to learn to read and write, it is torture for the soul that wants to develop and unfold in accordance with its own nature ... It is necessary to say such a thing, paradoxical though it may sound.[15]

Thus, assuming Steiner's insight to be reliable, we may extrapolate: early exposure to literacy prevents individuals from bringing their spiritual gifts from the past to expression in the present. And although this may not account for all the errors of the century through which we have ploughed, and the end of whose furrow this book is 'marking', the turn of the millennium offers an opportunity both poignant and pregnant for evaluation.

*

But how can the process of 'filtering out spiritual capacities' be understood? Having been alerted to the problem through the flight of Steiner's spiritual insight, can one approach it via a different route, accessible to the average, more pedestrian turn of mind?

Surely the method of teaching literacy that Steiner evolved—about which, while avoiding being prescriptive, he was so adamant—must have been, or at least contained, a prophylactic against at least some of the mal-effects of early literacy to which he points. Let us, therefore, look at how Steiner tackled the problem of literacy in education. But as a prelude to doing so, and before leaving the karma lectures, it should be noted that Steiner emphasized that the educationist could not ignore the trend of the day—e.g. by *not* teaching literacy when the children entered the first class (which was at age 7). Nor was it justifiable deliberately to circumnavigate the problem—a sort of twentieth-century pied piper, setting up some educational establishment in a forgotten valley, say, in Papua New Guinea. Nevertheless, Steiner must have been faced with finding a compromise upon which far-reaching consequences hinged. The solution to the problem that he advocated, so well known and widely practised in Steiner Waldorf schools, is therefore examined in what follows.[16]

After a few preliminaries, such as choosing letters of the alphabet and deciding in what order they are to be introduced to the class, the Steiner Waldorf teacher needs to become active in certain creative spheres: in the first place, connected with *sound* and *form*. Through inwardly listening to the sound that the consonant 'makes', the teacher arrives at what might be termed the 'creative essence' of the letter. From that, and from the images arising from words in which that essence is expressed (or, in which the sound is incorporated), the teacher moves from sound to form—from a creative *force* to something of a personified *image*. I am using the term broadly: personification usually implies a person. In a Steiner Waldorf teacher's introduction to a letter, inanimate objects may well assume a degree of personality. However, overriding this is the fact that a child's consciousness may well blur the edges between animate and inanimate more than we normally realize. Most people will not need to stop to think for long before recalling an example of this that they have witnessed.

To appreciate this 'creative essence' of a sound, let us take a common example: the sound *F* was clearly thought to be significant by our ancestral creators of language in words such as *fire, Feuer*/German, *fuego*/Spanish, *feu*/French; *flame, Flamme*/German, *fiammifero*/Italian=match) ... The gesture of flickering flames, flaring up, will-o'-the-wisping from the heart of a fire does seem to express the sound well and is a gesture that would lend itself to personification. However, given the sound *F* as a starting point, different individuals might choose other examples in which they feel intuitively that the *F* is a significant factor in the inner meaning of the word. *Fantasy, farce, farrier, father, feather, feminine, fern, fervour, festival, fiancé, flight, foam, folly, fool, form, fortress, fruit, fun, funeral, fur* ... are all food for thought in this respect. Not all of these will conjure forth an archetypal image that relates to the shape of *F* as readily, perhaps, as that of the flicker of flames. As it so happened, Steiner more than once chose *fish* (*Fisch* in German) as a ready-to-hand example for classroom use.[17] But he seemed equally happy with less animate instances, though to cite these would be peripheral to the present line of thought.

So the teacher has inwardly progressed from sound (force) to image (form). A step further in each direction now follows. Still at the 'hand' of the teacher, the personified image gains life and evolves into a story. From the story, which the teacher narrates to the class (another artistically cultivated activity), and in which the word beginning with the letter being taught is given prominence among the other *dramatis personae*, is extracted the shape (and name) of the letter.[18] Thus, through the abundance of the teacher's creativity, through which the child's first meeting with literacy is ushered in, the child is kept buoyant on the stream of the *spirit* of the letter. This means that, in the longer term, when finally the *letter* of the letter is arrived at, the teacher is less liable to have to deal with the leaden and frequently traumatic struggle of learning to read (which unfortunately is increasingly the case, as the age of early learning is forced down younger and younger, often killing the appetite for literacy in the process). But the main point at issue is that the buoyancy deriving from the spirit of the letter remains an abiding factor in the child's soul.

It is self-evident from the above that, before the stage of (passive) reading is arrived at, the child has embarked on a journey of (active) writing, from which activity it gradually alights towards the more cerebral occupation: reading. Emphasizing that active point of embarkation, not even is the form of the letter experienced purely as something static on the page—a mere formality, such as the adult would normally take it to be. The shape of the letter will be run or acted, by individual children or in groups;[19] so that even when it reaches its final 'resting place'—a letter crayoned by the child on to a piece of paper—the drawing/writing[20] is psychologically subtended by an active, realism-free attitude towards form that has been and is being nurtured all along through form-drawing,[21] where form for form's sake is what provides the motivation rather than some realistic end product. The letter is experienced not merely—not even primarily—through the clinical sense of sight, a black host of squiggly lines and curves—the printer's *font*—parading rank on rank in a school 'reader'; the letter lives in a *fount* of 'colour, movement, life, imagination, inspiration, dynamic form, vibrant orality...'[22]

Thus, when the child reaches the first stage of 'reading', something of the inner soul disposition that characterizes pre-literacy still prevails, even though literacy as such must needs more and more preside. The word SUN, for example, does not represent or resonate the shrivelled Copernican concept that we can neatly define as well as any dictionary, the measurable source of light and energy at the centre of our solar system, that we mostly take for granted. Rather, it enjoys an echo of that which earlier peoples, through their vibrant empathy, felt was embodied to some extent by the three sounds *S...U...N*—and here we shall have to bypass the way that Steiner recommended dealing with the vowels. (In other parts of the world different experiences of the sun have been 'inscribed' into language—e.g. *shemesh*/Hebrew; *aurinko*/Finnish; *ilyos*/Greek; *allunga, chintoo, thuyerloo, tonaleah, uuna, ykuko*/various Australian Aboriginal dialects!)[23] It is such echoes that have filled the child's soul through hearing and speaking the mother tongue up to this moment of its life. With Steiner's approach to literacy those echoes are not ever more efficiently vacuum-sealed off; they have a chance to vibrate on.[24] The breath of life still hovers over, wafts around the mummy that the spoken word becomes when encased within its sarcophagus of literacy.

And the corollary? Having concentrated mostly on how

not to vacuum-seal off the child's spirituality through its meeting with literacy, so that the incarnating individual is endowed with the fruits of the past—however exalted or modest the child's genius may be—is there something, as well as avoiding the *vacuum*, that might prove a good *conductor* also to be found in Steiner's method?

*

Whoever may be in the wings, the two actors on stage in this morality play are the teacher and the child. Let us therefore take one more look at the scene, and in particular the role of the teacher.[25]

In striving to discern the essence of the *sound* of the letter, the teacher is having to develop and exercise *Inspiration*. In striving to impart *being* (personification) to that essence which has been discerned, or discover being within it, the teacher is having to develop and exercise *Intuition*. And in striving to derive an *image* of that essential being (the focal point of the story, that is subsequently drawable on the board and in the child's book), the teacher is having to develop and exercise *Imagination*. Thus, even if only at a very elementary level, in attempting to introduce literacy in this way the teacher is having to aspire towards and activate within him- or herself those stages of consciousness described by Steiner as definite steps on the path to 'higher knowledge'.[26]

We may take it as empirical—thanks to the life work of Owen Barfield and others[27]—that these levels of higher knowledge were readily accessible to the human beings of ancient times, due to their pre-literal state of consciousness. We people of today have sacrificed this original, participative state as the price of freedom—and the child, being a child of today, is in the same boat. But—if I may risk a nautical analogy—whilst we twentieth-century adults, who have succumbed or at least are subject to the materialist's paradigm, are stowed away deep in the hold of the boat, unable to gain sight of those spiritual horizons whence we have journeyed, the child still enjoys something of that vision (even if partially impeded) being somewhere up in the shrouds. Teacher and pupil in the same boat, therefore, yes! But different ranking: the adult's being is enshrouded with the sense-world below; the child, to whatever extent (depending on the child's age), is still up-shrouded above—the dark 'light of common day' as against the still irradiated 'trailing clouds of glory'.[28]

But do not let this innate difference in rank deter us from trying to gain insight. Rather let us consider the inner effort that the teacher has to make, outlined above, to *achieve* the Waldorf way[29] in the approach to literacy, now by juxtaposing it alongside what Steiner termed the pedagogical law.[30] In that law he described how a higher member of the adult 'educates' (ostensibly through self education: 'what you are' or are in process of becoming) that member of the child that is one stage lower. This is suggestive of the 'conductor' that we hoped to detect. As the child descends from *original participation*, it meets the teacher who makes the attempt to climb a rung or two towards *final participation*. Through this, literacy—that has been described as the watershed between spirit and world[31]—is no longer the drastic watershed that it would otherwise be. The teacher's efforts towards final participation, through the working of the educational law, are transformed in the child into the prophylactic which—while still permitting freedom to take root, unfold and thrive in the growing human being—enables the ego to bring into play that spirituality to which it is heir, by virtue of its own past.

This, it seems to me, is what by implication is divulged by Steiner through his observation on Garibaldi; this is why he set such high stakes on the *way* literacy should be taught in the Waldorf School; why he exhorted the teachers to hold tenaciously to the Waldorf way as a key feature of their praxis ... and why the devil's advocate's client will do all in his power to prevent it and bring about the opposite, so that the human spirit is eclipsed, with human beings forced to act, not out of their higher, but out of their lower, easily diverted, easily hi-jacked, easily manipulated, anti-cultural, anti-social, anti-brotherly, clouded selves. Freedom, yes, lenient, even permissive, lashings of it: *except* the freedom to climb up again towards the heights of final participation.

Within the spiritual arena in which we find ourselves at the turn of the millennium, there are, however, signs that the results of the 'advocate's' subversive advice are being identified.[32] The outcry against early literacy led by Professor Josef Nagy, the Hungarian educationist, is a recent sign, even drawing forth a certain amount of condemnation of early literacy (and early learning in general) from within the 'establishment'.[33] Despite the fact that the reason for the outcry only reached as far as under-achievement, it is nonetheless welcome, for the first step must always be to identify the clouds of obscurity before setting about dispersing them.

Not that this gives cause for complacency, for, ironically, almost to the day, a year later than the above article, a 'new reading plan' was reported in the same newspaper by the same Education Editor.[34] In it, the British Government's favouring of 'analytic phonics' as a method of teaching literacy is criticized by a research team from St Andrews University, Scotland. The team found that a method described as 'synthetic phonics' produced much faster, 'staggeringly effective' results. This underlines the fact that the debate of whether or not early learning is a desirable educational aim is still likely to take time before it comes to any prominent place on the agenda. Doubly ironic, directly beneath that article the newspaper printed Article 26 of the Universal Declaration of Human Rights, marking its fiftieth anniversary, in which Clause (3) states: 'Parents have a prior right to choose the kind of education that shall be given to their children.'[35] Trebly ironic is the announcement, at the foot of the column that quotes the Article, that the proceeds of a pamphlet reprinting the Declaration will go to the Medical Foundation for the Care of *Victims of Torture* (my italics). Torture would, of course, be the wrong term for what we are discussing here (even, perhaps, for the personal trauma experienced by many young children who are put through this particular mill). Nevertheless, that should not tempt us to underestimate the consequences of teaching literacy—prematurely, seen from the spiritual standpoint.

Steiner is known to have waited until he was asked the 'right' question before revealing the results of his spiritual research. When we hear leading questions of such import being asked in our present time, it is surely imperative that those who have attempted to continue Steiner's work try and find the right form in which to share the results of what is known and has been achieved (both in an inner and outer sense) so that it can be recognized by contemporaries who are in the same boat—the boat that encompasses, enshrouds and enmeshes the human being down in the deepest hold of literacy—contemporaries, nonetheless, in whose hearts the future progress of humanity is also ready to leap at a chance.

3. A Response to the Claim that Anthroposophy is Racist

Bernard Nesfield-Cookson

During the past ten years or so Rudolf Steiner has been calumniated as a racist—particularly in Holland, Austria, Germany and Switzerland. The hard core of the virulent accusations of racism is addressed to statements Steiner made in six or seven lectures, that is, in approximately one thousandth of the total number of lectures he gave.[1] In those few lectures Steiner spoke about the American Red Indian, the Hottentot and the black people of Africa in terms which were generally accepted in Europe during the first quarter of the twentieth century. Certainly, though, if one were to make similar statements today about those races, and if such statements were to be taken at face value, they would be regarded as offensive.[2]

Those who accuse Steiner of racism refer to a number of other utterances by him which, though not in the same category as those just mentioned, can readily lead to misunderstanding if taken out of the context of his spiritual scientific conception of the evolution of mankind and the universe, of the involvement of spiritual beings in human destiny, and so forth.

*

The purpose of the present essay is to show that the central thrust of Anthroposophy is not only not racist, but, on the contrary, represents a powerful impulse by means of which racism can be overcome.

As far as the author is aware, Rudolf Steiner has not been accused in Great Britain of being a racist, but it must be obvious to everyone that racism is a serious issue in these isles.

Leitmotif

In the present and future ages of human evolution those who propagate ideals of race and nation are encouraging impulses which contribute to the spiritual decline of humanity.

'Nothing is more designed to take humanity into its decline than the propagation of ideals of race, nation and blood ... The true ideal must arise in what we find in the world of the spirit, not in the blood.'[3]

*

From 1913 onwards[4] Rudolf Steiner repeatedly drew attention to the significance of the spiritual being Michael. He emphasized, among other things, that Michael is the Time Spirit[5] of the age in which mankind has been living since 1879 and will continue to live until *c.* AD 2230.[6] He contrasted the present Michael Age with that which preceded it, which he designated the Age of the Archangel Gabriel (1510–1879). Whereas emphasis in the latter was on the stream of heredity, blood and racial relationships, on nationalism and on materialistic science,[7] emphasis in the former is on spiritual relationships (elective affinities), cosmopolitanism, and spiritual science.

Something of the quality of the Michael Impulse may be gleaned from a lecture Steiner gave a few weeks after the cessation of the 1914–18 war. Here he stressed the need to cultivate genuine human brotherhood, to nurture elective affinity instead of remaining confined to blood affinity. Expressed differently: we need to move out of the 'remnants' of the Gabriel Age and enter fully into the Michael Age.

Steiner did not suggest that we should deny the reality of blood affinity, but when elective affinities become reality—a realized consequence of the Michael Impulse—the boundaries of family, nation and race are crossed.[8]

During the course of human evolution what we could term 'blood-love' gradually spread from smaller to larger groups of human beings, from a family to a tribe and a people. A characteristic example of this can be seen in the Hebrew people which felt itself as a group that belonged together through ties of blood. With the Advent of Christ, through his Death on the Cross and his Resurrection, through what Steiner often described as the Mystery of Golgotha, the whole of humankind—all nations and races—was endowed with the seed from which could grow spiritual love. Such love embraces the whole of mankind with a bond of brotherhood.[9] This is a motif of paramount importance in Rudolf Steiner's Christo-centric spiritual science. He spoke of the significance of the Mystery of Golgotha in this connection in a lecture on the Whitsun Festival. '[Christ] died for *all* people.' Since the Deed of Golgotha a man might have a black, brown, red, white or yellow skin, and have no wish to know anything of Christ, 'nevertheless *Christ died for all men*'. Steiner then went on to say that it will be increasingly imperative in the evolution of mankind for *all* human beings, for *all* nations and races, to acquire real 'knowledge of spirit-being and of spiritual life. Such a knowledge as will lead *all mankind* into the world of spirit is the goal striven for by anthroposophical Spiritual Science'.[10]

In a lecture entitled 'The Spiritual Unity of Mankind through the Christ Impulse' Steiner described how, in the long distant past, it was the intention of the Spirits of Form

(Exusiai, Powers) to develop a uniform race in seven successive stages, and how this uniform human race was split up by the joint activity of Lucifer and Ahriman.

> They influenced the whole process in such a way that the various evolutions were shifted and displaced, so that whilst it was intended that in the main one form of human being should appear in the fifth Atlantean period[11] and be gradually transformed into another type of being, Lucifer and Ahriman preserved the form of the fifth Atlantean period on into the sixth and again that of the sixth Atlantean period on into the seventh, and yet again into the time beyond the Flood, so that what should have disappeared in the form, remained; and instead of the different characteristics of the races *developing one after the other*, which should have been the case, *the old racial types remained stationary and the more recent ones were introduced at the same time*. As a result, a simultaneous process was developed instead of a successive one ... And so it came about that physically different races peopled the earth and are still peopling it right into the present time.[12]

In the same lecture Steiner then went on to say that at the physical beginning of the earth's evolution it was intended that '*uniformity over the whole earth*' was to be imparted to the whole of mankind 'from without'. If this had taken place, if Lucifer and Ahriman had not acted in opposition to this *primordial* impulse, human beings would have been *obliged* to see themselves as uniform beings. They would have arrived at the experience of oneness in '*unfreedom*'. Without the

> interference of the luciferic and ahrimanic element human beings would have loved their fellow men without any effort on their part, without having any idea of the nature of the external force which compels them to do so. In order that spiritual love of one's fellow human beings—no matter what racial characteristics they may have—could be a *free deed*, could be born *within*, opposition to the primordial plan had to take place. First the

gods allowed human beings to be 'split up' as a result of opposing forces, in order that later, after the *bodily nature* had been thus split up, they could, in their *spiritual nature*, through Christ, again be brought into a unity.[13]

The attainment of such a unity 'from within outwards' is one of the fundamental meanings of the Mystery of Golgotha. *Externally*—even in the same family—human beings are becoming more and more different from each other. This growing diversity, rather than uniformity in *outer* physical appearance, brings with it the need to exert all the more force *within* in order to attain unity in brotherhood.

There will always be setbacks to this unity [for] groups of people will fight to the quick about all that concerns external life. Setbacks emanate from earlier epochs that take their course in opposition to the Christ Impulse.[14]

Anthroposophical Spiritual Science seeks to understand and to live in harmony with the Christ 'for whom there is no distinction of class, nation or race, but for whom there is only a single humanity'.[15]

*

With the Great War (1914–18) in mind, when nation was pitted against nation, blood against blood, Steiner drew an illuminating picture of the contrast between Jehovah and Christ Jesus. Christ appeared amongst a people who worshipped Jehovah, that God who is connected with all that

which lies at the basis of man's origin through the forces of nature and which is connected with the differentiation of men into classes, nations and races. Whereas it was the *one* Jehovah whom the Jews worshipped when Christ came, nations today turn to *many* Jehovahs. For what is worshipped today—even if it is no longer described by the ancient name—the powers to which men pay homage when they divide themselves up into nations and make war on each other as nations, they are Jehovahs.[16]

What is here spoken of in relation to nations, is equally valid in relation to races.

Under the regency of Michael the principles of both nationalism and racism have ceased to be in harmony with the spirit of our age. Nevertheless, whenever a new impulse in the evolutionary process begins to come to expression, adversarial, hindering forces—luciferic and ahrimanic[17]—also begin to become more active. It is these forces which, for example, transform a healthy patriotism into the 'evil' of virulent nationalism, racism and, in many quarters, opposing religious fanaticisms.

It has been mentioned already that Michael's task as Time Spirit is of quite a different nature from that of Gabriel. First and foremost, he has a special relationship with the Christ.[18] From him flows the impulse which we, as individuals, and in freedom, can take into ourselves and thereby create a personal relationship with the Christ. Michael 'wants us to be the spiritual hero of freedom; he lets us do'.[19] Through the Michael Impulse the opportunity is offered us to come together with our fellow human beings so that we can recognize not only our common humanity but also the Christ who lives within each one of us—no matter to which nation or race each one of us as individuals may belong.

We could ask ourselves: Why is it that such nationalistic and racist feelings are so obviously rife today when it is Michael who is the Time Spirit? One answer Rudolf Steiner gave to this question runs as follows: 'It is only by degrees that the impulse of Michael can make its way into what is, to a great extent, a legacy from the past reign of Gabriel.'[20] Steiner showed on numerous occasions that materialism was 'justified' in the nineteenth century, but that clinging to it now generates catastrophes.[21]

The spiritual being, Michael, is pivotal to Rudolf Steiner's conception of the life and evolution of mankind. Time and again he stressed that the anthroposophical conception of mankind's evolution is intimately connected with the Michael Impulse.[22]

That Steiner was not merely concerned with the idea but also, above all, with the realization of the Michaelic-cosmopolitan impulse in practical life is shown, for instance, in the fourth paragraph of the Statutes of the Anthroposophical Society, where it is clearly stated:

> Anyone can become a member, without regard to nationality, social standing, religion, scientific or artistic conviction, who considers as justified the existence of an institution such as the Goetheanum in Dornach, in its capacity as a School of Spiritual Science.[23]

Clearly any form of discrimination—including that of race—was rejected by Steiner in this all-important and far-reaching statement. Over the years he made many statements that endorse his view in regard to the need no longer to differentiate between races. For instance, in 1911 he stressed the importance of 'spreading ... Spiritual Science among men and women *without distinction* of race, nation or family'.[24] He made the same point the following year:

> It is contrary to every principle of true Spiritual Science to say that just as there was one leading race in each of the culture-epochs in the past,[25] so in future, too, there will be another such race, distinguished by physical attributes ... [A]lready today it is apparent that culture, instead of being borne by one specific leading race, spreads over all races. *And it is by Spiritual Science that culture—a spiritual culture—must be carried over the whole earth, without distinction of race or blood.*[26]

Earlier in the same lecture Steiner brought to our notice the fact that the further we go back in time, the more do we find that the outer physical form and characteristics of a child resembled those of its parents, that brother resembled brother, that there were marked resemblances between members of the same race and so on, whereas the further we go into the future, the more will the human being, in outer appearance, 'become an expression of the *individuality* who passes on from one incarnation to another'. Already today we can see considerable differences in outer form between parents and children, and between siblings. To emphasize the point he was making, Steiner re-stated the observation he had just made: 'The reason for this is that outer forms [including colour] will more and more no longer be the expression of family or race, but more and more the expression of the individuality.'[27]

We have noted already that under the influence of Michael there is today, counteracting the lingering force of nationalism and racism, a growing tendency towards cosmopolitanism. Steiner touched on this aspect of our theme in a lecture he gave during the First World War. He maintained that, in spite of the catastrophic times prevailing, the tendency exists in mankind 'to wipe out the various differences fostered by the blood'. He set this statement against a cosmic spiritual background. During the period from the beginning of the 1840s to the end of the 1870s Michael had to fight hard against certain opposing spirits, ahrimanic beings, who had hitherto had the task of splitting humanity into races. But, Steiner maintained, in our time 'it is not a tendency of the spiritual worlds to create further differences among mankind, but it is a tendency of the spiritual worlds to pour a cosmopolitan element over mankind'. To underline the point he was making, he went on to say that it is Michael, 'the Time Spirit of the modern age' who, from the 1840s, continues to fight against the Race Spirits.[28] Despite setbacks in the realization on earth of this impulse emanating from the spiritual world, from the Michael Impulse—the ahrimanic spirits, Race Spirits, are not easily overcome[29]—there are nevertheless clear signs throughout the world that the significance of race is slowly but surely waning.

*

Anthroposophy, Steiner insisted, must be developed out of the spirit, not out of the physical-corporeal, not out of racial characteristics.[30] In another lecture he spoke of the evolution of the human organization:

> This organization evolved ... until ancient Greek times. Then human bodies were as perfect as they can be during time spent on earth ... [Today] we are in bodies which are dying, increasingly crumbling and withering away. I am using fairly radical terms. The fact is, however, that anything we inwardly develop and inwardly are, will no longer become part of the outer physical body to the same extent as it did in the past.[31]

This fact is also decisive in respect of the colour of our physical skin—be it black, red, white or yellow, in respect of the race in which we as individuals incarnate. It is the inner qualities and impulses, not the outer, corporeal sheath, which are the real, true expression of humanness.

Steiner stated quite clearly on numerous occasions that it is no longer relevant, no longer 'fruitful', to attribute significance to differences between races.[32]

Reincarnation

Souls in the spiritual world seeking to incarnate in a physical body no longer do so, Rudolf Steiner maintained, on the basis of racial elements, but on that of geographical conditions, on the basis of forces which are active in one region of the earth or another.[33]

He often reminded us that the earth is not a lifeless body.[34] It is a living organism, permeated by hosts of elemental beings; ensouled by a great variety of spiritual beings who 'serve' the higher hierarchies in the spiritual world. The physical sense world is thus constantly under the influence of the spiritual world.

As a living organism, the earth works upon and influences the human beings who live on it. Just as man is differentiated with regard to the apportionment of the various organs of his body, so is the earth also differentiated with regard to that which it livingly develops and with which it influences those who live upon it.

> Our earth is not at all a being which everywhere pours out the same things on its inhabitants; but in the different regions of the earth, something entirely different is rayed out. And there are various forces in it, magnetic, electric, but also much more in the sphere of living, outstreaming forces, which come out of the earth, and which influence people in the most manifold ways at different points on the earth; that is, they influence the human being in various ways according to geographical formation.[35]

Since the fifteenth century, souls descending to earth have been less and less concerned with racial traits and characteristics and increasingly guided by the geographical conditions prevailing in the various regions of the living earth. There is, therefore, according to Steiner, a kind of chasm spreading

> through the whole of mankind today between the elements of heredity and race [i.e. the blood stream] and the soul-element coming from the spiritual world ... [I]f men and women of our time were able to lift more of their subconscious into consciousness, very few of them would—to use an ordinary expression—feel comfortable in their skins. The majority would say: I came down to the earth in order to live, for example, on flat ground, among green plants or upon verdant soil, in this or that kind of climate, and whether I have Roman or Germanic features is of no particular importance to me.[36]

Steiner spoke of the earth as being the 'Cosmos of Love' and of love as being what he called 'the mission of our earthly planet'.[37] For the incarnating soul, still in the spiritual world in which there is no racial differentiation, the earth is the body of the most exalted Being of Love, the Body of Christ.[38] In the light of the Michael Impulse the soul, 'gazing down' from the spiritual world towards the earth, harbours not only a longing to experience the spirituality with which Christ imbued the planet through the Mystery of Golgotha, but also the Michaelic Impulse to overcome, through the power of Christ-inspired spiritual love, the ubiquitous materialism ruling over human affairs today. The overcoming of materialism through such love for both the earth and for humanity as a whole inevitably leads to the overcoming of racism.

Materialism is the very ground upon which material-physical discrimination, racism, is founded. As long as corporality forms the basis upon which we consider and judge our neighbours, racism will persist. Rudolf Steiner's science of the spirit, in contrast, lays stress on the fact that each one of us *is* a soul-spiritual being who *has* a physical body. It is only the outer sheath which has one colour or another, not that which constitutes the core of human beingness.

In one of his many lectures on karmic relationships Steiner spoke of the future incarnations of those who receive the Michael Impulses through Anthroposophy. He made the point that today we attach importance to the fact that we can recognize the race and nation of those we meet. But for those who today receive anthroposophical spiritual science

with inner force of soul, with deep impulse and strength of heart—who receive it as the deepest force of life—such distinctions will have no more meaning when next they return to earth. People will say: Where does he come from? He is not of any nation, he is not of any race, he is as though he had grown away from all races and nations.[39]

In the lecture he gave on the following day, Steiner did not speak only of those who receive Anthroposophy. He broadened his canvas, as it were, to embrace all those 'who come to things of the spirit'.[40]

That racial distinctions, according to Rudolf Steiner, will increasingly be of no significance is borne out by a remarkable statement he made in a lecture he gave in London entitled 'Christ and the Metamorphosis of Karma'. Referring to the process of incarnation, he spoke of an important decision people have been able to make, since the beginning of the Christ-Michael leadership, just before they come down to earth. Today as yet only a few do so; a growing number will as time goes on. Through the present leadership of Michael and with the increasing spread of spiritual knowledge and the growing experience within the human soul of universal human love, the following realization will present itself to a human being at the point of descending into a new earthly life:

> Through something I did in former lives I see that I have gravely hurt some other human being ... The light of judgement as to what we have done to another person will be particularly vivid at this moment when we are still living only in our ether body, having not yet put on the physical. Here too in future time the light of Michael will be working, and the love of Christ.[41]

It is at this moment that a change in my decision to incarnate in a body of a particular race is made, namely, to give to the person whom I have injured the body I have been preparing, while I myself take on the body he has prepared, irrespective of the colour of that body. Steiner then went on to say: 'What we are able to achieve on earth will thus bring about karmic compensation in quite a new way.'[42]

Good and Evil Races

On a number of occasions Rudolf Steiner spoke of two future races—the Good and the Evil. Here he was clearly not using the term 'race' in the generally accepted sense. He was not referring to races distinguished by physical features but to two groups of people of contrasting moral qualities—good and evil. In an early lecture, 'Good and Evil—Individual Karmic Questions' he introduced the matter of the two moral races by mentioning two natural philosophers, Paracelsus and Oken,[43] who, when contemplating the kingdom of animals, stated that human beings should be aware of the fact that in the early stages of evolution they carried that kingdom within themselves and progressively cast it out from their own being. 'Thus,' Steiner continued,

> human beings once had within themselves a great deal that was later externalised. And today they still have within themselves something that later on will be outside—their karma, both the good and the evil. The good will result in a race of men and women who are naturally good; the evil in a separate evil race. You will find this stated in the Apocalypse, but it must not be misunderstood. *We must distinguish between the development of the soul and that of races.*[44]

In this connection Steiner made the significant statement that a soul may incarnate in the evil race, which he characterized as being 'on the down grade', but that if that soul does not itself 'commit evil' during that lifetime, it may incarnate next time in the good race, the race 'that is ascending'.

He then went on to say:

> With all this something of extraordinary interest is connected. Centuries ago, with the future development in view, secret Orders which set themselves the highest conceivable tasks were established. One such Order was the Manichean ... The Order

knew that some day there will be men and women in whose karma there is no longer any evil, but that there will also be a race evil by nature, among whom all kinds of evil will be developed ... they will practise evil consciously, exquisitely, with the aid of highly developed intellects. Even now the Manichean Order is training its members so that they may be able to transform evil in later generations.

What Steiner meant by 'races' being either on the 'down grade' or 'ascending' will become clear when we consider further statements he made regarding good and evil races in one of his lectures on St John's *Apocalypse*. Here he placed in the foreground the significance of the relationship the human being has with the Christ. In particular, we must learn to understand more and more the words St Paul wrote to the Galatians: 'Not I, but Christ in me.'

If the Michael-Christ Impulse enters into the hearts of men and women, if it becomes the impulse behind their activity and permeates their thinking,

then the ascent takes place, and all the souls who find union with this Christ-principle find the way upward. But all the souls who failed to find this union would have gradually to go down into the abyss. They would have gained the ego; they would have gained egoism, but would not be in a position to rise up again with the ego into the spiritual world. And the consequence for those who make no connection with the Christ-principle would be that they disconnect themselves from the spiritual ascent; instead of ascending they would descend and harden themselves more and more in their ego. Instead of finding in matter just the opportunity to develop the ego and then rise up again, they would descend deeper and deeper into matter ... Those who use the life in the body for anything more than an opportunity to gain ego-consciousness will descend into the abyss and form the evil race.[45]

A little later in the same lecture, looking towards the distant future, the seeds of which are already being sown today, Steiner made it crystal clear that it is the aim and task of Anthroposophy to embrace, *from all nations of the world*, those who hear and 'understand the call of the earth mission, who raise up the living Christ within themselves, who develop the principle of brotherly love over the whole earth; ... in the sense of true esoteric Christianity which can proceed from every culture'.[46]

4. Teenage Self-Development

Edward Warren

The brisk Norwegian wind refreshed my face as I walked carefully over the slippery school yard towards the high school building. Across the way two young girls approached me with eager steps, walking arm in arm. Smiles streamed from their countenances showing their inseparable friendship. Their eyes sparkled brightly. Something had made them very happy. And in addition it was the last day before Christmas vacation.

I greeted them and we walked to my classroom. We took seats around my desk, which was surrounded by gift wrappings, Coke bottles and other remains from the seventh grade vacation celebration. Lise spoke eagerly.

'We have something to tell you! We want to talk about a discovery we both made this week independently of each other. I know that it is true even if I cannot prove it to anyone else. It is a new experience and I wonder what you think about it. In our biology lessons our teacher spoke about the function of the heart. He compared it with other organic processes in nature which are self-maintaining. He told us that the blood going through the heart nourishes it at the same time. The coronary vessels not only take away the used substances but they also give nourishment to the heart. In the lungs, with their oxygen, the blood meets the outside world. The old, poisoned blood goes back from the lungs as regenerated, new blood. In this way, there is a constant dying and regeneration process that is peculiar to the heart.

'What I discovered was the fact that I have not only a physical heart but another, more profound heart with its centre near my physical heart. I experienced it and now I know it is a part of me. When I told my experiences to Leonora she said that she had a similar experience last week. We could not believe it! Do you know what we are talking about?'

This question points to the individuality. She asks for reinforcement of her experience in her heart region; the part of her being which carries her eternal individuality. At the age of 16 Lise and Leonora discovered their spiritual hearts—an experience they share with many teenagers throughout the world. But will they find their way to bringing the strength of their Self into the heart region? That will be entirely up to them.

Rudolf Steiner addressed this key area of teenage Self-development on 26 May 1922[1] just six months before his famous 'Youth Course'.[2] In the lecture entitled 'The Human Heart' he shared his research into teenage Self-development. At roughly the age of fourteen, he said, each teenager receives her etheric and her astral heart where forces from her life before birth and from previous lifetimes begin to concentrate. The Self grows forth year for year and strengthens its relationship to the heart region. This process is so essential for the entire lifetime on earth that Steiner created the Waldorf curriculum and the Section for the Spiritual Striving of Youth at the Goetheanum to support teenagers in their Self-development. He also took the first steps towards creating a new scientific discipline, 'Youth Anthroposophy', to help teenagers strengthen their Self-development.

Education and parenting in the twentieth century have taken large steps in the direction of helping youngsters tap into their physical and intellectual resources. But the incarnation processes in the heart region are essential areas of teenage development that will supplement that progress far into the future. During the teenage years every individual takes part in the process of discovering his resources, whether they be of an intellectual, an emotional, or a physical nature. But there is much more to life than that. I am convinced that teenagers not only develop their identity and personality according to their inherent talents and environmental conditioning but they strive for something more. Something which is more powerful than their personality, their identity and their daily self. They strive for their Self—that which is truly unique in their lives, that which goes beyond inheritance, genes, peer conditioning, cultural background, gender, personality, identity, and even their everyday self. They search for the Self which can work into the power of the personality from the maturity of the eternal individuality. The Self brings the teenager's ideas, ideals and intuitions into play.

I am convinced that adults who do not appeal to the search for the Self are not helping teenagers bring forth their most valuable resource. The same is true of our schools and other institutions that work with teenagers. In a society possessed by the advantages of the personality we often ignore the potential of the Self. The more I work with teenagers the more I realize how crucial the years between thirteen and twenty are for the entire lifetime. These are the years in which abilities are developed that will carry the teenager through her entire life. In the same way that supportive attitudes, independent thinking and social initiatives create the teenager's future, so do the unresolved issues during the teenage years continue to shape the quality of a person's life.

Educators and parents often ask themselves questions when they are working with the riddles of the teenage years:

How does he understand himself?

Does he have knowledge of himself or the first beginnings of such?

Does she experience herself as a pure product of her environment?

Is she playing a role? If so, does she fit the role?

The answers, if they come at all, are always temporary. Every day is a new day, especially for youngsters. The more I think deeply and consistently about these questions the more I am able to observe in the teenagers who cross my path. Then long-term questions appear:

How can teenagers tap into their true resources?

When do they discover their own personality?

Are they integrating their personality with the Self?

Few educators take the Self seriously. Many whom I have spoken with agree that teenage Self-development is extremely important for youngsters in the next millennium, but few know where they can start their work. I think this is the case because each individual has to figure out for himself what the Self really is. Such discovery does not come easily. It takes years really to grasp your own Self and observe the Self in others while working full-time as a teacher. There is an enormous amount of resistance involved.

Many scientists and educators deny the Self. For example, Dr Larry J. Siever gave his book the title *The New View of Self*, but he never mentions his concept of the Self. Instead he proposes that everything that makes us individual, our memories, hopes, emotions, talents, ideas—our entire personality and identity—is contained in the brain. According to Siever the brain also organizes behaviour, both conscious and unconscious. Whenever we speak, scratch an itch, sneeze, or glance up in surprise at some interruption, the impulse to do so originates in the brain. We can think of the brain as an organ of information—sensory data in, behaviour out, ourselves in between.

Siever and his colleagues try to create a science of the mind which covers the genetic influences upon the personality. They miss the mark, however, when they omit the self-conscious mind. I do not agree that all behaviour is ultimately mediated by the brain's chemical system. In this essay I will argue that behaviour is also mediated by the individual. Nor do I believe that differences in brain chemistry account for much of the differences in temperament.

The mind-body theme in psychiatry and education is far from solved. Scientists and educators in the genetic behaviourist camp strive for a science of the mind that covers anatomy, brain chemistry, child development, environmental factors and elements of psychoanalytical theory while denying the Self. Even if their experiments are correct in terms of biochemical data, clinical observations and daily experience they choose to omit the power of the Self.

Radical materialism or radical behaviourism is an important position which may not be neglected when considering the relationship between mind and body in the teenage years. It presents an easy solution to the problem when there is no mind, but only body. But teenagers have much more going for them than just their bodies. From an evolutionary point of view what matters, broadly speaking, is the ability to reproduce and for teenagers' offspring to do the same. But they also have much more going for them than their ability to procreate. They have minds. They are in a position to develop their Self-conscious minds.

One area in which we can bring the Self into focus is the daily sensory activities. This theme takes us to the heart of some of the most interesting questions concerning the teenage years. Each teenager has an enormous potential for sensory development. This is a vast area of opportunities for Self-development in education as well.

Late adolescents have well-developed sense-experiences. In many cases, their sensory abilities have reached their peak of performance and they have often learned how to tap their individual potential. Now is a time for finely tuning their sensory skills which will give them the essential competence they will need in their chosen field of work. At the same time, they will need to develop other sensory skills which will give them a healthy balance to their lifestyle.

We see teenagers developing their quality of performance in all areas of life from the arts to professional training. Dancers bring their sense of *balance* and *movement* on to the stage. Musicians work intensively with *touch* and *hearing*. Downhill-racers carve powerful turns at high speed while pushing their sense of *balance* to supreme tests. The Israeli Air Force takes five years to teach pilots, beginning at age 18, how to train their senses in order to manoeuvre 60-million-dollar F15s. A teenage violinist will spend 10 hours a day practising Tchaikovsky's Concerto for Violin and Orchestra in D major, Op. 35 in order to perform it at his debut concert. And when a class of 19-year-olds performs a play such as *Our Town* by Thornton Wilder, a very unique sensory experience streams from them to their audience. Their youthful talents can sometimes outdo even the best professional performances.

We can look into the unfolding of the senses while a teenager walks through a landscape on a quiet afternoon. She meets a whole symphony of sense-experiences performing for her simultaneously. On her walk she sees the colour of the sky, detects the motion of the clouds, identifies the shapes of the crowns of trees, gauges the distance to the hills and watches the changing speed of the swallows diving at low altitudes. Her sense of *smell* may be engaged by the roses, the drying hay or the muddy lake she passes. As the sun shines through the apple trees she may feel its *warmth* on her arms, her legs and her forehead. When she stands by a huge maple tree her sense of *touch* may be awakened by the rough bark. The crickets in the fields surround her with *sound* and the rustling of the breeze in the trees may echo in her ears.

The simple things in life can also be the most profound. A walk in nature is one of them. What is really taking place in our senses during an afternoon stroll? Can we understand our sensory experiences even better? According to neuroscientists, all of these sense-experiences are processed separately. They are transmitted to different parts of the brain where various senses are processed. What neuroscientists are still trying to understand is how the separate experiences are synthesized into the total experience of the afternoon stroll. We can ask ourselves how active the teenager is in the process. Just a simple walk through a landscape brings her directly into the area of science called mind-brain interaction. In simple words, this area describes how our mind relates to the physical activities of our brain. Of course, the teenager does not think about her mind-brain interaction when she is enjoying her walk. Her sense-experiences do not reach her *attention*. Nevertheless, this poses a major question.

Are her sense-experiences synthesized into a total experience by the instinctive reactions of her nervous system or is this process of integration carried out by her Self?

My experience convinces me that it is the power of Self that does so.

Unlike most neuroscientists, who believe that all aspects of mind, including consciousness and awareness, are explainable, materialistically, as the interaction of large sets of neurons, Sir John Eccles asserts that the soul is distinct from the body. He is certain that we exist as Self-conscious beings in a material world that includes our body and brain. The question of mind-brain interaction is essential for the teenage years. Just consider the vast areas of development that are available to a teenager who goes actively into his Self-conscious being and takes part in the integration of the sensory experiences, rather than closing the door to such creativity by assuming that the body's sets of neurons will automatically provide the integration. The Self-conscious mind is the highest mental experience a teenager may participate in. Because of it, she knows what she knows. It is the most fundamental characteristic of the teenage years. When such mental experiences take place over a longer period of time, they become the basis for mental unity in her memory. In this way, the Self-conscious mind provides continuity in her life. Knowing what she knows, in turn, strengthens her understanding of her Self.

Eccles goes even further. He also differentiates between the outer and the inner senses. He considers the outer ones to be: *light, colour, sound, smell, taste, pain, touch, perception.* And according to him, the inner senses are: *thoughts, feelings, memories, dreams, imagining, intention, attention.*

Normally we only consider five senses. Eccles names fifteen, but there may be even more. *Movement, warmth* and *balance* are certainly missing from his list. One of the twelve senses Rudolf Steiner describes is the *sense of Self.* With this sense we not only experience other people but we can experience their Self. This opens a vast new area of teenage Self-development. The inner senses may be explored by the teenager who is conscious of her Self in a healthy way. It is this Self that has the power to integrate the flow from the outer to the inner sense-experiences.

We can look into a very interesting double nature of the Self of every teenager. On the one hand, the Self is the central force in the core of the teenager's being in the other heart region. On the other hand it lives, simultaneously, in the periphery. An excellent picture of this relationship may be found in the astronomical symbol for the sun. The Self swings between the inner point of the other heart region to the bordering circle of the world. Roughly speaking, it moves in two separate directions—a centrifugal movement away from the centre and a corresponding movement towards the centre. Just how this movement takes place depends on the activity of the individual. Our outer and inner senses are instruments with which teenagers can work with the world of nature, the cities and their social lives. A schooling of perceptions accompanied by individual thinking with the Self-conscious mind can integrate the sense-experiences and further develop the experiences of the Self.

Let me give one example:

The girl walking in the landscape may decide to focus her *attention* on a waterlily floating on the lake. She sits quietly and observes the flower in as much detail as possible. Then she closes her eyes and tries to make an inner picture of the lily. With the power of Self, she tries to build up an inner picture of the lily she has been observing in nature. When she opens her eyes again and looks once more, she will correct her inner picture. This enables her to observe even better the next time. When she continues to observe the lily, her *perception* is sharpened and she begins to concentrate even more. By looking even more closely at the flower, she discovers new details. Then she actively engages her inner senses of *attention* and *memory* when she tries again to create a new inner picture of the flower. As we all know, these senses do not usually work alone. Her senses of *imagining* and *day-dreaming* may easily come into play and distract her creation of the inner picture of the lily she had decided to work with. It is easy to become distracted and float off into unrelated associations.

But when her power of *thought* helps her to redefine her

focus, she may come back to the inner picture she is trying to develop. Even more senses may be drawn upon when she opens her eyes again and looks closer at the *colours* she experiences in and around the lily on the lake. A clear sign of the fact that her efforts are working appears when her *perceptions* lead to new *feelings*. Subtle but powerful new *feelings* may appear. So far, she has only observed the flower as it appears above the water. What does the rest of the plant look like underneath the surface? From the muddy floor of the lake the stem of the water lily grows forth in the murky waters. Down here, there are no beautiful yellow and white blossoms and petals. But life in the underworld also belongs to the radiance of the flower resting on the lily pads. Without the stem flowing from the murky underworld, the flower would never open itself to the sun. And furthermore, the single flower she is observing belongs to the whole lake, to the air, the sun, the wind, the trees. By unfolding her senses this afternoon, she moves towards the connections of the living forces at play below, upon and surrounding the lake. She is taking place in the movement of her Self; from the centre to the periphery of the lake-landscape, and back again. In this way, the teenager does not remain merely in a subjective experience of her unfolding senses but the reality of the world provides an objective correction.

This work comes naturally to her. She has the need for contemplation. For her friends, however, it may be more natural to work on their motorcycles or sit by the swimming pool. Other girls prefer to jump off the edge of cliffs!

When the movement of the Self from the central point to the periphery is temporarily blocked, the teenager is especially vulnerable to numerous forms of sensory over-exposure, the result being a lack of integration. One example may be seen when the sense of *taste* may be so overbearing that the teenager eats constantly and becomes obese. Or, when teenagers start to drown in their appetite for sense-less experience, the uncontrolled need for consumption of sensory experiences takes over.

That is why Self-education is so important in the teenage years. When teenagers can educate themselves as to how they can bring their interest and enthusiasm from their Self into the world and then from the world back to themselves, they carry out an invaluable strengthening of their personality. This process will help them create inner freedom. The Self becomes clearer and clearer. It takes part in a process of sensory nourishment which strengthens mind, soul and spirit.

Why does a teenager feel refreshed when she experiences the wonders of nature, the joy of human contact or the power of thought? It is because her Self has interacted with the world in a productive way. Rather than leaving the mind-brain interaction up to physical coincidences, the teenager strengthens the flow of her life forces by carrying out healthy actions.

The vast majority of teenagers I meet, however, do not grasp their sense-experiences out of their Self-conscious mind, but take such a distance to their natural sense-experiences that they become alienated from their senses. Then they spend a lot of time filling themselves up with new artificial experiences—on the screens, in the earphones, and in the urban jungle. Their artificial sensory overload becomes a regular habit in their lives. In a bewildering variety of ways teenagers overdrive their nervous system. This is one of the major reasons why teenagers lack content in their lives. The natural flow of our senses is continuously interrupted in our daily lives. If you sit too long in one position your blood circulation in certain parts of your legs may stand still. Is it not the same with our senses such as *thinking, perceiving* and *feeling*?

An interesting experience for teenagers and adults is to

observe when your sensory apparatus shuts down on its own. Whether you like it or not, your senses have received so many experiences that all you can do is go to sleep, feel sick or get away for the weekend to recuperate. A sensory shut-down may be compared with a dam that is temporarily opened to lower the water level of the river. Huge, roaring waves burst upon the rocks below the dam. You hear the deep, thunderous drone of water exploding on the granite. An opening is made and all of the life forces rush out. The same situation occurs daily with teenagers who learn to observe when their sensory fields shut down and their life forces rush out.

A shut-down is nothing new to any of us. We experience it every day. We can observe a shut-down taking place when we come to a new city. As we walk down the streets we can observe how all of the impressions affect our senses. There is always a moment when overload appears. This moment is another important edge experience. It teaches the individual where her balance may be found. This is the point from which she can judge the abundance of energy she disposes. Her energy levels are constantly on the edge. Here she may find a starting point for experimentation—then the high-wire act of missing and finding her balance may be practised day after day!

Teenagers are generally aware of the connection between their sensory experiences and their life forces. The girl with the need to use her sense of *attention* in nature probably had a certain sensory under-exposure. She needed to expose her senses more to the world of nature in order to find her balance.

If the teenage senses become ill due to over-exposure, the capacity for mental awareness and feeling will be severely reduced. No healthy sense of judgement is then active and the teenager's inner life becomes weaker and weaker. The outside world no longer enriches her feelings and actions. There are scores of examples of this condition.

An extreme example of sensory over-exposure which devastates a teenager's energy levels may be experienced in the basement under the shiny fluorescent strobe flashing on and off through a whirling globe during a rave party. The laser shoots light over the liquid bodies dancing in the black air. They are all looking forward to getting lost, letting go, losing themselves in the dancing, laughter and coloured ecstasy of the party. These teenagers are out to sacrifice body and mind. When teenage hearing-receptors are under constant siege from extreme music, drugs and modern life, many of the 32,000 cilia in their ears stiffen because they are held too long in a rigid pose. The cilia eventually just keel over and die. There can be no doubt that 115 decibels of heavy metal strafes the ears! After years of this and other forms of self-abuse, it appears that one's facial bones may become more pronounced, one's teeth may rot, one's brain may melt and hallucinations disorientate one's consciousness.

Other teenagers are exposed to an assault upon their sense of sight when they spend hours indulging in nourishment of the consumer industry's sensory experiences. The superficial media-experiences create the desire for even more passive entertainment. They need more and more impressions because the senses are not being replenished and the life forces are not refreshed. It is much like car-sickness. Their strength withers and the senses are shut down until the paralysing effect can be overcome.

A far-reaching question any educator or parent may ask: Is my child receiving a healthy development of her senses, taking her lifestyle into consideration? Adults can help teenagers break into new energy levels in two ways. One is going into the details of the actual development of all fifteen senses of the child you are living and working with. This means asking questions like: How is your teenager unfolding her outer senses of *perception, touch, pain, taste, smell, sound, colour* and *light*? In what way is she in touch with her inner senses of *attention, intention, imagining, dreams, memories, feelings* and *thoughts*?

By asking such detailed questions and searching for the relevant answers you can further your understanding of the teenager. This can also help you take off some of your blinkers. The picture quickly becomes very complicated when the details arise and we start looking into the reality of her inner and outer sense-experience. You can start looking into the actual under-exposures or over-exposures the teenager is living with. This ultimately leads to two new questions: Which sensory skills does she need to unfold? How can I challenge her to reach new energy levels?

The other area which is opened up by the field of mind-brain interaction concerns teenagers at school or in the workplace. They may be developing their skills in a trade or in academics. And the question arises: How can my subject appeal to the unfolding of all fifteen senses?

Even a subject like grammar can promote the unfolding of teenage senses. As a grammar teacher I can focus on my subject as the sole goal of my teaching. Or I can step out of my present mind-set and learn to teach grammar in such a way that I also appeal to some of the inner and outer senses. In the case of grammar, the methods of teaching can promote the unfolding of senses such as thought, attention or perception. This is possible in all academic subjects as well as working skills. In my opinion this is what makes teaching and learning interesting. Then teaching not only helps the teenager to be excellent in, say, English, but it also promotes other sides of life. Which senses can be unfolded when teaching mathematics, botany, history or geography?

In the work place, teenagers will be faced with improving

their skills such as: gathering facts, completing analyses, managing activities, communicating, creating personal values and inspiring their co-workers. Will all of these activities merely take place or can they be developed in such a way that the fifteen senses are unfolded so that the individual becomes mature and self-reliant?

By the time the teenager has reached the age of 17, I believe that the individual has to unfold her senses in a process of Self-education. By then, each teenager will have areas of her sensory life that are either under-exposed or over-exposed. I meet more and more teenagers who already have the maturity to discover that they can take care of themselves and further develop their sense-experiences. It is hard work. Many realize how vulnerable they are and how much of their strength has already been wasted. Many of them are interested in new experiences in nature—on the ocean, in the mountains, on the glaciers or in the woods. Some enliven their senses through singing, dancing or playing music. Others learn how to fly aeroplanes or sail boats. They know how to involve themselves.

A very good example of a 19-year-old who was not over-exposed may be found in Lee Iacocca. In 1943 he enjoyed the advantage of small classes at Lehigh College because most of the men were at war. He had already been forced to put aside his athletic career as well as his service in the military during World War II due to a six-month bout of rheumatic fever as a 15-year-old. This challenged him to develop his ability to concentrate, to use his time well and to persevere. He played chess, bridge and poker. Iacocca joined a Latin club, a drama club and a debating society. In his way he developed essential skills, which only a teenager can develop by himself.

Just as the individual's need for Self-integration becomes so obvious at this age, the demands for career preparation are so intensified that teenagers have to neglect their individual

development in order to pursue distant goals. Teenagers
often spend these years being filtered out by career demands.
Those who make it through the filter become specialized.
Those who do not choose to put themselves through the
intellectual meat-mincer search for other lifestyles. Society
has set the guidelines by which they are evaluated and promoted. Most college and university education is not based on
an integration of the Self, but on extreme neglect of the Self.
The fear of not succeeding or the fear of making a mistake
replaces the confidence of Self-integration. Most often the
possibility of unfolding the senses in the teenage years is
passed over and the unbelievably colourful palate of inner
and outer senses remains to a large extent unused.

Modern education can promote teenage Self-development. The artistic element of her Self-education should not
be isolated in artistic subjects alone. It belongs together with
the scientific and religious elements of knowledge. The
teenager then searches for a field of activity. Whether she
goes into singing, dancing, painting, sculpting or any other
artistic process, the activities and products do not have to be
the goals in themselves. The arts may become media through
which the teenager unfolds her senses and develops mental
hygiene. I have observed a tremendous difference between
those who play an instrument or sing and those who do not
work with music as children and teenagers. Teenagers who
become anything from a rocker to a cellist often have a sense
of judgement that other teenagers do not have. They know
what it means to practise and to work hard. They learn how
to judge their actions as well as how to live with their results.
Barriers are constantly overcome due to their own initiative.
Their senses are awakened and formed as skills.

I have noticed how well they develop their sense of
gratitude and I have seen how many teenagers develop their
inner lives in a more distinguished way. Artistic work,

whether it be within the more traditional disciplines or in social life, helps the teenagers go beyond their sympathies and antipathies. It sets them in motion. Their perception is sharpened and, most importantly, they create new feelings. Being in motion, creating new feelings, sharpening their perceptions—these are some of the activities through which teenagers can get to know their Self.

5. *Freedom in Thinking*

Olive Whicher

At a time when materialism was dominating thinking more and more, the life's work of Rudolf Steiner was to awaken human beings to an understanding of their spiritual nature and background.

The names by which his teaching is known—Anthroposophy and Spiritual Science—make clear the fact that it is indeed a science and not a religion, even though the content of his around 30 books and over 6,000 lectures deals over and over again with both religion and science. Indeed, a true understanding of the Christ Being and of the forces of life and growth lies at the heart of his life's work.

Steiner based his work on that of Goethe the scientist, and named the building at Dornach, Switzerland, from which he worked, the Goetheanum. This centre is the birth-place of the anthroposophical movement, which is now world-wide, embracing the fields of agriculture, medicine, education and art.

In the past, humanity was guided by the various great world religions, which in their different ways raised men's minds beyond the day-to-day experience of practical life. Kings and Queens and Churchmen guided ordinary mortals in a manner similar to the way schoolchildren are brought up by parents and teachers. Literacy and numeracy were achieved by the few, who were the great individuals of whom history tells.

Looking back even only to the early decades of the

twentieth century, life was vastly different from what it is today as we face the new millennium. In those years, when motorcars were beginning to compete with the horse and trap, the roads were very different from what they are today.

My memory goes back to the time before saloon cars were to be seen on the roads, when my father, an organist, and the local vicar each owned one of the first Morris Cowleys. The vicar called his car Boanerges (Son of Thunder!). I also remember markings being introduced on the roads and my young brother shouting to my father, 'Daddy! Don't straddle the white line!'

Such memories describe how much the world has changed in less than a century, following the time of the Industrial Revolution, since when research into matter in all manner of materials has far surpassed a clear understanding of how the living forces function in living organisms.

How do plants grow? How do we stand upright? What is the basic difference between the gravitational forces and the forces at work in the living kingdoms of nature and in humankind? Is it true to think that such forces as those at work in compelling an aeroplane, laden with people and their luggage, to rise up from the earth and fly from one country to another, are in any way similar to the forces at work in a living organism?

What is taking place when in agriculture farmers resort to chemical fertilization of the soil, or when in medicine we resort to *in vitro* fertilization?

How can science today, while still maintaining clarity and integrity in thinking, without falling back into the mode of religious belief, come to terms with these essential questions?

The answer is at hand in Rudolf Steiner's spiritual science. What is, however, urgently necessary is that his way of approach should spread still more widely, so as to balance out the one-sidedly materialistic developments in science, preventing them from dominating in fields to which they do not belong.

Education is a prime example of where this task lies. Is it not obvious that if children and young people are only introduced to scientific concepts based one-sidedly on the idea of the force of gravity and its counterpart, the push and thrust forces of the sword or the gun, they will quite naturally resort to activities in which such forces work, even to the point of killing one another?

Rudolf Steiner was quite clear about this, when in the founding of the Waldorf School in Stuttgart he did not allow football to be part of the games. My experience in this field as a child was that of moving from a school where hockey was the main game to one where we played netball on dunes above the sea-shore. I experienced boundless relief, which was renewed when much later I met with eurythmy and then with Bothmer gymnastics.

These aspects of physical training, which in eurythmy, when achieved, become an art, are based on the experience of the threefold nature of the human body: head, rhythmic system and limb-system. Such movements bring to the human being an experience of the way in which the living body is poised between gravity and the force whereby all living forms rise upward, thus overcoming gravity.

Here we can understand why and how Rudolf Steiner based his life's work, spiritual science, on Goethe, and how essential it is in our time to take this work further.

Basic to the work of Johann Wolfgang von Goethe[1] in the eighteenth century and taken further by Rudolf Steiner in the twentieth century is the *metamorphosis of plants*. Fundamental here is Steiner's description of the laws whereby plants and other living beings stand upright, overcoming the downward pull of gravity and changing their shape as they do so. The so-called etheric or ethereal formative forces pour inward from sun and stars with *an upward suctional force,* which works contrary to the force of gravity.

It is of utmost importance that in the coming twenty-first century an understanding of the laws of the ethereal formative forces should come to the fore in science and education.

A beginning has been made by a number of scientists, among them George Adams, who was doing research in physics and chemistry at Cambridge when he met with the work of Rudolf Steiner.[2] He was immediately impressed and lost no time in going to meet Steiner at Dornach.

At the Goetheanum he was introduced to Edith Maryon, the English sculptress, who was helping Steiner to carve the great wooden statue.[3] (Adams was later one of those who helped save this work from the flames that demolished the first Goetheanum.)

Edith Maryon gave him hammer and chisel to cut away unwanted wood, and while he was doing this Rudolf Steiner entered and came up to the scaffolding, where they shook hands. Steiner had just come from the Waldorf School in Stuttgart and the first thing he said was, 'The children are rampageous; if a child does not enjoy a good romp it will not later become a capable human being.'

George Adams was able to have many quiet conversations with Rudolf Steiner and became his interpreter when he spoke to English audiences. He was able to put to Steiner his fundamental scientific question: Would he agree that the *idea of polar reciprocation in modern projective geometry* might be brought to bear on his [Steiner's] teaching concerning the laws of the etheric forces at work in all living processes? Steiner answered this question immediately in the affirmative.

In 1934 George Adams published a book in German with a title that translates as 'Radiant Forces of Creation' in which he described the historical development of mathematics in terms of perspective transformation and polarity.[4] Together he and I wrote *The Plant Between Sun and Earth*,[5] a fully illustrated book, which Adams looked upon as a sequel to his earlier work, even though that has never been translated into English.

In the coming twenty-first century science and education must generate a true understanding of the laws of living growth, those laws that Steiner called etheric, or ethereal formative forces, which work counter to the earthly gravitational forces in all realms of living development.

 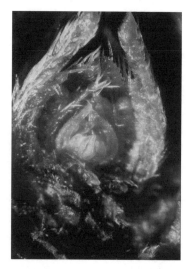

The illustration on the left is of a twelfth to thirteenth century icon or mandala in the Cathedral of Trento in Italy. The force of gravity in the space of earth is clearly pictured and at the same time is being overcome and held upward by the same Sun Being whose Blood entered the earth in order to save mankind from being bound to the earth. See the head of the Being standing upright and compare it with the magnified section of the young growing-point of a living plant. Surely both reveal a similar morphology, showing an inner space ready to receive the forces of light and warmth from the sun.

Today as we face the new millennium the heart of the matter is that—together with human beings the world over and in freedom of thinking—we should uncover and teach the true laws of living organisms, that science may become more and more able to be as efficient in the organic realms as it is in the realm of machines. This will be achieved, the more the living forces of Rudolf Steiner's spiritual science spread throughout the world.

6. Interpreting Life through the Eyes of Anthroposophy

Doré Deverell

When I stepped on to the campus of Rudolf Steiner College at Fair Oaks, California, a suburb of Sacramento, in April 1983, I knew I was home at last despite knowing almost nothing about Rudolf Steiner or Anthroposophy.

I was at the campus because on a bleak morning three days earlier during my meditation I had asked the spiritual worlds in desperation, 'What do you want from me?' I had reached an impasse in my life and I didn't know what to do. My son had committed suicide a few months earlier, and at the same time my work of lecturing, facilitating workshops, teaching classes and counselling about holistic health had come to an abrupt halt.

I felt responsible for my son's death and I knew that he was suffering terribly in the spiritual worlds because of his suicide. I didn't know how to help him except to pray for him.

When I asked the question, I received the answer, 'Perhaps you can help in the development of children.' This was strange indeed; I had never even considered working with children.

That evening I confided this cryptic message to a friend and she said to me, 'Rudolf Steiner College trains people to teach children according to their development. It is located in the Sacramento area. Let's go to Sacramento and investigate.'

A couple of days later we drove the 400 miles from Los Angeles to Sacramento, and as we walked around the deserted campus that Sunday afternoon I felt my excitement grow. I could hardly wait for my interview with the registrar the following day.

In the registrar's office on Monday I looked over the schedule of classes, and I couldn't believe that any college offered such classes: *Knowledge of Higher Worlds, Reincarnation and Karma, Evolution of Consciousness, Philosophy of Freedom* and many more. I enrolled immediately in the Foundation Year for fall 1983. I also bought Rudolf Steiner's five basic books.

I moved to Fair Oaks and waited impatiently for classes to begin. I knew this was a turning point in my life, but I had no idea what to expect. While waiting I read *Knowledge of Higher Worlds*, which was the only book out of the five that I could understand to some degree. I felt the book more than understanding its contents.

A few weeks after classes began, I learned from a classmate that Rudolf Steiner had said that the dead can be helped by reading spiritual books to them. This was blessed knowledge to me. I started immediately reading daily to my son and other members of my family who had died. For the first time I felt some relief from his suicide.

From the beginning of the Foundation Year I felt tremendous gratitude and wonder to find myself in Anthroposophy. I had been through many stages and many years searching for a spiritual path.

When I was 16 I had a burning desire to live for God. When I asked a Baptist minister in the small Bible belt town in Oklahoma where I lived, 'What can I do for God?' his only suggestion was that I could tithe 10% of my $16.00 a month salary, which I did.

At 21 I married a Catholic. I took instruction in Catholicism and was baptized at 23, and was a Catholic for 25 years. I loved attending Mass and receiving communion, and I liked to teach religion to Catholic children who attended public schools. I also started the first rudiments of meditation by saying the rosary prayers while imagining the scenes of Christ's life. I joined a perpetual adoration of Christ group and devoted an hour every month to this practice.

As life's problems piled up that I didn't know how to handle, I couldn't find any help in the Catholic church. Though daily mass was a comfort to me, I still slid into alcoholism. Conferences with Catholic priests provided no concrete answers or guidance. Indeed, a Jesuit priest sent me to a Catholic psychiatrist who insisted I take drugs. This compounded the problems.

Not until I joined Alcoholics Anonymous at age 46 did I finally find a way to start the long climb out of the abyss. AA with its 12 steps and 12 traditions has a powerful spiritual programme. I learned to take responsibility for my life and my actions. I gave my life to God, took a searching moral inventory of my actions, made amends wherever possible to people I had harmed, asked God to help me remove my character defects, prayed and meditated daily, forgave others, and tried to practise these principles in all areas of my life.

Through the unconditional love, acceptance and support from members of AA, and through working the 12 steps, I painfully gained self-knowledge slowly but steadily.

After seven years in AA I had to face cancer. Of necessity I had to take drastic steps to heal the cancer, accelerating the process of emotional catharsis, changing my lifestyle, and using my mind to change negative thoughts. Most of all, I was trying to find myself. With much research and help from alternative health providers and healers, I was able to overcome cancer and wrote the book *How I Healed My Cancer*

Holistically in 1976 (now out of print). This experience awakened me more and gave my life direction for several more years working with others through offering classes, counselling, workshops and lectures.

With my grandson, who was born after I had been in AA for 11 years, I was able for the first time to connect with another human being. I had no idea until that time that I had been disconnected from myself and others because of severe emotional abuse from babyhood. I was devastated to see that I had not been able to bond with my children, and the consequences of this in their lives. I blamed myself for their problems and I gave myself no mercy despite my abusive childhood.

Then, 13 years after I had come into AA, my son committed suicide at age 36, which led me to Rudolf Steiner College and Anthroposophy. By this time I was 60.

I started the two-year course, joined the Anthroposophical Society and poured myself into the branch work. I also attended every conference and workshop offered by the college and the branch.

During these years of study I constantly had jarring insights about my life's experiences. For example, my mother told me she hadn't allowed me to crawl. I had thought nothing of it at the time. But, in my Foundation Year in a remedial class I learned that not crawling causes great hindrances in a child's development. To help correct this, I started doing the Extra Lesson exercises.[1]

After I completed the Teacher Training I realized that I couldn't become a Steiner Waldorf teacher because of my undeveloped imagination and lack of arts. So, I took three years of the Arts Programme. Not until the second year was I able to put on a veil of paint without having to scrub some of it off. As I wrestled with the painting, I was further handicapped because I couldn't draw. And, I had no memory pictures of fairy tales to draw from. So, I read fairy tales every night for three years before I went to bed, and tried to imagine the scenes. The more arts I took and knowledge I gained, the more I realized how painful and bleak my life had been and how uncomfortable I still was with myself and others. Eurythmy was my favourite art. I could really touch into bliss during tone eurythmy classes.

Meanwhile, I read Anthroposophy to my son every morning and began to have experiences with him, which I duly recorded in my journal.

The summer after I completed the two-year training in my 63rd year, my health trials began. I had a shock to my system which caused a heart crisis. I then started taking anthroposophical remedies, curative baths, curative eurythmy, curative painting and curative speech. In addition to the physical crises I found hidden terrors in my soul which I had to transform. I was terrified of dying and wrestled with this many times. I finally solved that terror by realizing that the only thing that really mattered was my relationship to Christ. In Christ, we die. So, it didn't matter whether I was living, dying or dead; Christ would never abandon me and I certainly wasn't going to let go of him.

Other fears arose: the fear of poverty, the fear of having a stroke and being helpless, and even unnamed fears. Sometimes I had to spend an hour saying Rudolf Steiner's verse:

> What have you, Phantom Thoughts and Deceitful Visions,
> To do with the mighty task that is mine?
> The spiritual worlds expect it of me.
> Therefore will I drive the enemies out of my soul
> By taking hold of strong thinking;
> My heart serves me stoutly
> If only I so will.[2]

I would pace up and down the floor gesturing with my hands to drive out the enemies of my soul and then take up strong thoughts until calm once again descended. I also repeated like a mantra Rudolf Steiner's saying: 'Illness is not suffering. It is an opportunity to overcome an obstacle by uncovering the Christ power within.' I meditated on this constantly.

I continued to read to my son daily, and after five years I was elated when he moved from a place of dark despair in the spiritual worlds to a place filled with light. I continued to read to him and after two more years I was amazed when I experienced that he had returned in a new incarnation, and he pleaded with me to carry him spiritually in my consciousness. He told me he needed my spiritual support very much in his new incarnation. I agreed to do this and stopped reading to him at that time. I didn't know how to think about his return. I held it in my heart and planned never to mention it.

When a friend asked me when I was going to write a book about reading to the dead, I knew this was a destiny question. So, over a period of the next seven years I wrote the book *Light Beyond the Darkness*.[3] This book tells in detail my experiences with my son.

As I was finishing that book I realized that I couldn't omit my belief that my son had returned, because I didn't think by this time that this was just a personal experience. Though most reluctant to write about it, I was supported and encouraged to do so by my spiritual mentor, a wise anthroposophist of many years.

When Temple Lodge Publishing published the book and I went on a speaking tour in Europe, I began to see my life from a different perspective. Many people were delighted to hear about experiential Anthroposophy. For the first time in their life they shared their experiences with me. Several confided that they had also experienced a loved one's return after a few years, but they were not prepared to write about it.

Further insight came when a clairvoyant anthroposophist

who had read my book told me that what I had to give the
world was overcoming alcoholism, cancer and suicide. I told
him that I would rather teach *Knowledge of the Higher
Worlds*, but I knew he was right. So, I wrote a booklet
'Finding a Greater Good Out of the Greatest Evils: Alcoholism, Cancer and Suicide.' When I was in Europe I gave
several workshops on this theme in Holland, Germany and
England. When Temple Lodge Publishing saw the booklet,
they asked me to expand it into a book. That book is in
process now, and will include the effects of my childhood
abuse, too.

In Europe I also learned about 'the other Michael stream'
characterized by Ita Wegman in 'On the Work of Michael'
where one follows the evil without becoming evil.[4] I also
heard about the will stream, which comes to wisdom through
earth experiences in contrast to the stream which comes to
wisdom through thinking.

I started to have a shift in consciousness of what I had been
doing all those years. Maybe my life hadn't been stupid and a
failure. Perhaps I had been looking in the wrong places and
with the wrong perspectives for the meaning of my life.
Maybe my life had been about wresting the good from the
evils of child abuse, addictions, divorce, cancer and suicide.
Could my life be some of the ways a Manichean stream
manifests?

Carl Stegman, a Christian Community priest from Germany who came to California after he retired and helped
found Rudolf Steiner College, said that the scourge of
America was alcohol, child abuse and the strong ahrimanic
forces here. Isn't it possible that people in the Michael school
would come to America to help transform child abuse and
alcoholism? Isn't it startlingly interesting that Alcoholics
Anonymous was founded and developed by Bill Wilson in
1933–1935 just as Christ was appearing in the etheric and

after Bill Wilson had had a life-changing spiritual experience of meeting a being of light to whom he surrendered his life?

It seems evident to an anthroposophist who understands the esoteric significance of the 12 steps and AA that they belong to the greater Michaelic work. AA not only helps millions of people who are struggling with addictions, but the 12 steps are actually will exercises for the development of the ego. In addition AA gives people unconditional love, acceptance, understanding and support without judging them. Maybe having addictions was the only way some people could find a spiritual community in this desert of the consciousness soul age.

In *From Symptom to Reality in Modern History* Rudolf Steiner says:[5]

> On the other hand the finest and most important social attribute in the future will be the development of a scientific objective understanding of the shortcomings of others, when we are more interested in their shortcomings than in our concern to criticize them. For gradually in the course of the fifth, sixth and seventh epochs the individual will have to devote himself increasingly and with loving care to the shortcomings of his neighbour.

AA sees addiction as a spiritual disease which can only be healed through a spiritual awakening. What could be more objective than that perspective? On the next page, Steiner says regarding people with mental illness. 'We must not be repelled by them, but must develop an understanding for them.' AA members welcome newcomers regardless of what state they are in when they arrive.

The 12 steps have been applied to many other problems: overeating, drugs, gambling, sex addiction, child abuse, and programmes for family members who have suffered from living with an addicted person. Indeed, every aberration in our society has a 12-step programme. Millions of people world-wide belong to 12-step programmes.

Maybe in the fifth epoch, in which we have to confront evil, problems are not to be eliminated, but lived through. In the problems one sees the flaws in our society highlighted, and discovering the way through them enriches the community that is able to reintegrate the people who have overcome them.

Isn't it possible that the ones who do work through these problems and help others to do so could be forerunners of the fifth, sixth and seventh cultural epochs when 'the individual will have to devote himself increasingly and with loving care to the shortcomings of his neighbour,' as quoted in full above? It is healing, indeed, to receive this selfless devotion from another human being who can truly understand and help you because he's been where you are.

An ideal I have is for anthroposophists to become more open and be willing to provide a space where people can say who they are, and can share spiritual experiences if they wish without being judged. I experienced in Europe how many people are hungering for this. How refreshing it could be to hear how other anthroposophists interpret their lives through the eyes of Anthroposophy. Even the humblest experience would be heart-warming to hear.

I have written about the 12 steps because I think it is important for anthroposophists to recognize the spiritual significance of the 12-step programmes, and to be alert to other movements who are doing Michael's work outside of our movement. Then when we meet them we could recognize a kindred spirit.

After five years in AA I yearned for something beyond its scope, but it was another nine years before I found Anthroposophy. During those nine years I had explored many movements and had even travelled to India where I learned that I am my own guru. I felt increasingly homeless until I walked on to Rudolf Steiner College campus.

That was 16 years ago now, and my wonder and gratitude for Rudolf Steiner and Anthroposophy grows daily. I'm convinced that I would have died years ago without the healing I've received through Anthroposophy. My experience with my son through reading Anthroposophy to him is a miracle to me.

Only through Anthroposophy did I find the true meaning of my life.

In the beginning was the Christ,
And Christ was with God
And Christ was a God.
In each human soul
Being of Christ indwells.
In my soul too he dwells
And he will lead me
To the true meaning of my life.[6]

Appendix
When did Rudolf Steiner Expect the Incarnation of Ahriman?[1]

Hans Peter van Manen

Introductory remarks

As most people realize, the century now drawing to a close has been very dramatic. Headlong speed in scientific, technical and economic advance contrasts with the misery of war, oppression, genocide and ecological hazards, while the consequences of psychological and social crisis remain incalculable. What most are unaware of, however, is something spiritual science sees as the most positive and moving element in all this drama of the twentieth century, and that is the reappearance of Christ in the etheric realm.

Our eyes are opened to this most important event of our time in two ways: by Rudolf Steiner's descriptions of it, and by intimate experiences a good many of our contemporaries are having. Steiner mentioned this subject for the first time quite unexpectedly in 1910, and it remained one of his main themes until 1914. Thereafter he only referred to it briefly from time to time. In subsequent decades, especially since the Second World War, further work has been done on it, mainly by his pupils and often in the light of the above-mentioned experiences people are having.[2]

As he continued to elaborate his work on spiritual science—in this connection from 1909 to 1925—Steiner repeatedly described in detail the main opposition with which this contemporary Christ Event is confronted: the unfolding of the spiritual power of materialism or, more concretely, the work of Ahriman. In most of these cases he balanced his remarks by also mentioning the opposite spiritual aspect, Lucifer's seductive power which approaches 'I'-consciousness through the feeling life, fanning the flames of individual egoism as well as group egoism in all its forms of chauvinism and elitism. One could devote an entire life's work to elaborating the dual nature of evil present in Lucifer and Ahriman, and it is certainly one of the most comprehensive chapters in the whole of Anthroposophy. The ahrimanic aspect is the most topical now, for Lucifer's influence was more dominant in the past, during pre-Christian cultures and partly even up to the end of the Middle Ages. Ahriman's influence, i.e. materialism, has been on the increase since the fifteenth century and has become predominant during the nineteenth and twentieth centuries.

Shortly after the First World War, unexpectedly again, Steiner began to approach this whole theme from a new angle: the expected future incarnation of Ahriman. He did this in only six lectures given towards the end of 1919 in four different locations.[3] It is equally surprising to find that thereafter he never touched on the subject again, either verbally or in writing. In recent decades it has occasionally been taken up again by his pupils.[4]

The present article will summarize what Steiner said on this subject in those lectures and refer directly to the published texts.

The central event in human evolution is the incarnation of Christ with its culmination in the Mystery of Golgotha; and now Christ faces opposition from two quarters, from Lucifer and from Ahriman. This opposition is such that, in keeping with cosmic fairness, both these adversaries are offered an opportunity to incarnate. Lucifer went through a human incarnation in China quite near the beginning of the third pre-Christian millennium, while in the future Ahriman will be incorporated in 'the West' during the third millennium after Christ. Cosmic fairness decrees that in order to protect the development of human freedom both these adversaries must be given the opportunity, through having their own incarnation, to work against the effects of Christ's incarnation.

The incarnation of Ahriman in the West

Rudolf Steiner did not specify the place nor the exact time of Ahriman's incarnation. In anthroposophical circles it has become more or less customary to regard America as the place. This may be correct, but the very carefully expressed suggestions in the lectures make it impossible to be sure. In Steiner's terminology 'the West' can mean 'Western Europe and America', or simply 'America'. The following passage from the lecture given in Stuttgart on 28 December 1919 does appear to specify the English-speaking region:

> When one day Ahriman appears in incarnation, the local register will record the birth of John William Smith; well, that will not be the actual name. He will be regarded as a commonplace citizen like any other, and people will not be awake to what is actually going on. Our university professors will certainly not be the ones who will wake us up in this respect, for all they will see will be someone called John William Smith. The thing that will matter, though, will be for people in the age of Ahriman to know that John William Smith is only what appears before them outwardly, and that inwardly Ahriman is there; they must know what is happening and not succumb to any deception in the drowsiness of their illusions.

As far as a date is concerned, only the third millennium is mentioned. Reading these lectures it is easy to get the impression that the moment of incarnation will be well on into the third millennium, in the middle or at the end. There are two reasons that appear to emphasize this. Firstly the lectures say that Ahriman's influence will increase throughout the whole of the third millennium, which makes one assume that the culmination will come at the end. Secondly there appears to be a meaningful parallel in the Lucifer incarnation: Lucifer incarnates at the beginning of the third pre-Christian millennium, Ahriman at the end of the third post-Christian millennium, and right in the middle comes the incarnation of Christ.

A few more elements can be mentioned to round off this summary. Steiner spoke immensely seriously about the future incarnation of Ahriman. He stressed that there could be nothing meaningful in trying to prevent it. Just as with Lucifer, the effects of this incarnation could turn out to be for the good. But if—as happened with Lucifer—Ahriman were to remain unrecognized, then harm would result. Ahriman's incarnation will only have positive consequences if humanity recognizes him. Steiner then also listed a number of symptoms by which one will be able to detect his approaching appearance. I shall return to these symptoms later.

The moment in time

Anthroposophists differ considerably in their view of the moment in time Steiner had in mind when he spoke of the coming incarnation of Ahriman. Some are convinced that he was pointing unequivocally to the end of the twentieth century. Others, such as H. W. Schroeder, again basing their opinion on Steiner, reckon that Ahriman's incarnation is not expected until further on in the third millennium.[5] We shall now consider Steiner's utterances.

A passage in a Berlin lecture of 16 July 1918 is, understandably, often mentioned questioningly.[6] Here Enrico Dandolo, the blind doge of Venice—known as a commander

of the fourth Crusade (1204) which he manipulated into
becoming a Venetian conquest of Constantinople—is called
by Steiner an 'incarnation of the ahrimanic spirit'. What this
might signify is immediately the question. That it does not
signify an incorporation of the gravity spoken of in 1919 is
certain, but nevertheless this description given a year earlier
does remain remarkable.

Steiner spoke for the first time about the past incarnation
of Lucifer and also about the future incarnation of Ahriman
in the Zurich lecture of 27 October 1919. The description of
the luciferic incarnation is immediately followed in somewhat vague terms as follows: 'The luciferic impact on the
feeling life of humanity has gradually diminished in the
human soul. Instead, what we call the ahrimanic impulse will
grow stronger and stronger in more modern times—and it
will become stronger and stronger *towards the near future
and also continuing on towards the more distant future*.' The
words shown here in italics cover a period of at least 1000
years, so the question of the exact date of the incarnation
remains open.

Only a few sentences further on we read: 'Just as an
incarnation of Lucifer took place at the beginning of the third
pre-Christian millennium, and just as the incarnation of
Christ took place at the time of the Mystery of Golgotha, so
will there be a western incarnation of Ahriman *some time
after our present time on earth, also round about the third
post-Christian millennium*.' Having read this far we are
tempted to ask whether the very near future is meant. But
then comes the next sentence: 'So we can only understand the
course of humanity's historical development *over approximately six millennia* correctly if we consider it as having *at the
one pole* a luciferic incarnation and *at the other pole* the
incarnation of Ahriman.' This juxtaposition rather compels
us to reach the conclusion already mentioned above that

Ahriman's incarnation is not to be expected until the end of the third millennium.

We shall be looking more closely at the developments through which Ahriman is preparing his approach. Among these Steiner mentioned the complete intellectualization of social science. 'Ahriman would have the greatest success and experience the greatest triumph if it could be managed to prolong *into the third millennium* that scientific superstition which is today seizing hold of every level of society and in accordance with which people even want to establish their social science, and if he could *then* come to the earth as a human being in western civilization and find this scientific superstition awaiting him.' Taken on its own, and leaving aside the preceding remark about the polarity of the incarnation times, this sentence could once again lead us to ask whether Ahriman's incorporation might be expected in the relatively near future.

The second time Rudolf Steiner turned to this specific theme was in Dornach on 1 and 2 November 1919. The first of the two lectures describes in detail the after-effects of the Lucifer incarnation on pagan-gnostic wisdom. This is followed by a brief mention of the increase in Ahriman's influence since the fifteenth century and preparation for his incarnation. Then, all of a sudden, we read: 'And just as there was an incarnation of Lucifer in the flesh, and as there was an incarnation of Christ in the flesh, so will there be, *before even a part of the third post-Christian millennium will have passed*, an actual incarnation of Ahriman in the West: Ahriman in the flesh.'

An astonishing statement! And almost more astonishing than its content is the fact that hitherto almost no notice has been taken of it, as though it were being systematically overlooked. Even Schroeder cites this sentence without due appreciation. As in many similar situations, we do well to linger for a while and let the full effect of such a statement begin to work on us. What do the words 'before even a part of the third post-Christian millennium will have passed' signify? Studying them closely I can only reach two fairly similar interpretations. Either the very beginning of the third millennium is meant, i.e. the very beginning of the twenty-first century; or—even sooner! The latter interpretation would entail the actual incarnation taking place in the later years of the twentieth century, so that a culmination and conclusion would occur in the early years of the twenty-first century. The very carefully considered formulation does, in my opinion, point more towards the latter of these two possibilities.

In a summary such as this the question immediately arises as to how the sentence just cited can be understood in conjunction with the statement made on 27 October 1919 about the two poles. This question remains to be answered. First we shall continue to examine the other statements on this subject.

In the two November lectures Steiner discussed in detail the developments that are to be seen as direct preparations for Ahriman's incarnation. 'It is now time for some individuals to know which of the processes going on around them are machinations of Ahriman that are perhaps preparations—to his advantage—for his *soon to come incarnation on earth*.' In the same lecture we also read: 'In our time now, the traces of Lucifer are becoming less visible because an incarnation of Ahriman *is to come* in the third millennium ...' These sentences, too, could be interpreted as pointing to the very near future, yet this should by no means be taken as a foregone conclusion.

The third occasion on which Rudolf Steiner spoke about this subject was in Berne on 4 November 1919. He did not refer to the descriptions given in Zurich and Dornach but developed the content in a new although similar way. From the beginning the mood of the lecture is very serious. The belligerent character of the time is stressed, even with a hint of a possible 'war of all against all'. There is a detailed description of the circumstances of Lucifer's incarnation at the beginning of the third pre-Christian millennium. Following this we find the sentences: 'In addition to these two incarnations, that of Lucifer in olden times and that of Christ, which gives earthly evolution its actual meaning, there will be a third *in a not too distant future*.' And: 'What is being prepared now and will definitely happen on the earth *is an actual incarnation of Ahriman in the not all that distant future*.' These two statements again make one think that the future referred to will be sooner rather than later. And then, quite soon after the statement last quoted, we find a more detailed indication:

> Humanity must live consciously in expectation of the Ahriman incarnation amongst the shocks that will come about on the physical plane. Under the influence of constant wars and other troubles of the *near future of humanity* the human intellect will become very inventive in the realm of physical life. As a result of *becoming so inventive in the realm of physical life*—which is something that cannot be averted in any way by whatever kind of behaviour, for it will come about as a necessity—*it will be possible for there to be a human individuality of a kind in which Ahriman will be able to be incorporated.*

This statement, in which Steiner was referring to what were then future symptoms of Ahriman's appearance, seems extraordinarily apposite today! One cannot help thinking immediately of the fertilization techniques of recent decades and of the even more recent technology of genetic engineering. Steiner predicted these 'for the near future'—in which the present day can now be included—as instrumentally necessary conditions for the incarnation of Ahriman due at this time.

The fourth and final mention of the subject took place in Stuttgart in the lectures of 25 and 28 December 1919. Once again no exact time is mentioned. Perhaps his audience was surprised that he should take up such a theme during the Christmas period. Steiner countered this possible objection at the beginning of the lecture of 25 December by saying that especially when taking Anthroposophy as one's starting point one had no right to 'forget all the suffering of the times' at Christmas or during any other Christian festival. Rather one was 'obliged to allow' one's experience of the phenomena of decline 'to flow right up to the Christmas tree'. The rest of the lecture is more redolent of Michaelmas than of Christmas. The first mention of a point in time for the coming incarnation of Ahriman in the West states: 'We are approaching this time.' (25 December) And: 'When the time is ripe—*and it is preparing to be so*—Ahriman will simply incarnate in a human body in the western world.' Towards the end of the lecture of 28 December Steiner again referred to 'the western *incarnation of Ahriman in the not at all distant future* . . .'. These are the mentions of timing in those lectures.

Two things are made conspicuous by this summary. Firstly the statements about time are formulated very carefully and are thus usually quite non-specific. Secondly when we look closely there is an unmistakable sense that Rudolf Steiner was nevertheless referring to a near future. (Of course one must take into account that he was saying these things in 1919, 80 years before the end of the millennium. For him this was still a 'not too distant', relatively near future, whereas for us the moment has come much closer.) The partly veiled but, when you look closely, actually quite precise statement of 1 November is rather the exception and appears to contradict the remark about the polarity made on 27 October.

Let us look at this contradiction. The first statement, that

Lucifer's incarnation took place at the beginning of the third pre-Christian millennium, is definite. It resulted in that whole millennium, and indeed the following millennia as well, being strongly influenced by Lucifer. This influence had receded by the beginning of the fifteenth century. From then onwards the influence of Ahriman began to increase, and the third millennium will be very strongly ruled by this influence. One might initially feel obliged to think that in Steiner's view Ahriman's influence would continue to increase throughout the coming millennium as a preparation for his still distant incarnation which would happen as a culmination at the end of that third millennium. Another, perhaps more realistic, possibility would be that Steiner saw the polarity and parallel to mean that Ahriman would want to incarnate right at the beginning of 'his' millennium in order to be able to set the tone for it, just as Lucifer had been able to do for the third pre-Christian millennium. The diagram shows this:

```
3000 BC    2000    1000    M. of G.    1000    2000    AD 3000
.../  X      /....../.........+........./......./ X      /...
       Luc.inc.                                   Ahr.inc.
```

The parallel between the two incarnations and their balance with the Mystery of Golgotha in the middle would come about through Lucifer and Ahriman both appearing in the flesh at the beginning of the relevant millennium.

We cannot any longer put off asking why Rudolf Steiner did not speak more clearly about the point in time he was referring to. The answer may have something to do with the fact that he did not like to act as a prophet. Of course there are some prophetic elements in his lectures, for example his mention of a possibly premature war of all against all at the end of the twentieth century.[7] Prophecies of disaster like this have a threatening effect and do not leave people free. It was always Steiner's intention to stimulate people's own discovery of knowledge and allow them to form their own opinions on the basis of facts that anyone can check up on. In the lectures under discussion here this was very strongly his intention. The symptoms he pointed out in detail—which we have not yet discussed here—can be used by anyone to recognize how close we have come to Ahriman's incarnation.

Another factor plays into this as well. Rudolf Steiner's lectures were never pure monologues. As he spoke he had a direct perception of his audience's variations in interest, people's openness or partial lack of it and so on. This was partly what determined the content. Intense receptivity could make him go into greater detail. And the reverse also happened; lack of receptivity made him hold back. (Many speakers know this phenomenon at more of a feeling level. Steiner perceived it directly.) Are there phrases in these lectures that point to the receptivity of the audience? In the lecture of 2 November there certainly are. At the very beginning we read:

> Yesterday's considerations will have shown you that in order to look more deeply into what actually drives the coming into existence of humanity and the nature of the human being we must turn the eye of our soul very strongly upon the effects of the luciferic power, the Christ-Power, the ahrimanic power. These powers have of course already been effective in the process of world evolution hitherto accomplished. But they worked in spheres that made it unnecessary for the human being to have a clear awareness of the kind of effect they have. The very purpose of our fifth post-Atlantean epoch is that the human being should increasingly gain an awareness of what works throughout earthly existence because of him. In fact it would be necessary today to reveal much, much more of humanity's life secrets *if only humanity were more inclined to accept these things in a more sober and objective manner.* Without knowing certain things, especially of the kind shown yesterday, humanity will not be able to progress either socially or in the inner life.

One might think that this warning applied to the general attitude at the time and not so much to Steiner's actual audience. That it did apply to them, however, shows clearly in the way he expressed himself a few sentences further on: 'Today, though, there is still a strong tendency to cast a veil over the very things we were speaking about yesterday.' And some pages further on we then read: 'Most people today do not strive to penetrate things objectively or to recognize the proper manner in which historical matters ought to progress out of the depths of the world's becoming.' These passages give the impression that in Steiner's opinion his audience did not necessarily posses the alertness needed for taking in and working through what he had to tell them. Therefore he had to exercise great caution.

The type of preparation being made

Rudolf Steiner did not tire of emphasizing in these lectures firstly that the incarnation of Ahriman cannot and should not be prevented, and secondly that in the long run—with regard to materialism, i.e. the ahrimanic impulse as such—this incarnation can have a positive outcome. Thirdly he stressed that for this latter, positive outcome the decisive factor will be whether Ahriman is or is not recognized by human beings when he incarnates. If he remains unrecognized, the effect he has will be calamitous; if he is recognized the effect will serve the progress of humanity. 'The most important thing is that humanity should not sleep through the appearance of Ahriman.' Lucifer's incarnation was able to work positively without being publicly noticed. Christ's incarnation, too, went virtually unnoticed at first, and yet it had its effect. There must be full awareness of Ahriman's incarnation if its consequences are to be positive.

There must be certain criteria or symptoms that can enable

us to see for ourselves how close Ahriman's arrival is. From supersensible—or subsensible—realms Ahriman is systematically preparing his appearance. By promoting specific trends he is trying to make the circumstances of the times fit his impulse. We can recognize his approach by observing the direction in which his activities are going and how strong they are. Steiner described these preparations in varying ways in different places, with the most comprehensive survey being given in Dornach. We shall now summarize the various enumerations.

1. The mechanical conception of the universe that has become customary since Copernicus and Galileo. (Remarkably, Newton is not mentioned.) This mechanical world view is, Steiner said, a great illusion. Although humanity must pass through a stage of believing in it, it remains an illusion, 'a scientific superstition'.

2. The tendency to regard the whole of public life solely from the economic viewpoint without wanting to recognize the need for a threefolding of the social order. Ahriman will especially be able to use for his own purposes our rejection of an independent spiritual-cultural life. 'The ahrimanic power will feel an independent spiritual life to be a kind of darkness. It will feel any interest human beings have in this independent spiritual life to be a fiercely burning fire.'

3. The principle of nationality as a solution for the problems of humanity. Reference is implied to the programme of America's President Wilson.

4. Mentioned in the same breath is the system of party politics because, like nationalism, it creates divisions. An example mentioned is the founding and splintering of socialist parties, but only as an example; the party system as a whole is meant. For 'these ahrimanic powers are present wherever disharmony comes about between groups of people'.

5. The one-sided emphasis on 'simple evangelism' brought into being by evangelical, protestant liberal theology. This is the point about which Rudolf Steiner spoke in the greatest detail. Until the fifteenth century the heritage of luciferic gnosis continued to have its effect in Christian theology; though this had become rather diluted, it still meant that the spiritual significance of Christ continued to be appreciated to some extent. From the fifteenth century on this last remnant of luciferic influence ceased, and in the nineteenth century the ahrimanic influence infiltrated theology, especially in biblical criticism. What especially promotes Ahriman's effect is the one-sided emphasis on the 'simple man of Nazareth'. This interpretation turns the human being Jesus into an effective illusion, a 'hallucination' that covers up the reality of the etheric Christ seen by Paul in his vision. As Steiner said on 2 November 1919: 'If human beings could stop before pressing on to the real Christ, if they could press on only as far as the hallucination of Christ, this would best serve Ahriman's purposes.'

6. A purely intellectual cultural life in which libraries have a central function as 'canned wisdom', with social life threatening to become entirely intellectual. In some instances Steiner mentioned statistics as a separate method of preparation in the way its triumphal march leads it to become the decisive factor in questions of public concern.

7. One effect that is more difficult to observe than those mentioned so far is the 'unconscious absorption of spirit through eating'. As mentioned in the lectures of 1 and 4 November 1919, when the spirit is consciously rejected it creeps into the human being unconsciously through the food he eats. This is a luciferic effect that has great advantages for Ahriman.

8. In the lecture of 4 November Steiner said twice that in

the near future human beings would become 'very inventive'.
The first mention, already cited apropos of genetic engineering, refers to the 'realm of physical life'. The second
refers to foodstuffs that will promote people's ingenuity.
'And by making specific use of these things certain secret
societies, societies that exist, are today already making their
preparations for the incarnation of Ahriman to take place on
the earth in the right way.' (Steiner meant 'in the right way'
from the point of view of those societies.)

Rudolf Steiner gave his audience, the members of the
Anthroposophical Society, tasks to carry out. They were to
investigate the preparations he described and judge for
themselves how urgent the various threats were. From this
they would be able to estimate how close Ahriman was to his
incarnation. See the lecture of 4 November 1919:

> There is much in the spiritual and unspiritual streams of the
> present time that people ought to examine, and then adjust
> their behaviour, and especially their attitude of soul, accord-
> ingly. On whether human beings actually want to come to grips
> with this will depend the kind of impact Ahriman's incarnation
> will make on them and whether this incarnation will cause them
> to lose sight of the earth's goal entirely, or whether it will bring
> them to realize the utter narrowness of a life of intellect, a life
> without spirit. If people take in hand in the right way the things
> I have characterized as streams leading to Ahriman they will,
> simply through the incarnation of Ahriman in earthly life, see
> clearly what is ahrimanic on the one hand, and on the other also
> what is the polar opposite, namely luciferic. The contrast
> between ahrimanic and luciferic will then enable them to turn
> the eyes of their soul to the third element, that encompasses
> everything. Human beings must work their way consciously to
> this trinity of Christian, ahrimanic and luciferic. If they lack an
> awareness of this, human beings will be unable to live towards
> the future in a way that will enable them really to achieve the
> earth's goal.

Rudolf Steiner's final words on this matter

It is not too difficult to use these points as guides in a symptomatological investigation of the degree to which these tendencies have increased up to now (1996). One should look not only at today and tomorrow, but also at the recent past, which for Steiner was still the future. As regards nationalisms and party systems (points 3 and 4), linked as they are, one cannot help asking whether they have not long since reached their explosive culmination, specifically in the 1930s and in Germany. Studies of such things are urgently needed, but they go beyond the scope of this article which is focussed on trying to gauge Rudolf Steiner's view as to the time of Ahriman's incarnation.

A number of statements are mentioned above—not only those of 1 November 1919—which suggest that Steiner was thinking of a very near future. Can this also be deduced from the way in which he characterized the symptoms? Several examples have been given here that certainly point in this direction. There is another passage in a lecture we have not yet considered that is also very significant in this connection.

We stated earlier that this theme was only dealt with in six lectures given towards the end of 1919, and that it disappeared as suddenly as it had appeared. But Steiner did return to it briefly once more a year later on 28 November 1920.[8] In this lecture he once again contrasted the past effect of Lucifer with the present effect of Ahriman. The symptoms and times are weighted somewhat differently. According to this lecture Lucifer's effectiveness was enhanced to some degree towards the end of the second pre-Christian millennium by the way human beings consorted with the elemental spirits of nature. There was, this lecture says, a kind of luciferic 'contamination' of culture. 'On other occasions we have pointed towards this luciferic contamination from different points of view.' (Presumably this is a reference to the lectures of the previous year which we have been discussing here.) The lecture then continues: 'This luciferic contamination of the world is confronted by another, an ahrimanic one.' This refers to a description in that lecture of the way industrialization during the nineteenth and early twentieth centuries caused energy production to rise far beyond a human scale. The number of horsepower/years rose annually millions of times over.

> A sleepy, civilized individual of today cannot easily conceive of the huge speed with which a world that is inhuman and beyond the human scale has been created by human beings in recent decades ... We are living in the age of Ahrimanic contamination. People do not notice at all that they are standing back from the world, and that they are incorporating their intellect into the world, creating next to themselves a world that is becoming independent.

This is a description of the state of the world today, just as Rudolf Steiner described it in his last letter to the members 'From Nature to Sub-Nature'.[9] Such explosive development of industry boiled over initially in the catastrophe of 1914. The actual dehumanizing element, though, lies in the industrialization process itself.

> We are living in the age of Ahrimanic contamination. *People do not notice at all that they are standing back from the world, and that they are incorporating their intellect into the world, creating next to themselves a world that is becoming independent.*

Here again it is tempting to extend this observation to include our age and the significance of computer technology. By doing this we greatly increase the current validity of that sentence.

> Roughly since the second half of the nineteenth century a new world, what might be termed a mighty new geological stratum, is

covering the earth. To all the other strata of diluvium, alluvium etc. is added the ahrimanic stratum of mechanized forces that is forming like a crust across the earth ...

Here again it is a fact that this development is unavoidable, indeed necessary. 'Culture demands to be ahrimanized. But side by side with it we must put whatever works outwards from the inner human being, whatever draws wisdom, beauty, power, i.e. strength, from the inner human being in Imagination, Intuition, Inspiration.' Towards the end of the lecture Steiner repeated something he often said, which was that he did not like too easy a use to be made of the words 'period of transition'. *'Nevertheless, a period in which something as specific as ahrimanism has developed with such colossal speed as has been the case since the final third of the nineteenth century—such a period does not last forever.'* Thus far the content of the lecture of 28 November 1920.

When you consider this last passage against the background of what was said in 1919 it gains a very up-to-date dimension. It certainly appears to corroborate the view we have already posited, that Rudolf Steiner himself expected the culmination of Ahriman's offensive, i.e. his incarnation, to take place soon.

As regards Steiner's views, this simple yet important conclusion throws up new questions; or perhaps questions that appeared to have been settled already now require a new answer. This applies especially to further statements he made regarding the approaching end of the twentieth century. He spoke in greatest detail about this in the lectures on karma in the summer of 1924. He described how Ahriman would endeavour to increase enormously his influence on civilization. He would appear 'as an author'. This does not refer to an incarnation, however, but to *incorporations* in a number of individuals. (In an incorporation a being that is not incarnated mingles with the soul of an incarnated human being for a shorter or longer period. In most cases the incarnated person remains unaware, or scarcely aware, of this over-shadowing.) It is conspicuous that the incarnation unmis-leadingly announced in 1919 is not mentioned at all in 1924.

In connection with this question one should also as far as possible examine what exactly Rudolf Steiner meant by the word 'incarnation' in the case of Ahriman and also of Lucifer. During the life of the person in question, where is the point at which incarnation as such begins? Is it at birth, or is it later? In the case of Lucifer, full penetration into the chosen person is said not to have been completed until his fortieth year. When Christ incarnated in Jesus of Nazareth through the baptism in the Jordan, Jesus was 30 years old. In Soloviev's *Antichrist* the genial main character is over 33 when the 'spirit of the abyss' enters into him. Should these incarnations of Lucifer and Ahriman perhaps be regarded as particularly deep and long incorporations? If this is so, how does the incorporating being enter into the bodily sheath of the incarnated human being? These and other questions that arise remain to be answered.

Authors' Notes

FOREWORD (pages 1–3)

1 R. Steiner *Karmic Relationships, Vol. VIII*, Rudolf Steiner Press, London 1975, lecture of 27 August 1924.

INTRODUCTION (pages 4–16)

1 Rudolf Steiner speaking to the German Foreign Secretary Richard von Kühlman in 1917. From *Nachrichten der Rudolf Steiner Nachlassverwaltung*, No. 15, p. 9, quoted from *The Birth of a New Agriculture, Koberwitz 1924*, ed. A. von Keyserlingk, Temple Lodge Publishing, London 1999.

2 Ibid., Rudolf Steiner speaking to Count Polzer-Hoditz.

3 R. Steiner *Materialism and the Task of Anthroposophy*, Anthroposophic Press, New York 1987.

4 In his recent resignation speech as Welsh Secretary, the British Labour politician Ron Davies famously claimed that human beings are the sum total of their genes and experiences. However, the dramatic tension between what are usually seen as mutually exclusive viewpoints was expressed clearly in an editorial in *The Guardian* newspaper on 30 April 1998 about the murderer Mary Bell, which complained of her treatment by the popular press: 'All killers have to be demonised. Natural causes of crime, complex though they are already, are not enough. The supernatural is always invoked. It is not just irrational—with links right back to the medieval belief in the invasion of ordinary people by humuncole (evil little men)—but dangerous. If killing is the product of evil, then secular society can be excused its failures. There is nothing that can be done.'

5 R. Steiner *Evil*, Rudolf Steiner Press, London 1997, lecture of 26 October 1918.

6 Thus, for example, he spoke of forces within the human being that create an internal 'source of destruction' out of which our individual consciousness is formed. 'In this chaos—which must

be within man, this necessary source of evil in man—the human I, the human egoity, must be forged.' However, if this necessary internal 'destruction' is externalized, then evil results. 'Evil is nothing but the chaos thrust outside, the chaos that is necessary in man's inner being.' (R. Steiner *Cosmosophy*, Anthroposophic Press, New York 1985, lecture of 23 September 1921). He continued: 'What within the human being has a good purpose, without which we could not cultivate our I, must never be allowed outside ... If it is carried outside, it becomes wrong, it becomes evil.' (Lecture of 24 September, 1921.)

We find the same idea, expressed in quite a different way, from a much earlier period of Steiner's work. Here he stated: 'Evil and criminal behaviour originate in the fact that our better—not our worse—nature descends into the bodily element (which cannot of itself be evil), and there develops qualities that belong in the spiritual rather than in the physical realm.' (From a lecture of 15 January 1914, not translated.)

7 By considering these 'forces', we are getting to the heart of the mystery of evil—the actual ability to carry it out. Of course, there are outer *causes* (like the environmental, sociological factors mentioned earlier) which may influence a person to act in an evil way. And then there are evil *beings* that encourage people to commit evil acts. But it is only through these primary spiritual forces—which provide us with the critical *capacity* to act in an evil way—that we can actually carry out an evil deed.

From this perspective, the 'evil beings' as such (Ahriman, etc.) are simply agents of evil. It is we who allow them to incarnate into the space which is left when our spiritual forces are not used for higher development. These beings themselves, however, are not intrinsically 'evil', but only perform a particular function—ultimately for our own progress. For more on the task of the evil beings, and the suffering experienced by certain of them in fulfilling their roles, see S. O. Prokofieff *The Occult Significance of Forgiveness*, Temple Lodge Publishing, London 1995, and *The Encounter with Evil and its Overcoming through Spiritual Science*, Temple Lodge Publishing, London 1999.

8 Sergei Prokofieff suggests exactly this in his book *The Spiritual Origins of Eastern Europe and the Future Mysteries of the Holy*

Grail (Temple Lodge Publishing, London 1993) when he says that the Eastern European peoples absorbed the karmic consequences of western materialism of the nineteenth century through the establishment of Bolshevism in their culture.

9 The inevitable consequence of the decadent view of karma mentioned above—which can be found in many new age teachings, but also in the anthroposophical movement—is the caste system which still exists in Indian culture. The true Christian view of karma can never be judgemental, and is always based on compassion—as typified by Christ's parable of the Good Samaritan.

Shortly after I finished writing this article, the England soccer coach Glen Hoddle was widely condemned in the media for stating his reflections on karma, and was eventually forced to resign. He is alleged to have said: 'You and I have been given two hands and two legs and half-decent brains. Some people have not been born like that for a reason. The karma is working from another lifetime.' Hoddle appears here to be making the assumption that a person's suffering is necessarily a result of misdeeds in a previous lifetime. As I have tried to show, it is not possible to make such a judgement without exact clairvoyant perception of an individual's karma.

10 In his historical analysis of this period, Sergei Prokofieff further suggests that the failure to institute Steiner's threefold social ideas led indirectly to Bolshevism in Russia and the rise of Nazism in Central Europe. See *The Spiritual Origins of Eastern Europe and the Future Mysteries of the Holy Grail*, op.cit.

11 D. Brinkley with P. Perry *Saved by the Light*, Piatkus, London 1994.

12 See further in R. Steiner *The Temple Legend*, Rudolf Steiner Press, London 1997, lecture of 11 November 1904.

13 D. Brinkley, *Saved by the Light* (op.cit.).

14 See R. Steiner *The Book of Revelation and the Work of the Priest*, Rudolf Steiner Press, London 1998, lecture of 19 September 1924.

15 See R. Maikovski *Schicksalswege auf der Suche nach dem lebendigen Geist*, Verlag die Kommenden, Freiburg 1980, quoted from J. Ben-Aharon *The Spiritual Event of the Twentieth Century*, Temple Lodge Publishing, London 1996.

16 See for example M. and E. Kirchner-Bockholt *Rudolf Steiner's Mission and Ita Wegman*, private printing, London 1977, and S. O. Prokofieff *Rudolf Steiner and the Founding of the New Mysteries*, Temple Lodge Publishing, London 1994. I am indebted to Prokofieff for his excellent presentation of Rudolf Steiner's key incarnations, on which I have drawn.

17 O. Mandelstam *Journey to Armenia*, George F. Ritchie, San Francisco, 1979.

PART ONE, CHAPTER 1 (pages 19–39)

Quotations from Rudolf Steiner in this chapter have been translated by S. Blaxland-de Lange. Where a complete lecture is available in another translation, the English title of the volume is given below. Untranslated titles are shown by GA (Complete Works) number only.

1 R. Steiner *Karmic Relationships, Vol.VI*, Rudolf Steiner Press, London 1989, lecture of 18 July 1924.

2 R. Steiner *Karmic Relationships, Vol.III*, Rudolf Steiner Press, London 1977, lecture of 8 August 1924.

3 R. Steiner *Karmic Relationships, Vol.VIII*, Rudolf Steiner Press, London 1975, lecture of 12 August 1924.

4 For example in GA 260a, lecture of 16 April 1924.

5 R. Steiner *The Christmas Conference for the Foundation of the General Anthroposophical Society 1923/24*, Rudolf Steiner Press, London & Anthroposophic Press, New York 1990, lecture of 25 December 1923.

6 GA 260a, lecture of 6 February 1924.

7 R. Steiner *The Easter Festival Considered in Relation to the Mysteries*, Rudolf Steiner Press, London 1968, lecture of 22 April 1924.

8 See Note 5.

9 See Note 6.

10 See Note 5.

11 See, for example, R. Steiner *The Anthroposophic Movement*, Rudolf Steiner Press, London 1993.

12 See Note 5, lecture of 26 December 1923.

13 R. Steiner *The Fifth Gospel. From the Akashic Record*, Rudolf Steiner Press, London 1995, lecture of 2 October 1913.

14 R. Steiner *Occult Science. An Outline*, Rudolf Steiner Press, London 1969.

15 R. Steiner 'The Sermon on the Mount and the Return of Christ', lecture of 20 February 1910, Typescript Z 295.

16 R. Steiner *The Reappearance of Christ in the Etheric*, Anthroposophic Press, New York 1983, lecture of 1 October 1911.

17 See also S. Prokofieff *The Cycle of the Year as a Path of Initiation. An Esoteric Study of the Festivals*, Temple Lodge Publishing, London 1995, Part XII 'The Modern Mysteries of the Etheric Christ'.

18 R. Steiner *The Etherisation of the Blood*, Rudolf Steiner Press, London 1971, lecture of 1 October 1911.

19 See Note 16.

20 R. Steiner *Cosmic and Human Metamorphoses*, Anthroposophical Publishing Co., London 1926, lecture of 6 February 1917.

21 See further in S. O. Prokofieff, *The Encounter with Evil and its Overcoming through Spiritual Science*, Temple Lodge Publishing, London 1999.

22 See Note 5, lecture of 1 January 1924.

23 R. Steiner *The Temple Legend*, Rudolf Steiner Press, London 1985, lecture of 22 May 1905.

24 See Note 1, lecture of 28 January 1924.

25 See Note 6.

26 R. Steiner *Anthroposophical Leading Thoughts*, Rudolf Steiner Press, London 1973.

27 See Note 1, lecture of 19 July 1924.

28 See Note 5, lecture of 26 December 1923.

29 See Note 6, lecture of 25 May 1924.

30 See Note 5, lecture of 1 January 1924.

31 Ibid.

32 See further regarding this in S. O. Prokofieff *Rudolf Steiner and the Founding of the New Mysteries*, Temple Lodge Publishing, London 1994, Chapter 7.

33 See Note 3, lecture of 27 August 1924.

34 See Note 1, lecture of 19 July 1924.

PART ONE, CHAPTER 2 (pages 40–62)

1 L. Thomas *The Lives of a Cell: Notes of a Biology Watcher*, Penguin Books, New York 1978.

2 L. R. Brown et al *A Worldwatch Institute Report on Progress Toward a Sustainable Society*, W. W. Norton & Co, New York 1998.

3 *The Human World Report*, 1997, published by the UN.

4 Barnet & Cavanagh *Global Dreams—Imperial Corporations and the New World Order*, Simon & Schuster, Touchstone Editions 1995.

5 A. Arato & J. Cohen *Civil Society and Political Theory*, MIT Press, Cambridge, Mass. 1997.

6 J. T. Mathews 'The Power Shift' in *Foreign Affairs* magazine, Jan./Feb. 1997.

7 Editor of *Foreign Policy* magazine, 'Global Impact—NGOs in the field'.

8 *International Herald Tribune*, 16–17 January 1999.

9 Nicanor Perlas, president of the Center for Alternative Development Initiatives (CADI) and head of the Anthroposophical Group in the Philippines. He is the author of 7 books and numerous articles and has served as plenary speaker and resource person at many international conferences in Europe, Latin America, North America and Asia. He has recently been awarded the UN Environmental Programme (UNEP) Global 500 Award for Sustainable Agriculture, and The Outstanding Filipino (TOFIL) Award. He was one of the technical writers of the Philippine Agenda 21 (PA 21), which has had a decisive influence on development in the Pacific region. In 1997, over 80 countries adopted the PA 21 way of involving Civil Society, Business Life and Government into programmes for sustainable development. The UN Commission on Sustainable Development started in 1998 to implement a PA 21 innovation, the involvement of the three actors in society—Civil Society in culture, Government in polity, Business and Labour in economy—in creating sustainable development and programmes. The Philippines is the first country in the world consciously to adopt and work out the full implications of a threefold image of society. Address: Anthroposophical Group in the Philippines, 110 Scout Rallos Street, Timog, Quezon City.

10 N. Perlas (with D. Lynch, J. Sharman & D. Hey-Gonzales) *Philippine Agenda 21 Handbook*, The Center for Alternative Development Initiatives (CADI), Philippines 1998.

11 The eastern, northern and southern conferences are part of a new 'tradition' of Michael School conferences. The themes are:

1. *'Elite Globalization, Anthroposophy and Threefoldness'* (Tagaytay City, near Metro Manila, The Philippines, 25–30 October 1998).

2. *'The Anthroposophical Society and its Living Relation to the Esoteric Christ and the Present Social Intentions of Michael'*, (Gothenburg, Sweden, 29 December 1999—3 January 2000).

3. *'The Re-Christianizing of the World and the Development of Brother/Sisterhood—Ubuntu'*, Cape Town, South Africa, January–February 2001.

These conferences can be said to cover West—East—North—South. They therefore constitute a basis for a broad and deep work on establishing Anthroposophy as a decisive force at the Turn of the Millennium.

Ralph Shepherd has written the following in connection with the Southern Conference in South Africa.

The conference programme will be developed and shaped around the theme 'The Re-Christianizing of the World and the Development of Brother/Sisterhood—Ubuntu'. This will be taking the Northern Conference further, so that there will be a direct developmental process from Manila to Gothenburg to Cape Town.

The main features of the esoteric intentions of this South African Conference can be described with a spiritual experience of the General Secretary of the Dutch Anthroposophical Society, Willem Zeylmans van Emmichoven, a few days before he died in Cape Town in 1961.

During November 1961, Willem Zeylmans came to South Africa on a lecture tour. Whilst driving through the Swartberg Pass 200 km from Cape Town, he was given a vision in which he saw the 'World Cross' described by Plato in the sky above South Africa in which the great foot of the Cross rested upon Table Mountain. The Swartberg Pass is a very dry and arid landscape with very ancient and twisted rock formations very similar to the area between Jerusalem and the Dead Sea.

Shortly after his arrival in Cape Town, Zeylmans called the small anthroposophical group together and told them of his vision. He believed this meant that the re-Christianizing of the earth would begin at the Cape in Africa. The stature of Zeylmans, and his life-long service to Anthroposophy, begs us to consider this spiritual picture in the light of the great attack against humanity by the forces of opposition and also the attack against the future development of 'Ubuntu' in South Africa. Ubuntu is an African word which contains the qualities described by Rudolf Steiner as being essential to the coming into being of the sixth cultural epoch. An important step in this direction during later years is the development of the Truth and Reconciliation Commission which has been heard and experienced throughout South Africa, in which the victims and the operators of the apartheid system have been given the possibility of receiving amnesty for crimes committed through political motives. The spirit and the true essence of this attempt, with all its human faults and lacks, is a Christian impulse, a unique manifestation of forgiveness in which an attempt has been made to create conditions in an atmosphere of openness and forgiveness for a fresh start. Among all weaknesses and inhuman patterns of behaviour there is the evident presence of the Etheric Christ, creating these new human conditions through his presence in all dark situations. The attempt means a concrete step to the coming into being of the sixth cultural epoch. And it is an essential contribution for understanding or feeling of the deeper conditions of the re-Christianizing of the world. This development and the concept of Brother/Sisterhood developing out of the new Ubuntu promoted through civil society could give a foundation to Zeylmans' vision.

The part that Nelson Mandela has played in South Africa—and the world—is also an important consideration. Here is a man who, after spending 27 years in gaol, not only forgives his enemies but is able to demonstrate 'servant leadership' in a way that has become inspirational to others. Forgiveness and servant leadership are the two main ingredients for a true Brother/Sisterhood to develop. South Africa now has to demonstrate that it can, as a nation, rise to the two great examples that it has received; Nelson Mandela's leadership and the Truth and Reconciliation Commission.

12 See note 11.

13 J. Ben-Aharon *The New Experience of the Supersensible*, Temple Lodge Publishing, London 1995; and *The Spiritual Event of the Twentieth Century*, Temple Lodge Publishing, London 1993.

PART ONE, CHAPTER 3 (pages 63–74)

1 R. Steiner *Karmic Relationships. Vol.IV*, Rudolf Steiner Press, London 1977, evening lecture of 5 September 1924 in which he spoke for the last time about the significance of the Christmas Foundation Conference.

2 R. Steiner *Esoteric Lessons for the First Class of the School of Spiritual Science at the Goetheanum, Vol.3*, Anthroposophical Society in Great Britain, London 1994 (private printing), lecture of 6 September 1924.

3 R. Steiner *Education for Special Needs*, Rudolf Steiner Press, London 1998, lecture of 7 July 1924.

4 R. Steiner *The Christmas Conference for the Foundation of the General Anthroposophical Society 1923/24*, Anthroposophic Press, New York 1990, p.118.

5 R. Steiner *Knowledge of the Higher Worlds. How is it Achieved?*, Rudolf Steiner Press, London 1985.

PART ONE, CHAPTER 4 (pages 76–78)

1 R. Steiner *The Occult Significance of the Bhagavad Gita*, Anthroposophic Press, New York 1968, lectures of 28 May and 5 June 1913.

2 R. Steiner *Human and Cosmic Thought*, Rudolf Steiner Press, London 1991, lectures of 20 to 23 January 1914.

3 R. Steiner *The Philosophy of Spiritual Activity*, Rudolf Steiner Publications, New York 1963.

4 R. Steiner *Human and Cosmic Thought*, op. cit.

PART ONE, CHAPTER 5 (pages 79–90)

1 F. Schiller *On the Aesthetic Education of Man* translated by R. Snell, Fred. Ungar Publishing Co., New York 1954, 4th letter.

2 R. Steiner *Knowledge of the Higher Worlds. How is it Achieved?*, Rudolf Steiner Press, London 1985.

3 R. Steiner *The Philosophy of Spiritual Activity, A Philosophy of Freedom*, Rudolf Steiner Press, Bristol 1992, Second Appendix.
4 R. Steiner *Occult Science. An Outline*, Rudolf Steiner Press, London 1969, in the chapter 'Knowledge of the Higher Worlds'.
5 Ibid.
6 Ibid.
7 R. Steiner *Art as Spiritual Activity*, Anthroposophic Press, Hudson 1998, lecture of 9 November 1888.
8 R. Steiner *The Archangel Michael. His Mission and Ours*, Anthroposophic Press, Hudson 1994.
9 R. Steiner *The Search for the New Isis, Divine Sophia*, Mercury Press, Spring Valley 1983, lecture of 25 December 1920.
10 R. Steiner *Towards Social Renewal*, Rudolf Steiner Press, London 1977.

PART ONE, CHAPTER 6 (pages 91–107)

1 R. Steiner, *Awakening to Community*, Anthroposophic Press, New York 1974, lecture of 23 January 1923
2 Ibid.
3 Ibid.
4 This anecdote was related to me by Dr Ernst Lehrs.
5 For further discussion, see G. Childs *Truth, Beauty and Goodness: Steiner-Waldorf Education as a Demand of our Time. An Esoteric Study*. Temple Lodge Publishing, London 1999.
6 Slightly adapted from R. Steiner *Verses and Meditations*, Rudolf Steiner Press, Bristol 1993, p.119.
7 R. Steiner 'The Nature of Egotism' in *Metamorphoses of the Soul*, Rudolf Steiner Publishing Co., London, n.d.
8 R. Steiner *The Anthroposophical Movement. Its History and Life-Conditions in Relation to the Anthroposophical Society. An Occasion for Self-Recollection*, Rudolf Steiner Publishing Co., London 1933. Note: I am here using the terminology of Rudolf Steiner, which must not be confused with that referring to the being 'Anthroposophia' mentioned in other contexts, notably by Sergei O. Prokofieff in his book *The Heavenly Sophia and the Being Anthroposophia*.
9 *Awakening to Community*, op. cit., lecture of 28 February 1923, and *passim*.

10 Note: The noun 'purity' (*hagnotes*) is rarely employed by New Testament contributors. As adjectives, both *hagnos*, which bears connotations of holiness or godliness, and *katharos* are used, the latter more commonly with wider implications.

11 R. Steiner *Love and Its Meaning in the World*, Anthroposophical Publishing Co., London 1960.

12 R. Steiner *Guidance in Esoteric Training*, Rudolf Steiner Press, London 1994, p.48f.

13 R. Steiner *Love and its Meaning in the World*, op. cit.

14 Ibid.

15 R. Steiner *Anhroposophical Ethics*, Anthroposophical Publishing Co., London 1928, lecture of 28 May 1912.

16 Ibid.

17 R. Steiner *Awakening to Community*, op. cit., lecture of 13 February 1923.

18 R. Steiner *Anthroposophical Ethics*, op. cit. lecture of 30 May 1912.

19 R. Steiner *Earthly and Cosmic Man*, Rudolf Steiner Publishing Co, London 1948, lecture 6, 14 May 1912.

20 Slightly adapted from R. Steiner *Verses and Meditations*, Rudolf Steiner Press, Bristol 1993, p.191.

21 R. Steiner *Earthly and Cosmic Man*, op. cit., lecture of 14 May 1912.

22 Ibid.

23 R. Steiner *Waldorf Education for Adolescence*, Kolisko Archive Publications, 1980. Closing remarks in lecture of 19 June 1921.

24 R. Steiner *Truth-Wrought Words*, Anthroposophic Press, New York 1979, p.17.

25 R. Steiner *Karmic Relationships, Vol.IV*, Rudolf Steiner Press, London 1997, at the end of lecture of 28 September 1924 'The Last Address'. Another translation of this verse appears on p.93 in *Verses and Meditations*, op. cit.

PART ONE, CHAPTER 7 (pages 108–111)

1 The information for this article comes from R. Steiner *The Challenge of the Times*, Anthroposophic Press, New York 1941, lecture of 8 December 1918.

2 R. Steiner *The Four Mystery Dramas*, Rudolf Steiner Press, London 1997.
3 R. Steiner *Towards Social Renewal*, Rudolf Steiner Press, London 1999.

PART ONE, CHAPTER 8 (pages 112–118)

1 R. Steiner *Occult Science. An Outline*, Rudolf Steiner Press, London 1979.
2 *Life in the Anthroposophical Society—Anthroposophy World-wide*, published monthly in Switzerland by the G.A.S.
3 *New View. Anthroposophy Today*, quarterly journal published by the Anthroposophical Association Ltd on behalf of the Anthroposophical Society in Great Britain.
4 R. Steiner *How Can Mankind Find the Christ Again?*, Anthroposophic Press, New York 1984, lectures of 27 and 28 December 1918; *Occult Science and Occult Development*, Rudolf Steiner Press, London 1983, lecture of 1 May 1913.
5 R. Steiner *Ideas for a New Europe*, Rudolf Steiner Press, Sussex 1992, lecture of 22 February 1920.

PART ONE, CHAPTER 9 (pages 119–131)

1 T. Meyer *Der unverbrüchliche Vertrag—Roman zur Jahrtausendwende* (The Unbreakable Contract—a novel for the turn of the millennium), Perseus Verlag, Basle 1998.
2 Daniel Nicol Dunlop (1868–1935); Ludwig Graf Polzer-Hoditz (1869–1945); Walter Johannes Stein (1891–1957).
3 Around 1777, Cagliostro 'discovered' in London a system of Egyptian Freemasonry, the ultimate authority of which was supposed to be the Grand Copht. Subsequently he claimed to be the Grand Copht himself.
4 Caroline von Heydebrand (1886–1946), a teacher at the first Steiner Waldorf school in Stuttgart.
5 See R. Steiner *Karmic Relationships, Vol.IV*, Rudolf Steiner Press, London 1997, lecture of 28 September 1924 'The Last Address'.
6 Helmuth von Moltke (1848–1916), German Chief of General Staff at the outset of the First World War. See T. Meyer *Light for the New Millennium. Rudolf Steiner's Association with*

Helmuth and Eliza von Moltke, Rudolf Steiner Press, London 1997.

7 R. Steiner *Karmic Relationships, Vols. I—VIII*, Rudolf Steiner Press, London, various dates.

PART ONE, CHAPTER 10 (pages 132–135)

1 German text in R. Bind (Ed.) *Wissenschaft, Kunst, Religion*, Dornach 1998.

PART TWO, CHAPTER 1 (pages 139–156)

1 J. Laughland *The Tainted Source—The Undemocratic Origins of the European Idea*, Warner Books, London 1997.
2 Ibid., p.204.
3 Ibid., p.105
4 I have argued elsewhere that the much-vaunted Third Way, loudly trumpeted by Blair and Clinton, is but a chimera. There is no space here to discuss this. See my article in the magazine *Transintelligence Internationale* (inaugural issue Feb–Mar 1999).
5 The last Michaelic Age was *c.* 600–200 BC.
6 P. Tradowsky *Kaspar Hauser. The Struggle for the Spirit*, Temple Lodge Publishing, London 1997, p.225.
7 In this development of Man in the Christian era, of the new Christian humanity, one might say, we can see parallels with the unfolding life of the child at ages 4, 7, 9, but elaboration of this is beyond the scope of this essay.
8 R. Steiner *The Cycle of the Year*, Anthroposophic Press, New York 1984.
9 *The Guardian*, 25 February 1998.
10 See T. Boardman *Mapping The Millennium—Behind the Plans of the New World Order*, Temple Lodge Publishing, London 1998.
11 Except in the realm of ideas, as mentioned above.
12 The significance of the ninth-year crisis has been discussed by many anthroposophical childcare specialists; see, for example H. Koepke *Encountering the Self—Transformation and Destiny in the Ninth Year*, Anthroposophic Press, Hudson 1982.
13 Joel Wendt http://www.tiac.net/users/hermit/thpts.html.

14 The ideas of Ben-Aharon mentioned here are drawn from a lecture given by him at Tagaytay, Philippines, on 25 October 1998.

15 At the 1997 Annual General Meeting of the Anthroposophical Society in Great Britain.

16 R. Steiner *The Archangel Michael. His Mission and Ours*, Anthroposophic Press, Hudson 1994, lecture of 30 November 1919.

PART TWO, CHAPTER 2 (pages 157–173)

1 Some of the material in this article derives from research undertaken by the author in the early 1960s (which becomes apparent during the course of the article); more recently, he has had the opportunity of taking the theme further and giving it the present karmic slant through research preparatory to lectures in London (March 1997) and Cape Town (February 1998). An opportunity for bringing some of this out in print occurred in the July 1988 issue of *Steiner Education*, in which the theme was 'Literacy'. Some of the very valuable research carried out by other authors on the theme is mentioned both in the text and in the references below.

2 M. Rawson 'Writing and Cultural Memory' in *Steiner Education*, July 1998, Vol.32, No.2, pp.24–31, 42.

3 R. Steiner *Conferences with the Teachers of the Waldorf School in Stuttgart*, Vol.2, p.51, Steiner Schools Fellowship Publications, Forest Row 1987.

4 The present essay, weaving as it does anecdote and straightforward argument, could be taken as an attempt to dress partially familiar concepts in new garb.

5 R. Steiner *Conferences with Teachers*, op. cit., p.53.

6 Ibid., pp.58f.

7 This is one instance among many where Steiner's vigilance over the independent nature of Waldorf education is asserted (q.v. *Freie* Waldorfschule).

8 R. Steiner *Karmic Relationships, Vol.I*, Anthroposophical Publishing Co., London 1955, lectures of 22 and 23 March 1924 are those referred to in this essay.

9 This was at Nutley Hall, Sussex, then known as Perevale. It was founded in 1959, two of the founder members (Misses M.

Buckeridge and M. Bridger) having been trained at the Sunfield Children's Homes in the 1930s. The latter was the first anthroposophical home of its kind in the UK putting into practice that approach to curative education that had been developed at the Sonnenhof in Switzerland under Dr Ita Wegman's medical supervision. Thus evolved, from the workshops, from the cultural life and from the social life that staff and 'residents' all shared, an interpretation of curative education that seemed justified in the way it met the needs of those concerned in harmony with Steiner's ideas.

10 The Waldorf age-related curriculum going up to Class 12 (age 18) does marginally overlap with this age group. However, four years out of an age range of 36 did not seem to justify any direct borrowing.

11 G. M. Trevelyan *Garibaldi and the Thousand*, Longmans, Green & Co., London 1909.

12 G. Garibaldi, *Autobiography*. Trans. A. Werner. Walter Smith & Innes, London 1889.

13 See Trevelyan, op. cit. Map III.

14 Ibid.

15 R. Steiner, *Karmic Relationships, Vol.I*, op. cit. lecture of 23 March 1924.

16 See B. Masters 'What's the Problem? Steiner Education Theory and the Teaching of Literacy' in *Steiner Education* July 1998, Vol.32, No.2, pp.18-21 for a detailed and less philosophically ensconced account than the present one.

17 Incidentally, although giving ample scope, it should be noted that the above examples are restricted to where *F* occurs as an initial letter.

18 The intermediate steps taken by the children are pedagogical details that have been elaborated frequently by Steiner/Waldorf practitioners and in any case are less germane here. For one very common example, see B. Masters 'What's the Problem', op.cit., referring to the fairy story and its 'picture of the upright king, striding out with one arm raised and sword in hand ... to battle against evil', from which is derived the letter K.

19 A description of this classroom activity is referred to by B. Henderson 'Move Along Please: The Need for Movement in the Teaching of Literacy' in *Steiner Education* July 1998, Vol.32, No.1, pp.14–17.

20 See R. Steiner *The Child's Changing Consciousness*, Anthroposophic Press, New York, lecture of 18 April 1923.

21 See R. Steiner *Practical Advice to Teachers*, Rudolf Steiner Publishing Co., London 1937, lecture of 21 August 1919.

22 B. Masters 'What's the Problem', op. cit.

23 See A. W. Reed *Aboriginal Words of Australia*, Reed Books, Balgowlah, NSW 1965.

24 See R. Steiner *Adolescence: Ripe for What?* Tr. M. Stott. Steiner Schools Fellowship Publications, Forest Row 1996, lecture of 22 June 1922, in which Steiner hints at the fact that the teaching of literacy is tied up with the child's 'recapitulating' of the general consciousness experienced by humanity in former civilizations.

25 See B. Masters *An Appraisal of Steinerian Theory and Waldorf Praxis: How Do They Compare?* Ph.D. Thesis, University of Surrey 1997, pp.115–124, in which the author redefines educational theory so that the role of the teacher is made a separate component; i.e. in addition to the standard four components: Aims, The Nature of the Child, Curriculum and Pedagogy, is a fifth: *The Teacher*.

26 R. Steiner *Occult Science*, Anthroposophic Press, New York, 1950, Chapter V.

27 See O. Barfield *Saving the Appearances*, Faber & Faber, London 1957, Chapters IV & XX.

28 Wordsworth not only divined this state but, of course, expressed it infinitely more poetically in his *Ode on Intimations of Immortality from Recollections of Early Childhood*.

29 B. Masters *An Appraisal of Steinerian Theory*, op. cit., pp.274–276.

30 R. Steiner *Curative Education*, Rudolf Steiner Press, Bristol 1993, lecture of 26 June 1924.

31 See N. Skillen 'The Uses of Orality' in *Steiner Education*, July 1998, Vol.32, No.2, pp.5–9.

32 See J. Judd 'Children sent to formal schooling too early, says minister' in *The Independent*, 9 December 1997.

33 'Dispatches' on ITV's *Channel 4*, 29 January 1998.

34 J. Judd 'New reading plan "staggeringly good"' in *The Independent*, 7 December 1998.

35 Moreover, Clause (1) states that education should be 'free at least in the elementary and fundamental stages'.

PART TWO, CHAPTER 3 (pages 174–188)

1 See H. Schmidt *Das Vortragswerk Rudolf Steiners*, Philosophisch-Anthroposophischer Verlag, Dornach 1978.

2 It is pertinent to note that there were black members of the Anthroposophical Society as early as the 1930s (perhaps even earlier). See S. Leber's essay 'Schwarzmagisches Sektierertum und geistige Verführung. Neue Versuche, Anthroposophie und Waldorfschulen zu diskreditieren', in the supplement to the journal *Das Goetheanum*, No.44, 2 February 1997.

3 R. Steiner *The Fall of the Spirits of Darkness*, Rudolf Steiner Press, Bristol 1993, lecture of 26 October 1917.

4 See lecture of 18 May 1913 in Typescript Z 136, and that of 20 May 1913 in *Anthroposophical News Sheet*, Vol.IV, Nos. 23 and 24.

5 According to Steiner, Michael has gradually risen from the rank of an Archangel to that of a Time Spirit, an Archai, since the beginning of the 1840s. See R. Steiner *The Mission of the Archangel Michael*, Anthroposophic Press, New York 1961, lecture of 17 February 1918.

6 See R. Steiner *Karmic Relationships, Vol.VI*, Rudolf Steiner Press, London 1971, lecture of 19 July 1924, and Vol.III, 1977, lecture of 28 July 1924.

7 See, for example, R. Steiner *Manifestations of Karma*, Rudolf Steiner Press, London 1984, lecture 9 of 26 May 1910; *The Occult Movement in the Nineteenth Century*, Rudolf Steiner Press, London 1973, lecture of 16 October 1915; *The Driving Force of Spiritual Powers in World History*, Steiner Book Centre, Toronto 1972, lecture of 11 March 1923.

8 See R. Steiner *The Challenge of the Times*, Anthroposophic Press, New York 1941, lecture of 7 December 1918.

9 See, for example, R. Steiner 'Notes on eight lectures on St John's Gospel', Typescript EN 50, lecture of 19 November 1907.

10 See R. Steiner *Man's Being, His Destiny and World Evolution*, Anthroposophic Press, New York 1952, lecture of 17 May 1923. (Author's italics.)

11 See R. Steiner *Occult Science. An Outline*, Rudolf Steiner Press, London 1969 Chapter IV, 'Man and the Evolution of the World', Rudolf Steiner Press, London 1979.

12 R. Steiner, lecture of 9 January 1916 'The Spiritual Unity of Mankind through the Christ Impulse' in *Anthroposophical Quarterly*, Vol.13, No.1, 1968. (Author's italics.) Elsewhere, Steiner stated: 'All that is connected with the idea of race is still a remnant of the epoch preceding our own, namely the Atlantean. We are now living in the period of cultural ages. Atlantis was the period when seven great races developed one after another. Of course the fruits of this race development extend into our epoch, and for this reason races are still spoken of today, but the sharp distinctions of Atlantean times are already blurred. Today the idea of culture has superceded the idea of race.' See *The Apocalypse of St John*, Rudolf Steiner Press, London 1977, lecture of 20 June 1908.

13 Lecture of 9 January 1916 in *Anthroposophical Quarterly*, op. cit. (Author's italics.)

14 Ibid.

15 R. Steiner *The Search for the New Isis, Divine Sophia*, Mercury Press, Spring Valley 1983, lecture of 23 December 1920.

16 Ibid.

17 See R. Steiner *Influences of Lucifer and Ahriman*, Rudolf Steiner Publishing Co., London 1954.

18 See, for instance, R. Steiner *The Destinies of Individuals and of Nations*, Rudolf Steiner Press/Anthroposophic Press 1986, lectures of 17 & 19 January 1915; *The Cosmic New Year*, Rudolf Steiner Publishing Co., London 1938, lecture of 25 December 1919; *Man's Life on Earth and in the Spiritual Worlds*, Anthroposophical Publishing Co., London 1952, lecture of 19 November 1922; *Anthroposophical Leading Thoughts*, Rudolf Steiner Press, London 1973, lecture of 9 November 1924.

19 R. Steiner *World History in the Light of Anthroposophy*, Anthroposophical Publishing Co., London 1950, lecture of 1 January 1924.

20 R. Steiner *Karmic Relationships, Vol.VI*, op. cit., lecture of 19 July 1924.

21 R. Steiner *Materialism and the Task of Anthroposophy*, Anthroposophic Press/Rudolf Steiner Press 1977, lecture of 2 April 1921.

22 R. Steiner *Karmic Relationships, Vol.III*, Rudolf Steiner Press, London 1977, lecture of 3 August 1924.

23 *The Christmas Conference for the Foundation of the General Anthroposophical Society 1923/24*, Anthroposophic Press, New York 1990, as discussed in lecture of 24 December 1923.

24 R. Steiner, lecture of 2 December 1911 in journal *The Golden Blade*, 1964. (Author's italics.)

25 Steiner was referring here to the Ancient Indian, Ancient Persian, Egypto-Chaldean and Greco-Latin epochs; see R. Steiner *Occult Science. An Outline*, op. cit.

26 R. Steiner *Earthly and Cosmic Man*, Spiritual Science Library, Blauvelt 1986, lecture of 20 June 1912. (Author's italics.)

27 It is enlightening in this connection to note the different renderings in paintings of the human face, figure, gesture, posture, and so forth, by Duccio di Buoninsegna, *c.*1255–1319, on the one hand, and Masaccio (Tommaso di ser Giovanni di Monc), 1401–*c.*1428, on the other.

28 R. Steiner *The Mission of the Archangel Michael*, op. cit., lecture of 17 February 1918.

29 One could think here of the neo-Nazi movement in Germany, of the Far Right in Britain and France, and, until a few years ago, Apartheid in South Africa, and so on. It is apposite to note in the present context that the Steiner Waldorf schools in South Africa began to count black children among their pupils a few years after they were founded (early 1960s).

30 See Typescript Z 390 of a lecture entitled 'Colour and the Human Races' given by Steiner on 3 March 1923.

31 Steiner was speaking here of the human physical body as a totality and the various processes which take place within it; processes which, well 'organized', as it were, act in harmony with one another. R. Steiner *The Fall of the Spirits of Darkness*, op. cit., lecture of 7 October 1917 'Changes in Humanity's Spiritual Make-up'.

32 See, for instance, R. Steiner *Theosophy of the Rosicrucian*, Rudolf Steiner Press, London 1981, lectures XI & XII, both of 4 June 1907; *The Gospel of St John* (Hamburg), Anthroposophic Press, New York 1933, lecture of 30 May 1908; *The Influence of Spiritual Beings upon Man*, Anthroposophic Press, New York 1961, lecture of 1 June 1908; *The Apocalypse of St John*, op. cit., lecture of 24 June 1908; *Universe, Earth and Man*, Rudolf Steiner Press, London 1987, lecture of 16 August 1908; *Rosi-*

crucian Esotericism, Anthroposophic Press, New York 1978, lecture of 12 June 1909; *The Ego*, Rudolf Steiner Publishing Co., London n.d., lecture of 4 December 1909; *Occult Science. An Outline*, op. cit., Chapter IV; *The Mission of Individual Folk Souls in Relation to Teutonic Mythology*, Rudolf Steiner Press, London 1970, lecture of 10 June 1910; *Faith, Love, Hope*, Steiner Book Centre, Toronto n.d., lecture of 2 December 1911; *The Mission of the Archangel Michael*, op. cit., lecture of 17 February 1918; 'Spiritual Emptiness and Social Life', lecture of 13 April 1919 in *The Golden Blade* 1954; *The Search for the New Isis, Divine Sophia*, op. cit., lecture of 23 December 1920; Typescript Z 390, op. cit.

33 Lecture of 13 April 1919 in *The Golden Blade* 1954, op. cit.

34 See, for instance, R. Steiner *The Cycle of the Year*, Anthroposophic Press, New York 1984.

35 R. Steiner *Geographic Medicine*, Mercury Press, Spring Valley, NY, no date, lecture of 16 November 1917.

36 Lecture of 13 April 1919 in *The Golden Blade* 1954, op. cit.

37 R. Steiner *The Influence of Spiritual Beings upon Man*, op. cit., lecture of 24 March 1908. See also Typescript EN 50, op. cit.

38 See, for instance, R. Steiner *The Gospel of St John* op. cit., lecture of 26 May 1908.

39 R. Steiner *Karmic Relationships, Vol.III*, op. cit., lecture of 3 August 1924.

40 Ibid., lecture of 4 August 1924.

41 R. Steiner *Man's Life on Earth and in the Spiritual Worlds*, op. cit., lecture of 19 November 1922.

42 Ibid.

43 Paracelsus (Theophrastus Bombast von Hohenheim) 1493–1541, German physician; Lorenz Oken 1779–1851, German naturalist.

44 R. Steiner *At the Gates of Spiritual Science*, Rudolf Steiner Press, London 1970, lecture of 29 August 1906. (Author's italics.)

45 R. Steiner *The Apocalypse of St John*, op. cit., lecture of 24 June 1908.

46 Ibid.

PART TWO, CHAPTER 4 (pages 189–205)

1 R. Steiner *The Human Heart*, Mercury Press, Spring Valley 1985, lecture of 26 May 1922.
2 R. Steiner *The Younger Generation*, Anthroposophic Press, New York 1984. See also J. C. Eccles *Evolution of the Brain, Creation of the Self*, Routledge, New York 1989, p. 232.

PART TWO, CHAPTER 5 (pages 206–211)

1 Johann Wolfgang von Goethe (1749–1832).
2 George Adams (Kaufmann), MA (Cantab.) (1894–1963).
3 Edith Maryon, English sculptress (1872–1924).
4 G. Adams Kaufmann *Strahlende Weltgestaltung*, Mathematisch-Astronomische Sektion, Goetheanum, Dornach 1934.
5 G. Adams & O. Whicher *The Plant Between Sun and Earth*, Rudolf Steiner Press, London 1980. See also O. Whicher *The Heart of the Matter*, Temple Lodge Publishing, London 1997.

PART TWO, CHAPTER 6 (pages 212–221)

1 A. E. McAllen *The Extra Lesson*, Steiner Schools Fellowship, Forest Row 1985.
2 Adapted from R. Steiner *Verses and Meditations*, Rudolf Steiner Press, Bristol 1993, p.53.
3 D. Deverell *Light Beyond the Darkness, the Healing of A Suicide Across the Threshold of Death*, Temple Lodge Publishing, London 1996.
4 I. Wegman 'On the Work of Michael' in *Anthroposophy*, Vol.5, No.3, 1930.
5 R. Steiner *From Symptom to Reality in Modern History*, Rudolf Steiner Press, London 1976, lecture of 25 October 1918.
6 Adapted from R. Steiner *Verses and Meditations*, Rudolf Steiner Press, Bristol, 1993, p.161.

APPENDIX (pages 222–240)

1 This essay is based on two articles which were first published in *Das Goetheanum*, Nos. 46 & 47, 25 February and 3 March 1996. For the purposes of the present book, most of the first article—which focused largely on the incarnation of Lucifer—has been

omitted. Although for health reasons Hans Peter van Manen was unfortunately not able to write a new contribution, we are grateful to him for suggesting the inclusion of this essay. While it was first published some years ago, it remains very relevant and deserves further attention.

2 R. Steiner *The Reappearance of Christ in the Etheric*, Anthroposophic Press, New York 1983, lecture of 25 January 1910; T. Stöckli (Ed.), *Das ätherische Christuswirken*, 3 vols., Dornach 1991. H. W. Schroeder, *Die Wiederkunft Christi heute*, Stuttgart 1991. Both the latter contain references to further works.

3 R. Steiner *The Ahrimanic Deception*, Anthroposophic Press, New York 1985, lecture of 27 October 1919; *The Influences of Lucifer and Ahriman*, Rudolf Steiner Publishing Co, London 1954, lectures of 1, 2 and 4 November 1919; *The Archangel Michael. His Mission and Ours*, Anthroposophic Press, Hudson 1994, lecture of 21 November 1919 (mentioned only in passing); *The Cosmic New Year*, Rudolf Steiner Publishing Co, London 1938, lectures of 25 and 28 December 1919.

4 E. von Houwald, 'Menschheitszukunft—Menschheitsver-antwortung', in *Mitteilungen aus der anthroposophischen Arbeit in Deutschland*, 1953, p.63; and 'Studiengrundlagen zur Frage der Luzifer-Inkarnation in der Vergangenheit, der Ahriman-Inkarnation in der Zukunft', in ibid, p.67. H. W. Schroeder in Vol.1 and A. Floride in Vol. 3 of T. Stöckli (Ed.), *Das ätherische Christuswirken*, op.cit.

5 In: T. Stöckli (Ed.), *Das ätherische Christuswirken*, op. cit.

6 R. Steiner, Typescript C 50, lecture of 16 July 1918.

7 R. Steiner, Typescript NSL 228, lecture of 6 August 1921.

8 R. Steiner *Die Brücke zwischen der Weltgeistigkeit und dem Physischen des Menschen*, Dornach 1993, lecture of 28 November 1920.

9 R. Steiner *Anthroposophical Leading Thoughts*, Rudolf Steiner Press, London 1973.

Further Reading

If you liked the essays in this book, you might want to read further works by the various authors. (All titles published by Temple Lodge.)

Jesaiah Ben-Aharon:
The Spiritual Event of the Twentieth Century, An Imagination. The Occult Significance of the Twelve Years 1933–45 (1993, 2nd ed. 1996)
The New Experience of the Supersensible (1995)

Mario Betti:
The Sophia Mystery in Our Time (1994)

Terry Boardman:
Mapping the Millennium, Behind the Plans of the New World Order (1998)

Peter Bridgmont:
Liberation of the Actor (1992)

Gilbert Childs:
Truth, Beauty and Goodness, Steiner-Waldorf Education as a Demand of Our Time, An Esoteric Study (1999)

Doré Deverell:
Light Beyond the Darkness, the Healing of a Suicide Across the Threshold of Death (1996)

Michaela Glöckler:
Medicine at the Threshold of a New Consciousness (1997)

Sevak Gulbekian:
At the Grave of Civilization? A Spiritual Approach to Popular Culture (1996)

Brien Masters:
Meteor Showers and Us (1989)
A Round of Rounds for the 52 Weeks of the Year (1990)

Patter-Paws the Fox (2nd ed. 1996)
Trumpets of Happiness (1998)

Thomas Meyer:
Clairvoyance and Consciousness, The Tao Impulse in Evolution (1991)
D.N. Dunlop, A Man of Our Time (1992)
The Bodhisattva Question, Krishnamurti, Rudolf Steiner, Annie Besant, Valentin Tomberg, and the Mystery of the Twentieth Century Master (1993)

Bernard Nesfield-Cookson:
Michael and the Two-Horned Beast, The Challenge of Evil Today in the Light of Rudolf Steiner's Science of the Spirit (1998)

Sergei O. Prokofieff
Rudolf Steiner and the Founding of the New Mysteries (1986, 2nd ed. 1994)
The Twelve Holy Nights and the Spiritual Hierarchies (1988, 2nd ed. 1993)
The Cycle of the Year as a Path of Initiation Leading to an Experience of the Christ Being, An Esoteric Study of the Festivals (1991, 2nd ed. 1995)
The Occult Significance of Forgiveness (1991, 3rd ed. 1995)
Eternal Individuality, Towards a Karmic Biography of Novalis (1992)
Prophecy of the Russian Epic, How the Holy Mountains Released the Mighty Russian Heroes from their Rocky Caves (1993)
The East in the Light of the West, Two Eastern Streams of the Twentieth Century in The Light of Christian Esotericism, Part 1: Agni Yoga (1993)
The Spiritual Origins of Eastern Europe and the Future Mysteries of the Holy Grail (1993)
Rudolf Steiner's Research into Karma and the Mission of the Anthroposophical Society (1995)
The Cycle of the Seasons and the Seven Liberal Arts (1995)
The Heavenly Sophia and the Being Anthroposophia (1996)
The Case of Valentin Tomberg, Anthroposophy or Jesuitism? (1997)
The Encounter with Evil and its Overcoming through Spiritual Science (1999)

Richard Seddon:
The End of the Millennium and Beyond (1993)
Europa, A Spiritual Biography (1995)
Mani, His Life and Work, Transforming Evil (1998)

Nick Thomas:
The Battle for the Etheric Realm, Moral Technique and Etheric Technology, Apocalyptic Symptoms (1995)

Peter Tradowsky:
Kaspar Hauser, The Struggle for the Spirit (1997)
Christ and Antichrist, Understanding the Events at the End of the Century and Recognizing Our Tasks (1998)

Hans-Peter van Manen:
Transparent Realities, The Anthroposophical Impulse in the Environmental Movement and the 33-Year Rhythm in the History of the Anthroposophical Society (1994)
Marie Steiner, Her Place in World Karma (1995)

Edward Warren:
Freedom as Spiritual Activity (1994)

Olive Whicher:
The Heart of the Matter, Discovering the Laws of Living Organisms (1997)